A Practical Guide for Writers

A Practical Guide for Writers

DIANA HACKER
BETTY RENSHAW

with a section on research writing by
LLOYD SHAW

Winthrop Publishers, Inc.
Cambridge, Massachusetts

Library of Congress Cataloging in Publication Data

Hacker, Diana
  A practical guide for writers.

  Includes index.
  1. English language—Rhetoric.   I. Renshaw,
Betty, joint author.   II. Title.
PE1408.H27   808   78–10775
ISBN 0–87626–647–2

Interior design by Sandra Rigney/Nancy Earle
Cover design by David Ford

To our students

—*and to*   Betsy
            GJH
            Lynn
            Mary Jo
            —BR

CONTENTS

Capitalization   256

Spelling   259

PREFACE

A Practical Guide for Writers is a rhetoric/handbook for college students. Today's college students, whether they attend a four-year university or a community college, are a diverse group. They include grandmothers and sixteen-year-olds, dorm residents and commuters, disabled veterans and returning housewives. Many, but not all, read on the college level. A few are budding writers, but the goals of most are more modest. We have attempted to reach all of these students—with a book that is readable, but not simplistic; supportive, but not patronizing.

Furthermore, we have attempted to make *A Practical Guide for Writers* adaptable to a variety of teaching styles. The rhetoric section can be used either with or without further elaboration; the supporting exercises suggest many different kinds of activities, for both in and out of class; the handbook invites classroom discussion, if desired, or it can be used exclusively for reference.

Other features include:

- an emphasis throughout on writing as a process—an often chaotic process, but one that can be learned
- a focus on the writing situation, to encourage awareness of purpose and audience
- recognition of writing as a real-life pursuit
- a section on finding a writing voice and choosing appropriate language
- a step-by-step discussion of how to support a point in writing
- separate chapters on describing, narrating, and informing
- rhetorical principles illustrated by student writing
- a thorough discussion of research writing, with a sample paper

- hundreds of writing topics that encourage students to write about what they know
- a collection of student papers—so that students can see what has worked for other students
- a variety of stimulating exercises
- a nonthreatening, thorough approach to problems in mechanics and usage
- an analysis of "dialect interference" problems, to help students become skillful copyreaders
- an informal, friendly style throughout
- avoidance of unnecessarily difficult vocabulary and syntax
- a careful attempt to avoid ethnic, class, and sexist bias

An instructor's manual is available too.

We hope that A *Practical Guide for Writers* will reflect, throughout, our general approach to the whole process of writing: that learning about it is a human exchange between student and teacher, and that its results are a human exchange between writer and reader. To this end, we strive to be as sympathetic toward and supportive of the budding student writer as possible. We hope that he or she can, by using this book, become more and more comfortable when confronted with that most complex and challenging of human activities—trying to communicate on paper with other human beings.

ACKNOWLEDGMENTS

For their help in creating A *Practical Guide for Writers*, our special thanks go to the following persons.

To James C. Davis of Monroe Community College, Lynn Z. Bloom of The College of William and Mary, C. Jeriel Howard of Bishop College, and Donald S. Tighe of Valencia Community College, for constructive and often enlightening suggestions. And to our own colleagues at Prince George's Community College for what we have learned from them over the years, and for their support and encouragement while we worked on the book.

To the following students, whose writing appears in A *Practical Guide for Writers:* Steve Alexander, David Allen, George Andrews, Lisa Bennett, Henry Bertagnolli, Emily Boyle, Dale Brennan, Yvonne Bridges, Dorothy Broussard, Jill Broughton, Michael Buongiorne, Judith Burgin, Linda Cestari, Frank Cohee, Donna Cooper-Bey, Donna Corbin, Marie Dabbs, Juanita Davis, Joe DiBattista, Sharon Donohue, Robert Ducharme, Doris Duncan, Joan Easterling, John Egan, Helen Eisenberg, Michael Elmore, Steve Fitzgerald, Deborah Fletcher, Charles Ganley, Paul Glascock, Authella Gross, Mike Harrison, Melody Hill, Gussie Hopkins, Thomas Insley, Brenda Jenkins, Beverley Johnson, Sharon Jones, Margretta Kennedy, Mary Kenny, Renee Klar, Bill Leith, Martha Long, Andrew McCoy, H. C. McKenzie, Pam Mitchell, John Moore, Pat Napolitano, Mark Parker, Ruth Parker, Richard Peters, Kim Pleasant, Nancy Powell, Nolan Presnell, Peggy Purves, Irene Rabun, Johnnie Randolf, Marnita Riley, Brian Roache, Daryl Roe, Laurie Roehrich, Catherine Salsbury, Karl Schmidt, Jon Singleton, George Snellings, Cynthia Sofranko, Margaret Stack, Jefferson Stewart, Karen Sutton, Tom Weitzel, Belinda Whitehead, Gerolyn Whittemore, Sam Williams, Clevester Wimbish, Sharon Wultich, Andrew Woycitzky.

To Alice Hobbs for being the most competent and patient manuscript typist imaginable; and to Robert Hacker, Pat McPherson, and Robert Morris for support in duplicating.

To Bridget Broderick, Alison Mills, Herb Nolan, Sandra Rigney, Nancy Reilly, Janet Schreiber, William Sernett, Richard Superty, and Margery Williams of Winthrop Publishers for their skill and advice. And, finally—and most especially—to Paul O'Connell, who has proven himself, throughout, the ideal mentor, by being there when we needed him and by leaving us alone when we didn't.

Note: We would welcome suggestions from other instructors for improving our book.

Diana Hacker
Betty Renshaw
Prince George's Community College
Largo, Maryland

A Practical Guide for Writers

PART I
The Writing Process

If I start very early in the morning, with a fresh pot of coffee, sharp pencils, plenty of paper, a cat on my lap and total silence, I might come up with something.

—a student

CHAPTER 1
GETTING STARTED

Some people think they should be able to sit down at a desk, take out a clean sheet of paper, pick up a pen or pencil, and begin to write. They feel that the writing should just come off the top of their heads, cold, unpremeditated. But the experience of just about everybody we know or have read about, including ourselves, says that is just not the way good writing happens.

What has to happen first, often long before you sit down to write, is a less consciously directed, more random kind of thinking. You begin by musing, exploring, discovering—by letting your ideas go where they want to. You give yourself time for creative thinking.

CREATIVE THINKING

The creative thinking involved in writing can occur almost anywhere, often while you are doing something else. It is important to get your brain working on a piece of writing as soon as possible, to give yourself time for this "free thinking" to happen.

Agatha Christie, creator of mystery stories that have delighted generations of readers, found that the best time for planning a book was while doing the dishes. American novelist James Gould Cozzens says of his free-thinking time: "I meditate and put on a rubber tire with three bottles of beer. Most of the time I just sit picking my nose and thinking." Virginia Woolf, a British writer, did most of the serious planning for her writing during long bubble baths. And one of our students says, "Many ideas come to mind before I fall asleep when it's quiet and restful."

If you lead a busy life, you'll want to do your creative thinking while you are driving to work, or cleaning house, or taking a walk—or engaged

3

in some other activity that does not require much concentration. Toni Morrison, a contemporary American author, tells us, "When I sit down to write I never brood. I have so many other things to do with my children and teaching that I can't afford it. I brood, think of ideas, in the automobile when I'm driving to work or in the subway or when I'm mowing the lawn. By the time I get to the paper something's there—I can produce."

SCRIBBLING ON SCRATCH PAPER

While you are doing your creative thinking, make some random notes on whatever scratch paper is available at the moment. Don't worry about organizing your thoughts at this stage; just be sure to write down enough so you can decode it later.

Getting this much down on paper at once, as the thoughts are flowing, will help you later when you finally sit down to write. Professional writers scribble ideas on the backs of envelopes, on recipe cards or paper bags or cocktail napkins or scraps of cardboard—whatever happens to be handy at the time. Anne Tyler, a writer and mother of two, remarks: "In the evenings, occasionally—between baths and other sorts of chaos—a sudden idea will flash into my mind . . . I write it down on an index card and take it to my study."

One of our students says: "I sometimes have to write on anything I can get my hands on when my thoughts are running quickly. I must write them down so I can return to them later." Another student comments: "Sometimes things pop into my head just before I go to sleep. Then I have to jump up and jot them down right away. I just scrawl, but if I don't do it then, I'll lose them." Not surprisingly, bedtime, when the mind is free to wander, is a popular time for free thinking.

This thinking on scratch paper will make your blank paper look less empty and less intimidating when you sit down before it to write, for you will already have done some of the hardest work involved in writing.

YOUR WRITING ENVIRONMENT

If there is any magic connected with writing, it may come from your writing place. The more at home you are in the place where you write, the more free and easy you will feel. And there is likely to be a particular time of day, or night, when writing will come most easily for you. Observe yourself and try to figure out when your best writing time is.

Statements by famous writers as well as our students clearly support the importance of finding your writing place and of being there at your best writing time. Carson McCullers did her writing "in a quiet room in the early morning hours." Van Wyck Brooks, on the other hand, believed: "As against having beautiful workshops, studies, etc., one writes best in a cellar on a rainy day." One of our students reports: "I write in the quiet of night, when the children are sound asleep." Another says he writes "whenever there's free time, wherever there's free space . . . and lots of coffee."

Certain items—coffee, cigarettes, coke, milk, a favorite pen, a legal pad, music—seem to be essential to some persons as they write. Surround yourself with whatever you need to get started. Carson McCullers says that she took a thermos of tea to her quiet room. Ernest Hemingway wrote his more poetic descriptive passages with a pencil; he said he needed to hear the lead move on the paper. But he typed out his more sharp-edged action sentences while standing at a chest-high desk. Thomas Wolfe, another American novelist, did much of his writing while leaning on top of a refrigerator; he was so tall that he was most comfortable in that position.

Another writer we know does all her first-draft writing seated in the corner of a worn sofa, with containers of both hot coffee and iced water at hand. She writes on a beat-up clipboard, with a large supply of freshly sharpened yellow No. 2 pencils close by. She cannot write very well anywhere else. Nor can she write at night. On the other hand, one of our students says she can write anywhere she can get comfortable: "in the tub, in bed, on the floor, in a semidark room, almost anywhere."

TOOLS OF THE TRADE

To do anything well, you need the right tools—and writing is no exception. Beyond plenty of paper and the writing instrument that feels best to you, you will need some items to help you be *flexible* as you write. With these you can cut and paste and rearrange what you write in numerous ways as you work toward your final draft. We recommend that you have handy: sharp scissors; a stapler or transparent tape; and more paper, to attach your clipped pieces to as you cut and tape and rearrange your work.

Certain books will help you as you develop your writing skill. In addition to this book, we suggest that you have at your elbow at least two more paperback reference books: a good, reasonably current dictionary; and a dictionary of synonyms and antonyms (or thesaurus), which you will find an invaluable mine of words to enrich your writing. If you have serious spelling problems, an inexpensive spelling book that lists thou-

sands of words (the words only, so you don't have to wade through definitions) will be a must for you.

Here are the titles of some paperback reference books that we and our
students like:

1. *The American Heritage Dictionary of the English Language,* Dell
   Publishing Company, 1973
2. *Webster's New World Dictionary,* Popular Library, 1975
3. Devlin, Joseph, *A Dictionary of Synonyms and Antonyms,* Popular
   Library, 1975
4. *Webster's Synonyms, Antonyms & Homonyms,* Barnes & Noble,
   1974
5. *The New American Roget's College Thesaurus in Dictionary Form,*
   New American Library, 1973
6. *Webster's New World Thesaurus,* Popular Library, 1974
7. *Instant Spelling Dictionary: 25,000 Words,* Career Institute, 1967[1]
8. *Webster's New World 33,000 Word Book,* Collins, Williams &
   World Publishing Company, 1971

ACTUALLY GETTING STARTED

If you're like most writers, you'll do almost anything to avoid writing
that first sentence. Suddenly your car needs washing, your refrigerator
has to be defrosted, your closet demands a thorough cleaning. Even
when you've all but chained yourself to your desk you find ways to avoid
that blank sheet of paper. Your typewriter ribbon must be changed, the
desk has to be cleaned, and your notes must be arranged in an elaborate,
color-coded outline. Writer Jaques Barzun advises us at this point to
"suspect all out-of-the-way or elaborate preparations. You don't have to
sharpen your pencils and sort out paper clips before you begin."

Professional writers have discovered ways of forcing themselves to get
started. Barzun, who assures us that "no writer has ever lived who did
not at some time or other get stuck," begins by letting his first sentence
"be as stupid as it wishes." Another author we know of types or scribbles
gibberish, just to warm up his cold brain and get his fingers moving.
Both these professionals simply assume that their first sentence will be
thrown away; knowing this, they're not afraid to write it.

Flannery O'Connor, a Southern writer, had a method of getting
started that you might consider adopting. She set aside a regular time

---

1. Career Institute, Department 899–66, 555 East Lange Street, Mundelein,
Illinois 60060.

period for writing. As she told a group of students, "Every morning between nine and twelve, I go to my room and sit before a piece of paper. Many times I sit for three hours with no ideas coming to me. But I know one thing: if an idea does come between nine and twelve, I am there ready for it."

If you're attracted to Flannery O'Connor's method, try modifying it to fit your own writing needs. We would guess that you won't sit for hours without writing a thing. Sitting is too boring. And besides, you will have all those notes on scratch paper to help you get started.

EXERCISE 1   FOR THOUGHT AND DISCUSSION

Professional writers have had a lot to say about "how I write." Mull over the following comments by professional writers, to see what ideas you might pick up from them.

a. My working habits are simple: long periods of thinking, short periods of writing.

—Anonymous

b. One takes a piece of paper, anything, the flat of a shingle, slate, cardboard and [writes] with anything handy . . . The blankness of the writing surface may cause the mind to shy . . . [but] Write, write anything . . . it is absolutely essential to the writing of anything worthwhile that the mind be fluid and release itself to the task.

—William Carlos Williams, *American poet*

c. (on free writing, in a diary): . . . written rather faster than the fastest typewriting . . . the advantage of the method is that it sweeps up accidentally several stray matters which I should exclude if I hesitated, but which are the diamonds of the dustheap.

—Virginia Woolf, *British novelist and essayist*

d. I just sit at my typewriter and curse a bit.

—P. G. Wodehouse, *American writer*

e. When you start to write, you perceive many more relationships in your material than you were aware of at the start.

—Albert D. Van Nostrand, *professor of English*

f. Get it down. Take chances. It may be bad, but it's the only way you can do anything really good.

—William Faulkner, *American author*

g. I don't type [when I write] because . . . I often have the feeling that everything flows directly from my right hand.

—Anne Tyler, *American novelist*

h. The more you write, the more you can write.

—Anonymous

i. Writers kid themselves—about themselves and other people. Take the talk about writing methods. Writing is just work—there's no secret. If you dictate or use a pen or type or write with your toes—it is still just work.

—Sinclair Lewis, *American author*

EXERCISE 2   WRITTEN

Our students have come up with some choice comments about the writing process as they experience it; some of these are quoted below. Try commenting on your writing process in a similar concise statement.

1. I just sit at my typewriter and talk to myself.
2. Quiet music makes my head spin. As it is spinning, the ink flows swiftly from my pen.
3. I write better under pressure of a deadline.
4. When writing about the forest, I go into the forest; when writing about the ocean, I go to the beach. Environment is everything.
5. I find a comfortable place to relax, fix something to drink, have my cigarettes handy and begin to put my thoughts together.
6. I swear a lot.
7. When I begin to write, that's exactly what I do—begin to write.
8. I must be alone, where there are no distractions.
9. I write either clothed or nude. Sometimes being nude allows me to be more open.

EXERCISE 3   FOR THOUGHT AND DISCUSSION

Much has been written in recent years about the functions of the right and left hemispheres of the human brain. The theory is that the "right brain" is the seat of intuition, flexible thinking, and creativity generally, while the "left brain" controls our more systematic, analytical, rational thinking. One might say that the left brain is intellectual and the right brain intuitive. If this is true, then we need to be able to free up our right brains as much as possible during the initial exploratory phase of the writing process, saving our left brains for later when we organize and clarify our thinking and writing. The following quotations might help you figure out how to open up your right brain and let it play around more freely:

a. There are few experiences quite so satisfactory as getting a good idea. You've had a problem, you've thought about it till you were tired, forgotten it and perhaps slept on it, and then flash! When you weren't thinking about it suddenly the answer has come to you, as a gift from the gods. You're pleased with it, and feel good. It may not be right, but at least you can try it out.

—Lancelot Law Whyte, *British philosopher and engineer*

b. You can't think too much about these pictures that shimmer [in your mind]. You just lie low and let them develop. You stay quiet.
—Joan Didion, *American essayist and novelist*

c. There may be fortunate writers with the ability to whip out a totally organized and coherent paper in as little time as it takes to write their thoughts down. I'm not one of those fortunate people. After I select my topic and before I start writing, I contemplate, by letting random thoughts about my idea just flow through my mind. This process helps me become better acquainted with the content of my paper and saves me the frustration of starting over and over.
—a student

d. . . . . I could show how a passage originally shaped itself when [I was] in bed, how it became transformed upon arising, and again transformed at the moment of sitting down to record it.
—Henry Miller, *American author*

e. I think about my topic and try to play it through my mind. If I like it, I write it down.
—a student

f. You lose friends who can't understand why you never seem to recognize them in the supermarket. (Supermarkets are good places for letting your mind wander.)
—Anne Tyler, *American novelist*

Observe yourself for several days and notice when your right brain seems to be most active: perhaps when you're driving, or sitting in the bathtub, or just before you go to sleep or right when you wake up. Then, think of something you might be interested in writing about and set your mind to thinking about that topic. Keep a pad of paper and pencil handy, and jot down several pages of random notes as ideas come to you, to see how productive your right brain can be.

EXERCISE 4   FOR THOUGHT AND ACTION

Virginia Woolf says that to write, you need a "room of your own." Do you have that kind of privacy for the writing you need to do? If you don't, think about what you might do to make your writing place more isolated, and hence a better environment for the kind of concentration writing requires. Can you rather easily do something about whatever ideas you come up with? If so, will you?

EXERCISE 5   FOR THOUGHT AND ACTION

How good are you at dealing with intrusions on your writing time? Let's say you are a mother of young children who is going to school at night, and one of your friends wants you to watch her children from 9 till 4, "since you're just sitting home all day." Or your boss wants you to work overtime three nights a week, although overtime work was not mentioned when you took the job. Or a friend, who knows you have a major paper due in sociology class tomorrow, calls up and pushes you to go out for a hamburger. Can you say "no" when you need to work on your writing? If not, how can you train yourself into that kind of self-discipline? How much do you want to do so? How does how you feel about your writing affect all this?

EXERCISE 6   FOR THOUGHT AND ACTION

How one goes about writing is likely to reflect, in some ways, certain personality traits. Certain traits can stand in the way of one's being able to write. For example, perfectionism can lead one to try *too* hard; a high level of physical energy can make one too restless to sit down for very long; being interested in a wide range of diverse things can make it difficult to settle down to the single activity of writing; and so on. Think about whether any of these or something like them might make writing hard for you. If you hit upon any insights during this writing self-analysis, can you think of ways to overcome your particular obstacle? Make a list of whatever ideas occur to you and try to apply them the next time you need to write.

EXERCISE 7   FOR THOUGHT

If you have a hard time remembering to jot down ideas for a piece of writing, try to imagine going into a large supermarket to buy a week's worth of groceries without a grocery list. There you are, in that huge world of the supermarket—and you don't know where to begin, nor where to go after that, you can't remember what you need, you're so confused you feel almost paralyzed, maybe you panic. Right in the middle of your fantasy, remember that all this can also happen to you when everything else important in your world is competing for your attention—and you need to write. Those jottings you might have done would then help you out, in the same way a grocery list would have helped you out in the supermarket.

I used to worry considerably about my writing. Yes, I used to fret, but that was out of fear. Now, though, I have enormous confidence because I know that I can always rewrite it.

—Toni Morrison

CHAPTER 2
WRITING AND REWRITING

WRITING: SITTING DOWN TO IT

Let's get you into your writing place, at a good writing time, surrounded by whatever makes you feel at home. You have your supplies and reference books at hand. And before you is that blank sheet of paper. . . .

But you have something else, too, if you have been heeding our advice. Remember those bits and pieces of paper on which you've been jotting down ideas? Now you can congratulate yourself for collecting them, for all those "notes to yourself" are about to become a content list for your paper.

Pull your scattered ideas together on a sheet or two of paper, so you can think about them all at once. Don't worry about making a neat list; keep yourself free to play around. On page 12, for example, is what one student's list looked like.

Once this student had pulled her scattered ideas together, she was ready to begin to focus and organize her material. As she began to see the point she wanted to make with her content, she scratched out items not related to that point and added any new, related items she could think of. Then she rearranged the items by numbering. When she had finished, her list looked like the one on page 13.

This kind of informal "thinking in ink" will give you control as you write your rough draft, and it will make that blank sheet of paper look a lot less threatening.

Sometimes you may not have a collection of scratch-paper items to work from. Then how will you get underway? One way is to plunge right in. If the idea you have for a paper has not been generating bits and pieces for you, try some "free writing." You may be surprised at what happens once you get your pen or pencil *moving* on that piece of paper.

W. S. Merwin speaks in one of his poems of all that lies hidden and

Causes of child abuse--unwanted births
                          frustration with
                            small children
                        poverty
                        alcohol
                        others--??

Kinds of CA--physical
              emotional/psychological
              sexual

Extent--all social classes
          not ethnically determined
          all economic levels
          may vary according to socioeconomic
            level

How prevent--pre-parent education
              counselling of parents
              improve social conditions,
                generally

              legal implications in
                attempts at prevention
              difficulty in getting pre-
                parents and parents to
                cooperate

Use: example(s) from my ambulance runs to
      emergency room of hospital--plus
      stories I hear from my coworkers

Focus: (*Physical*)
Focus: Child abuse: Causes and methods of prevention

① Causes of child abuse--unwanted births
   frustration with
      small children ← *handle together*
   poverty
   ⎡alcohol
   ⎣others--??
   emptiness of lives of some parents
   projection- anger from work
   gets displaced on children

   Kinds of CA-- (physical) ← *restrict to this*
      emotional/psychological
      sexual
   Degrees - ranges from bruises (from beating)
      to broken limbs to cuts, third-
      degree burns, etc.   *use vivid examples as an opening device*
   ~~Extent--all social classes~~
      ~~not ethnically determined~~
      ~~all economic levels~~   *— off my focus*
      ~~may vary according to socioeconomic~~
      ~~level~~

② How prevent--pre-parent education (*a*)
      counselling of parents (*b*)
      improve social conditions,
         generally (*d*)

      ~~legal implications in~~   *would make*
         ~~attempts at prevention~~   *my*
      ~~difficulty in getting pre-~~   *discussion*
         ~~parents and parents to~~   *too long*
         ~~cooperate~~
      impose a fine on
         abusive parents - ? (c)

Use: example(s) from my ambulance runs to
      emergency room of hospital--plus
      stories I hear from my coworkers   13

unknown in a pencil. You can find out what may be hiding in your pencil (or pen) through free writing. Write down anything associated with your idea that comes into your head. Such free-association writing may yield words and phrases from which you can build a content list. And thus you are well on your way to a whole paper, from a different kind of start.

Now you're ready to write—whether you started from a scratch-paper list or by free writing. At this point, treat your paper as a *rough draft* that will be improved later. Don't worry about neatness and spelling and precise word choice, or even about sentence structure and grammar. Go with the flow, roughing out the paper, leaving blanks when you get stuck, moving forward without stopping. You can always fill in the blanks later, after the paper has begun to take shape. The trick, says writer Gene Olson, "is to keep the words flowing, rolling, sliding onto the paper. You're *creating* at this stage, not being picky-picky. Go with the flow, then push it a little, just sort of nudge it along. Before your eyes, a few words turn into a sentence, a sentence into a paragraph and a paragraph into a composition . . . in the rough."

As you write your rough draft it's a good idea to double space if you're typing or to write on every other line if you're writing longhand. That way you'll have room between the lines for small changes you may want to make later. And you should leave margins, again so you'll have space in which to experiment with improvements.

GETTING DISTANCE

A first, rough draft is seldom an acceptable piece of writing. Even professional writers cannot control their rough drafts perfectly, so they take their writing through several drafts, or revisions. You will need to do so too.

But how do you decide what revisions your rough draft needs? Like most writers, once you have finished a rough draft you probably feel too close to it to view it objectively. So you'll need to get "distance" from your writing. You'll need, somehow, to begin to see your paper as if you hadn't written it—as if you were your reader.

Getting distance from one's own writing is not easy, even for professionals. But you will be able to achieve some objectivity toward your writing if you try. One way to get distance is to allow your paper to cool off, preferably overnight, or even for a few days. After this cooling-off period, go back and read your paper as if it were someone else's. The hard-to-read parts will confuse even you; you'll begin to see what changes are needed.

Another way to get distance is to read your paper aloud, or better yet, have someone else read it aloud to you. When you hear your own words spoken by another voice, it's easier to pretend that someone else wrote the paper. Problems with clarity and with sentence flow will show up vividly when your reader stumbles over a sentence, or misreads it.

One of the best ways to get distance from your writing is to ask some-one else—a friend, spouse, parent, or teacher—to serve as your reader. Choose someone whose judgment you trust, preferably someone who will level with you, who is not afraid of losing your friendship by re-sponding honestly to your writing. Ask this person to be hard on you, to tell you where your paper is unclear or sounds awkward or is otherwise hard to read.

At this point, right before you are ready to begin rewriting your rough draft, you should probably ask yourself a tough question: "Is my paper *worth* rewriting?" Nothing is more depressing than trying to "perfect" a paper that you don't respect to begin with. If you feel sure you can't turn your rough draft into a paper that's worth reading, just throw it out and begin again. One professional writer claims that the most important piece of furniture in her office is a ten-gallon wastebasket. Her mistakes go into the wastebasket, sometimes with a dramatic hook shot. What doesn't go into the wastebasket is good enough to be rewritten.

REWRITING

Let's say that your paper is good enough to be rewritten. As you begin to rework the rough draft, make sure you have cutting and taping equip-ment close by, in case you need it: scissors and tape, or a stapler, and lots of clean paper. That way you won't have to waste time rewriting your rough draft over and over. You can cut up what you have and make a new rough draft by fastening the pieces to clean paper.

First decide whether you should delete anything from your paper. One of the hardest parts of rewriting is throwing out material that doesn't really belong. Train yourself to be merciless here. As Sir Arthur Quiller-Couch puts it, be prepared to "murder your darlings." No mat-ter how interesting a detail or an example or an idea may seem to you, if it is not clearly related to the main focus of your paper, then it must go.

Now that you've scratched out any material that doesn't belong, check to see if the remaining sentences and paragraphs are ordered in the best possible way. If not, reach for your scissors and tape or stapler. Cut apart the pieces and reassemble them until you get the order you want. Then read over your cut-and-taped version in search of possible gaps—places where new material may need to be written. And get to work on that.

Let's see how the rewriting process worked for one student as he wrote a paper in favor of the legalization of marijuana. We'll look at just one paragraph from the paper, a paragraph arguing that marijuana does not lead to hard drugs. Here is the student's rough draft version of the paragraph:

> As an argument against legalizing marijuana, it has been said that marijuana usage leads to hard drugs such as heroin, LSD, and cocaine. This is a myth. A marijuana user doesn't necessarily turn to hard drugs any more than an alcohol drinker necessarily becomes an alcoholic. You do not build a tolerance to marijuana, so it is not necessary, after a period of time, to move to stronger drugs to obtain the same effect you received smoking marijuana. As a matter of fact, the stronger drugs give totally different effects than marijuana. Some marijuana users do move on to use harder drugs, whereas some drug addicts have never smoked marijuana at all. It depends on the individual and is a matter of preference. Just as some drinkers prefer beer, wine or hard liquor, some drug users prefer hard drugs because of the different effect. Using marijuana has little connection with the use of hard drugs.

As he read over his rough draft with a critical eye, the student decided that this paragraph was not likely to convince people who did not already agree with its main point. He decided that his rambling comparisons between alcohol and marijuana were especially unconvincing. So he began revising the paragraph by crossing out the weak parts:

> As an argument against legalizing marijuana, it has been said that marijuana usage leads to hard drugs such as heroin, LSD, and cocaine. This is a myth. ~~A marijuana user doesn't necessarily turn to hard drugs any more than an alcohol drinker~~

~~necessarily becomes an alcoholic.~~ You do
not build a tolerance to marijuana, so it is
not necessary, after a period of time, to
move to stronger drugs to obtain the same
effect you received smoking marijuana. As
a matter of fact, the stronger drugs give
totally different effects than marijuana.
Some marijuana users do move on to use
harder drugs, ~~whereas some drug addicts have
never smoked marijuana at all. It depends
on the individual and is a matter of
preference. Just as some drinkers prefer
beer, wine or hard liquor, some drug users
prefer hard drugs because of the different
effect. Using marijuana has little connection with the use of hard drugs.~~

Having crossed out much of his original paragraph, the student next
decided that he needed to add new material to support his point. There
was not enough space on the page to write in this new material, so he
cut out the sentences he wanted to keep and taped them to clean paper.
He then set about writing a stronger, more convincing finish for the
paragraph:

As an argument against legalizing
marijuana, it has been said that marijuana
usage leads to hard drugs such as heroin,
LSD, and cocaine. This is a myth.

You do
not build a tolerance to marijuana, so it is
not necessary, after a period of time, to
move to stronger drugs to obtain the same
effect you received smoking marijuana. As
a matter of fact, the stronger drugs give
totally different effects than marijuana.
Some marijuana users do move on to use
harder drugs, *but this does not
prove that smoking marijuana
caused them to turn to
harder drugs. After all, some*

drinkers experiment with hard drugs, but no one suggests that drinking leads them to these drugs. It is true that marijuana smokers, since they must buy illegally -- usually from sources that can also supply heroin, LSD, and cocaine -- have a unique opportunity to purchase hard drugs. But if marijuana were legalized, this would no longer be true.

Although we've shown you the rewriting of just one paragraph, the same process works for rewriting a whole paper. First decide what to get rid of; next arrange what's left; and finally write in whatever new parts seem needed. You may want to take your paper through the "getting distance" procedure again after rewriting it, to check your new version for clarity and general readability.

SOME FINAL NOTES

Obviously there is much more to writing and rewriting than we have covered in this short chapter. All the rest of this book is intended to help you as you write and rewrite. As you learn more about focusing and organizing and paragraphing, you'll be better able to cut and paste your efforts into a workable rough draft that may need only polishing and proofreading. In the meantime, even before you've read the rest of the book, we suggest that you keep an imaginary reader looking over your shoulder whenever you write. That reader will tell you what to delete, what to rearrange, and what to add.

We have tried to discuss the writing/rewriting process so that you can follow it step by step. But we know you won't always follow the steps in just the way we've presented them. Because writing is an act unique to each individual, there are as many different ways to go about putting a piece of writing together as there are writers. We like what Ezra Pound has to say here: "It doesn't matter which leg of your table you make first, so long as the table has four legs and will stand up solidly when you have finished it." You will discover which leg it is easiest for *you* to make first, as you write—and write. We say "as you write—and write" because you will soon realize that nothing reinforces good writing like writing.

EXERCISE 1 CLASSROOM ACTIVITY

As a class, select a topic from part 7 and brainstorm the topic on the blackboard. Call out everything you can think of about the topic, with no one commenting on any items at this point. Once everyone's ideas are on the board, study the list, and consider whether anything should be deleted. Consider also whether anything needs to be added to the list. Then discuss in what order the items might be used in a paper and number them accordingly. If some items should be used as minor details to develop major points, letter those items to show their relationship to the paper as a whole.

EXERCISE 2 FOR THOUGHT AND DISCUSSION

If the idea of *rewriting*—perhaps even several drafts—sounds like just too much trouble to you, maybe the following comments by both professional writers and successful student writers will help to convince you. Think about the comments and be ready to talk about them in class.

a. What is written without effort is in general read without pleasure.
   —Samuel Johnson, *British writer and critic*

b. The best reason for putting anything down on paper is that one may then change it.
   —Bernard de Voto, *American writer*

c. There is no such thing as good writing, only good rewriting.
   —Louis Brandeis, *Supreme Court Justice*

d. I read my paper over and over. I think about it a lot. I use a great deal of paper. I rewrite and rewrite until it says what I want it to say.
   —a student

e. I have never thought of myself as a good writer. . . . But I'm one of the world's great rewriters.
   —James Michener, *American writer*

   f. Easy writing makes hard reading.
                               —Ernest Hemingway, *American novelist*

   g. My goal in everything I write is simplicity. I'm a demon on the
      subject of revision. I revise, revise, revise, until every word is the one
      I want.
                        —Ben Lucien Berman, *American author*

   h. I can't write five words but that I change seven.
                          —Dorothy Parker, *American writer*

   i. I keep rereading what I have written, making changes where needed.
     I do this about six or seven times until I feel it is right.
                                   —a student

   j. Writing and rewriting are a constant search for what it is one is
    saying.
                     —John Updike, *American novelist*

   k. He would scratch and then put in a word and scratch and work and
    then paste on another piece of paper and the whole thing would be
    new. And then when the typed script would come he was still working
    on it.
                  —Raphael Hamilton, about J.R.R. Tolkien

EXERCISE 3   FOR DISCUSSION AND ACTION

Professional writers tell us that rewriting is an essential part of the writing
process. But in spite of all the talk about the importance of rewriting, most
writers—especially beginning writers—are tempted not to rewrite. If you find
yourself tempted to skip the rewriting stage, try to discover *why*. Our students, when urged to be honest on an anonymous poll, came up with this
list of reasons. Are any of these *your* reasons?

    1. I wait until the last minute, so there's no time to rewrite.
    2. My first draft is the best I can do. I can't improve it.
    3. I don't know whether my first draft is any good or not, so how can I
       improve it?
    4. I don't know where to begin, and I wouldn't know when to stop.
    5. Well, frankly, I'm lazy.
    6. When I tinker with my sentences, they just turn out worse.
    7. I don't really care about what I'm writing, so I just want to get it
       over with.
    8. Rewriting is too messy. I like to work with clean looking pages.
    9. I'm such a bad writer I hate to read my own writing.
   10. Rewriting is my instructor's responsibility.
   11. Rewriting is painful. I can't stand the agony.
   12. If I can't get it right the first time, I must be stupid.

What can you *do* to overcome the temptation not to rewrite? Will you do
that?

EXERCISE 4 FOR WRITING AND DISCUSSION

The famous French writer Stendhal once said: "I see but one rule: To be clear." What do you think of Stendhal's remark? Is it possible that a single such rule could be applied to test one's writing? If not, what else would you require of "good writing," and why? Write out your answer and bring it to class for discussion.

EXERCISE 5 WRITTEN

The next time you hand in a paper, attach to it a list of your own concerns about the paper, for your instructor to respond to during his or her evaluation. Making such a list can help you to get distance from your paper. Handing in this page of questions and comments can be helpful to both you and your instructor, as it establishes a sort of mini-dialogue about the paper.

EXERCISE 6 JUST FOR FUN

I've always tried out my material on my dogs first. You know, with Angel, he sits there and listens and I get the feeling that he understands everything. But with Charley, I always felt that he was just waiting to get a word in edgewise.

—John Steinbeck, *American novelist*

Blot out, correct, insert, refine,
Enlarge, diminish, interline;
Be mindful, when invention fails,
To scratch your head, and bite your nails.
—Jonathan Swift

CHAPTER 3
FINISHING UP

POLISHING

When your reworded paper says pretty much what you want it to say,
you are ready to think about some finer points—ready to "polish" your
writing. We suggest you work on polishing only after dealing with the
larger problems we discuss under writing and rewriting in chapter 2; if
you try to do your polishing too early, you will probably neglect something really important in your first, major revisions.

Polishing consists of a variety of improvements in sentence structure
and wording. Here, for example, are two rough-draft paragraphs from
our first chapter as they appeared after they were polished:

While you are doing your creative thinking,
While ~~you are thinking creatively,~~
~~your content is playing around in~~
~~your head during any of these times, you~~
random
~~will find it useful to~~ make some ~~little~~
whatever scratch paper are is
notes on ~~bits and pieces of whatever writing~~
~~surface is~~ available at the moment, ~~oso keep~~
~~something available.~~ Don't worry ~~here~~ about
at this stage;
organizing your thoughts; just be sure to

write down enough so ~~that~~ you can decode it

~~when you need it~~ later. ~~Most of us forget~~

~~quickly.~~

     Getting *this much* ~~something~~ down on paper at

once, *as the thoughts are flowing, will help you* ~~may prove invaluable to you~~ when you *later*

finally sit down to write. Professional

writers ~~know this, so they~~ scribble ideas

on the backs of envelopes, on recipe cards

or paper bags, *or cocktail napkins* or scraps of cardboard--on

whatever happens to be *handy* ~~around~~ at the time.

Anne Tyler, a writer and mother of two,

remarks: ~~says:~~ "In the evenings occasionally--

between baths and other sorts of chaos--a

sudden idea will flash into my mind. . . I

write it down and take it to my study."

    An important part of polishing is deleting excess words. In our sample rough-draft paragraphs, for example, this word-heavy sentence appeared:

    While your content is playing around in your head during any of these times, you will find it useful to make some little notes on bits and pieces of whatever writing surface is available at the moment, so keep something available.

Without losing an ounce of meaning, we cut the sentence in half:

    While you are doing your creative thinking, make some random notes on whatever scratch paper is available at the moment.

This shorter sentence, relieved of the clutter of excess words, is easier to read. It is also more pleasing to the ear.

Following are several student sentences that have been revised for wordiness:

The bus driver had already made the

blacks ~~get up and give~~ *relinquish* their seats to

whites. I took one look at the weary old

black woman and ~~asked~~ *offered* her ~~to take~~ my seat.

Through the years I have come to enjoy

several ~~different~~ kinds of sports. ~~or exercise~~

~~type activities.~~

Was the water ~~really~~ colored in the

"COLORED ONLY" fountain or did it taste

~~entirely~~ different?

My first time at bat I struck out, and

every time after that, *because* ~~This was probably~~

~~due to the fact that~~ I would swing at any-

thing that came my way.

As you work to delete excess words, you'll probably notice words that need changing for one reason or another. Maybe you used the word "attire" when the more ordinary word "clothing" would have sounded better; or perhaps you wrote "friend" when "benefactor" would have

been more precise. You may have any number of reasons for deciding
to change a word, as you can see from the examples below:

1. The ~~instance~~ *incident* with that evil-looking

   person on the train left me speechless

   with fear. (incorrect word choice)

2. Already the gale-force winds ~~came~~ *roared*

   through the walls. (more vivid verb)

3. Until recently, ~~those individuals~~ *college graduates*

   ~~fortunate enough to further their~~

   ~~knowledge with a college education~~ were

   always in demand. (pretentious language

   --and wordy too)

4. The ~~loud~~ *raucous* cry of the seagulls greeted us

   as we neared the shore. (more precise

   adjective)

5. The nurse is our ~~middleman.~~ *link with the doctors.* (sexist

   language)

6. The plainclothes officers ~~reinstated~~ *restated*

   their demand that we leave with them.

   (incorrect word choice)

7. The ~~pecking~~ *rat-a-tat-tat* of a woodpecker, mixed with

    ^*the buzzing of* insects, ~~dashing about,~~ woke me early

    during our mountain camping trip.

    (eliminates awkward repetitions of

    "peck" and unlikely image of "dashing"

    insects)

8. According to my psychology textbook,

    there are *reasons* ~~components in why~~ we tend to

    like one person better than another.

    (jargon)

9. The doctors I worked with all had very

    lucrative ~~expensive~~ practices.   (incorrect word

    choice)

10. *Tension* ~~Emotion~~ began to build as the union

    committee debated the wage-and-inflation

    spiral.   (more specific word for exact

    emotion felt)

Just as you may have different reasons for changing words, you may
have a variety of reasons for deciding to restructure sentences. A restructured sentence might be clearer, or more forceful, or more emphatic, or
more rhythmic than the original. A restructured sentence might connect
more smoothly with the sentences that came before, or point more

clearly to the sentences that come after. To give you a feel for the variety of reasons you might have for changing sentences, we print the following "polished" sentences from students' rough drafts:

1. We agreed ~~to the idea it~~ *that the arrival and departure of the Concorde* must have been

   an impressive sight ~~to have seen the Concorde arrive and depart~~. (more

   forceful, more rhythmic--and less wordy)

2. ~~The thunderous roar of~~ The waves ~~can be heard as they~~ crash into the stone

   breakers / *with a thunderous roar.* (more vigorous, more

   emphatic)

3. This is the first day of Carnival in

   Trinidad, West Indies // ~~This~~ *-- a* celebration

   that occurs two days prior to Ash Wednesday

   each year. (deletes full repetition of

   "This" as sentence opener; emphasizes

   second half of new sentence)

4. Many people think that ~~all that has to~~ *to reforest*

   ~~be done to have a forest to regrow is to~~

   you can just stick some trees in the ground, ~~and~~ come

back in a couple of years, and ~~the~~
find a full-grown forest.
/~~forest will be there.~~   (smoother, more

balanced)

5.   Slowly *I realized* ~~the realization had taken place~~

that this was something I could not

control.   (more direct)

6.   The exhausted merrymakers drag them-

selves home, thinking about what
they will portray
character/or whose band they will ~~be~~

play~~ing~~ in next year.   (added words

needed to make sentence complete and

clear)

7.   The officers told us that someone ~~was~~
in our seating section)
~~throwing particles of~~ ice from the
had been
~~vicinity of our seats,~~ pelting the

innocent fans ~~down~~ below.   (more

straightforward, less pretentious)

With polishing done, you are ready to type or hand write your final
draft. Then, only one task remains before your paper is finished: It is a
very important if not a very exciting task—proofreading.

PROOFREADING

Proofreading is a slow and careful reading in search of errors that you
overlooked when you were struggling with more important matters. As

you proofread you will look for mispunctuation, spelling mistakes, words left out, word endings left off, capital letters misused, and such problems as subject-verb misagreement, faulty pronoun references, misplaced modifiers, and so on.

Many students have difficulty proofreading. Several times a semester we hear comments like this one, from a frustrated student: "I've tried proofreading, but I just don't see my own errors. When they're pointed out, the problems seem so obvious—so stupid. Why can't *I* catch them?"

One answer is that proofreading requires special reading skills. Your tendency when reading is to scan individual words quickly in search of the meaning of a whole passage. To proofread, you need to fight your ordinary reading habits. Since the purpose of proofreading is not to grasp meaning, but to spot errors, you need to pay more attention to surfaces than to content when you proofread. This special kind of reading is difficult, because your usual reading habits keep pulling your attention away from the errors you are trying to spot. Professional proofreaders become skilled only through practice, and with practice you too can improve.

The best way to proofread is to read your paper out loud, making yourself say aloud *exactly* what is on the page—not just what you intended to write there. If you read this way, slowly and deliberately, word by word, your ear will often tell you that you've added an unnecessary comma, dropped a letter from a word, or left out an entire word. When you read silently, these errors can slip right past you.

It helps, when you're proofreading, if you know what you're looking for. If you make a great many mechanical and grammatical errors, you may have trouble proofreading because you have to look for too many things at once, and because you're probably not sure when you've made an error. If this is your problem, talk to your instructor about it. The two of you working together can identify your most common errors and invent a style of proofreading that will work for you. You may decide, for example, to proofread several times, perhaps once for spelling, once for punctuation, and once for omitted words or word endings.

The handbook section of this book will serve as a "reference book" to help you as you proofread. There you will find a more detailed explanation of how to proofread for punctuation and for spelling, as well as much information about correcting other kinds of mechanical and grammatical errors. We suggest that you scan the handbook carefully enough now that you will know just what you can find there when you need help.

As we mentioned earlier, proofreading is not the most exciting part of the writing process, but it is nevertheless a very important part. The errors that careful proofreading can catch often jumble your meaning, thus confusing readers and quickly diminishing their respect for your writing. They suggest too much haste and too little care. Such errors say to a reader: "Apparently the writer did not have much respect for this piece of writing, so why should I?" If you are interested in what you have to say and proud of how you say it, you won't allow distracting errors to mar your writing.

We know that the writing process may not occur quite as systematically as we have suggested in the last three chapters. We have deliberately divided the procedure into definable steps, so that we could talk about everything that might need attention as you rework your early drafts. But certainly you may spot a misspelled word at the same time that you are considering reorganization. So much the better. But we would caution you against consciously trying to deal with all the big questions and all the little errors at once. That can get to be overwhelming and counterproductive.

LETTING IT GO

After so much serious talk about reworking your paper, we want to be sure to warn you against perfectionism. It is possible to worry a paper to death: Are my sentences varied enough? Shall I use this word or that one here? A comma or not there? A writer needs to know when to quit —when to release his or her writing to the world, to let it go.

Perhaps there is a fine line between not caring enough about your writing and caring too much. We don't know how to help you draw that line. But it is only fair to warn you that if you are a perfectionist in other areas of your life, you may tend to be the same way toward your writing. Our best advice here: Just remember that there is no such thing as a perfect piece of writing; there will always be alternative ways to handle every part of it. Just try to make your writing clear, readable, and at least somewhat interesting—a piece of work you yourself can reasonably respect. Then, let it go.

EXERCISE 1 FOR WRITING AND ACTION

Analyze exactly how you go about doing a piece of writing. Try to look at every separate step in your writing process and list all of this on paper. Then, go back over your list to see if there are any places where you might usefully experiment with some different ways of working. What might you change and how? Will you make any of these changes?

EXERCISE 2 CLASSROOM ACTIVITY

Bring to class the list you made in exercise 1. Talk with another person or in a small group, exchanging ideas about how each of you writes and how each might improve his or her writing process.

EXERCISE 3 CLASSROOM ACTIVITY

Interview someone you know who does quite a lot of writing, either on the job or in college. Find out from this person in as much detail as possible how he or she approaches writing tasks. In conducting your interview, you might use the following questions as guides:

1. Do you type rough drafts, write them in longhand, or dictate them to a secretary or into a machine?
2. Are you addicted to any sort of paper and pen?
3. How do you organize your ideas—in your head or on paper? Do you use outlines, and if so, how formal are they?
4. How do you go about rewriting, if you do rewrite? Do you use "scissors and paste"?
5. Do you have someone read what you have written, get advice, and then rewrite? Or do you handle it all on your own?
6. How do you go about editing your writing? Or do you do this at all?
7. Do you use a dictionary, a book of synonyms, a thesaurus, a grammar handbook, or any other kind of writer's reference book?

Bring the results of your interview to class and be prepared to share them with the group. If possible, also bring a page or two of rough copy from the person you interviewed, so other members of the class can get some sense of what your writer's in-process writing looks like. Be prepared to tell why, for what exact purpose, your writer writes.

EXERCISE 4 CLASSROOM ACTIVITY

Bring the rough draft of a paper you are working on (a paper in process) to class. Then, working with one other student, read each other's rough drafts aloud and try to spot sentences in need of polishing, either for clarity or for smoothness. As your partner reads your paper aloud, mark any problem sentences. Then go off by yourself to polish those problem sentences. Ask your partner to read your new version to check on its clarity and smoothness.

EXERCISE 5 FOR THOUGHT AND DISCUSSION

The following story circulates around Washington, D.C.: Shortly after a certain assistant was hired in the State Department, he was assigned to write a position paper on a particular subject. On the due date, the assistant delivered his paper to the then–Secretary of State, who immediately wanted to know whether the paper was the assistant's best work. The assistant had to confess that it might not be, and was told by his boss: "I want your best work. Bring it in tomorrow." On the second delivery, he was greeted by the same question. This time he answered: "I don't honestly believe I can write a better paper on this subject." "Fine," said the Secretary of State. "In that case, I'll read it." Question: Is it reasonable for any reader of any piece of writing to expect to be reading the writer's very best possible work? Or is that an unrealistic expectation in some writing situations? If so, what are some of these situations?

PART II

Writing with a Voice

The personality I am expressing in this written sentence is not the same as the one I orally express to my three-year-old who at this moment is bent on climbing onto my typewriter. For each of these two situations, I choose a different "voice," a different mask, in order to accomplish what I want accomplished.

—Walker Gibson

CHAPTER 4
CHOOSING A VOICE

Each time you write you will need to choose a voice. The right voice will be one you're comfortable with, one that suits your personality. But more than that, it will be a voice appropriate for your *purpose* in writing and for the particular *audience* you have in mind. As Walker Gibson says, a writing voice is the "mask" you put on to accomplish what you want accomplished.

Before you can don the right mask, you need to know what you want to accomplish. Only when you understand why you are writing (your *purpose*) and who you are writing to (your *audience*) will you be able to choose an appropriate writing voice.

Your writing situation usually provides you with both a purpose and an audience. Think of on-the-job writing situations, for example. Usually your audience will be quite clear: Perhaps it is your supervisor, a client, a board of directors, or your coworkers. And you will nearly always know why you are writing: Maybe to inform your supervisor about a workshop he or she did not attend; to ask a client to pay an outstanding bill; to present next year's budget request to the board of directors; or to encourage coworkers to cooperate with you in implementing an affirmative action plan.

For such writing situations, with a given purpose and audience, common sense tells you what writing voice to adopt. You might decide to sound businesslike in the memo to your supervisor; diplomatic, but firm, in the letter to the client; impersonal and objective in the budget request; personable and persuasive in the letter to your coworkers.

A PROBLEM WITH FRESHMAN ENGLISH

Freshman English presents you with a special problem because you are not automatically supplied with a purpose and an audience, as you are in most real-life writing situations. And without a purpose and audience, you will have no way of determining your writing voice.

You may seem to have a specific audience—your instructor—and a clear purpose—to impress that instructor with your writing ability. But that is not the sort of purpose and audience that will help you write with a distinct voice. If you write papers merely to impress your instructor, you'll almost always write with a confused voice.

Consider, for example, the following paper, written for freshman English class at the very beginning of the semester. From the student's point of view, the paper didn't have a real purpose; it was just an assignment, after all. And there was no real audience; it was written for an instructor. The result is a paper with a confused voice:

> *Psycho*, directed by Alfred Hitchcock, is an excellent movie. This contemporary classic is seen occasionally on television and is re-released to movie theatres quite often. Probably the most well-known scene from *Psycho* is the one in which Janet Leigh is murdered. In this scene and throughout the entire film, Hitchcock combines suspense, symbolism and an ingenious plot.
>
> It is advisable to see *Psycho* more than once. Many seemingly obscure details will become important after the second viewing. Hitchcock's twists and turns make *Psycho* a truly exciting movie.

The voice in this paper is confused because the writer hasn't decided on a specific purpose and a real audience. Think about it for a minute. What audience do you think the writer had in mind as she wrote the paper? Was she writing for a general audience interested in hearing about an exciting, suspense-filled movie? Or was she writing for intellectual readers interested in the film's artistic merits? It's hard to tell. She tells readers that *Psycho* is an excellent movie; a famous classic; an artistic film with suspense, symbolism, and an ingenious plot; a film so complex it requires several viewings; and an exciting movie. But notice that none of these messages has been developed. Readers truly interested in hearing about the film's complexity, or those who'd like a vivid description of the "well-known scene in which Janet Leigh is murdered" are disappointed. The paper mentions these points and others, then drops them all.

The writer couldn't decide what to tell her audience because she's not sure who her audience is. Nor did the writer have any clear understanding of her purpose in telling readers about *Psycho*. Was she trying to get them so excited about the film that they'd rush out to see it? Or was she analyzing the film for them so they'd understand it better, the way you might analyze a poem by Emily Dickinson or a play by George Bernard Shaw?

SUPPLYING A PURPOSE AND AN AUDIENCE

Unless you supply a purpose and an audience for each paper you write, you'll have trouble writing with a distinct voice. So if you're writing about the junk food in the vending machines at your child's school, don't tell your instructor about it. Aim your paper at other parents, and write with a real purpose—to get the parents to help you take action against the junk food. Or, if you're contrasting the merits of the Suzuki and the Harley-Davidson, write to readers who are interested in buying motorcycles; help them decide how to spend their money. When you write to real readers, for a real purpose, you'll be writing with a voice.

When we say you should supply a real purpose and a real audience, we are asking you to imagine a writing situation. If you're giving advice on the care of hanging ferns, imagine readers who don't know how to care for them but want to learn. Or, if you think you have the secret to success in tennis, imagine that your readers are tennis players eager to improve their game. Don't worry if your instructor is not a plant lover or a tennis nut. Your instructor is interested in your ability to communicate purposefully, not in your ability to figure out what he or she is interested in.

In part 7 of this book there are over two hundred writing topics. Some of these topics supply you with a purpose and an audience and thus help you to write with a distinct voice. For example: "If you know of some especially good community program for senior citizens, describe that program to readers who might be interested in taking advantage of it." This topic gives you a definite purpose for writing, and a specific audience. With that purpose and audience in mind, you'll have little trouble finding just the right voice for your paper. Here are a number of similar writing topics:

1. Inform your reader about some particular nutritional issue he or she is unlikely to know about—such as the dangers of nitrites or the need for fiber in the diet.
2. Take your reader on a tour of an art museum you have visited. Write the paper to encourage your reader to visit.
3. If you are very good at a team sport, summarize your qualifications to impress a coach or a scholarship committee.
4. If you have firsthand experience with some non-Protestant or non-Catholic religion in America (for example, Quaker, American Indian, Black Muslim, Jewish), explain some of the basic tenets of your religion to someone who knows nothing about it.
5. Show your reader that he or she can save money and be better off

nutritionally by substituting fresh foods for canned, frozen, or ready-mix foods.

6. Write an objective letter to one of your instructors suggesting changes he or she should make in his or her teaching. Assume that the instructor is interested in improving.

7. *The Coming of Age*, a book by Simone de Beauvoir, contains an interesting chapter on "old age in historical societies." Read this chapter and summarize it for someone who hasn't the time to read it.

8. Explain to someone who is skeptical of some type of avant-garde art, literature, or music why you feel certain works have merit.

Not all topics in part 7 supply a precise purpose and audience. Some are more open-ended, leaving room for your own invention. When you choose open-ended topics, you'll need to supply your own purpose and audience—in other words, to invent your own writing situation. For example, using the topic "Is Little League too competitive?" one writer aimed his paper at the parents involved in his son's local Little League team. For the topic "Interview someone who has an interesting or exciting job," another student directed her paper to readers who were considering police work as a career. Supplying real purposes and audiences helped these students to write with distinct, instead of confused, voices.

WRITING WITH A VOICE

Earlier in this chapter you read a student paper written in a confused voice, a paper without a specific purpose or a real audience. Now we invite you to listen to the voices of several students who were not just doing assignments. In each of these papers the student has found a distinct voice appropriate to a particular purpose, a voice that speaks directly to real readers.

In this paragraph you hear the voice of a person who wants to tell you all about a museum exhibit she enjoyed:

> Grab your most comfortable jeans and your tennis shoes. Pack a bag lunch and bring a deck of cards. You'll be waiting a long time.
> Where are we going? Why, we are going to see the King Tutankhamen exhibition at the National Gallery of Art.

Another student, who spent several years in Japan, plans to show us Westerners that our ways aren't always the best. Specifically, he'll use a persuasive voice to show us that the Japanese hot bath is much superior to the Western style of bathing:

For centuries the ritual of bathing in Japan has been second to none in the world. The Japanese word for hot bath is "ofuro," and until you have sampled this aspect of Japanese life, you really don't know anything about good healthy bathing habits. Once you have engaged in the art and the ritual of Japanese bathing, I'm sure you will never want to take a dirty Western bath again. You will be addicted to the clean Japanese "ofuro."

A third student writes, in a serious but friendly voice, about a new style of learning that he has experienced. His purpose is to show other students that this new "self-teaching" method has advantages:

Since this was my first semester in college, I was surprised to find that two out of my six classes were self-teaching courses. I had never attended, or even heard of, a self-teaching course before. But now that the semester is nearly over, I can give the self-teaching method a favorable evaluation.

Here is a writer who plans to entertain readers—in a lighthearted voice—with an honest glimpse of her secret afternoon activity:

Every afternoon that I am home and not otherwise occupied, I sneak down into the basement at one-thirty and hide there in the semi-darkness until three o'clock doing something that I really don't like to talk about. I have been doing this for more years than I care to say, and, I am forced to admit, there is no end in sight. I am a "closet viewer" of television soap operas.

And finally we hear the voice of a writer who wants to inform readers about her religion—not to persuade them to join it but to discourage them from stereotyping her faith.

You've heard of "Moonies" and "Jesus Freaks." Well, here's a religion you don't hear a lot about. It's called "Spiritualism." Spiritualism is not a current fad, but an old and misunderstood faith.

Like these students, you will be able to write with a voice once you've determined your purpose and your audience. But don't expect to sound like the same person every time you write. You might be an experienced mountain climber in one paper, an outraged victim of discrimination in another, the devoted parent of a retarded child in still another. Your writing voice, like your speaking voice, depends on your purpose and audience. When telling uninformed readers how to change a tire, you'll write with a straightforward, no-nonsense voice. But when sharing a hilarious adventure with readers, your voice will sparkle with personality. Whatever topics you choose, try writing for real. Try writing with a voice.

EXERCISE 1 FOR THOUGHT AND DISCUSSION

Writers often speak of the importance of the human voice behind a piece of writing. Here is what some have said. Think about their observations, in relation both to writing you have read and to your own writing.

a. False starts in writing are often failures to discover the right voice.
—Gerald Levin, *writing teacher*

b. . . . style usually means some form of fancy writing—when people say, oh yes, so and so is such a "wonderful stylist." But if one means by style the voice, the irreducible and always recognizable and alive thing, then of course style is everything.
—Mary McCarthy, *American author*

c. The audience fails to understand the writer because the writer has failed to understand the audience.
—Anonymous

d. The ideal reader of my novels is a lapsed Catholic and failed musician, short-sighted, colorblind, auditorily biased, who has read the books that I have read. He should also be about my age.
—Anthony Burgess, *British writer*

e. Who touches this book touches a human being.
—Walt Whitman, first page of *Leaves of Grass*

f. I've enjoyed writing in a course where I've been encouraged to experiment with my own voice. I didn't think I would because I never did enjoy English. I found out that I can do some things in writing that I never thought before I could.
—a student

EXERCISE 2 SMALL-GROUP ACTIVITY

This exercise is intended to help you find writing topics that will encourage you to write with a voice. Working with one or two other students, turn to the topics under one subject area in part 7—perhaps "violence and stress" or "parents and children" or "religion" or "sports." Choose a topic area that is of interest to all members of your group.

Starting with the first topic, discuss possible purposes and audiences for each topic. If you can't think of a purposeful approach to a topic, skip it and move on. Discuss as many topics as time allows. Keep your pace brisk so group members don't become bored. Remember, your goal is very practical. Each member of your group should leave this session with new ideas for writing with a voice.

EXERCISE 3 FOR CLASS DISCUSSION

Read the following student papers printed in part 8. Then identify the purpose and the audience of each paper.

So He's Driving You Crazy (#9)
"Popsicle" (#4)
Water-skiing to Signals (#10)
Light Action Today in South Viet Nam (#17)
A Dangerous State of Mind (#13)

EXERCISE 4 WRITTEN

From part 7 choose three topics that you think might work well for you. Then write a brief explanation of why you think these three topics would encourage you to write with a voice.

EXERCISE 5 FOR THOUGHT

Unless you can find writing topics that will work for *you*, you'll have a hard time writing with a voice. Wayne C. Booth, an English professor, tells a story that makes this point very well:

> Last fall I had an advanced graduate student, bright, energetic, well-informed, whose papers were almost unreadable. He managed to be pretentious, dull, and disorganized in his paper on *Emma*, and pretentious, dull, and disorganized on *Madame Bovary*. On *The Golden Bowl* he was all these and obscure as well. Then one day, toward the end of the term, he cornered me after class and said, "You know, I think you were all wrong about Robbe-Grillet's *Jealousy* today." We didn't have time to discuss it, so I suggested that he write me a note about it. Five hours later I found in my faculty box a four-page polemic, unpretentious, stimulating, organized, convincing. Here was a man who had taught freshman composition for several years and who was incapable of committing any of the more obvious errors that we think of as characteristic of bad writing. Yet he could not write a decent sentence, paragraph, or paper until . . . he had found a definition of his audience, his argument, and his own proper tone of voice.

When this graduate student finally found something he wanted to say—to someone who wanted who wanted to hear it—he could write with a voice.

"How am I to know," the despairing writer asks, "which the right word is?" The reply must be . . . "The wanted word is the one most nearly true. True to what? Your vision and your purpose."

—Elizabeth Bowen

CHAPTER 5

CHOOSING APPROPRIATE LANGUAGE

As a speaker, you command several varieties of English. When applying for a job or speaking to the congregation at church, you speak formally; but when you relax with friends on Saturday night, you relax your language as well. When explaining to your little brother, who knows nothing about the inner workings of automobiles, your latest modification of a VW engine, you use easy-to-understand, nontechnical English. But explain the same thing to your best friend, who has just modified his Corvette, and your language is suddenly filled with cams and crankshafts and cc.'s.

Among strangers you keep your language distant, but with your ingroup—people of your age, or your social class, or your ethnic or geographic background—you use language common to that group. If you're from Appalachia, you might talk one way to people from your part of the country and a slightly different way to outsiders. If you're an Afro-American or a Puerto Rican–American or a Mexican-American, you may have the ability to shift, depending on the situation, between an ethnic language and a more neutral language common to all.

Perhaps you come from a highly educated family around whom your grammar is perfect. If so, you probably tone down that perfect grammar when hanging out with friends from a different background. Or maybe you're a middle-aged veteran who has returned to college. On campus you make friends with a crowd of younger vets, and before long you find yourself picking up all their latest slang. When you get together socially with people your own age, you may throw in just enough of the new slang to be interesting, but not so much that you'll look like you're showing off.

42   In speaking, then, you have an amazing ability to choose, on the spot,

from a number of language varieties. It's as if you were computerized to judge every complex social situation in which you speak. Your computer gives you the answer immediately: it tells you how formal, how technical, how slangy, how ethnic, how intimate, how youthful, how class-conscious, how personal, how regional. Sometimes you may make mistakes; for example, you may speak too informally for the situation, or you may choose language too technical for your listeners. But on the whole your instincts—and those instincts of almost all native speakers of our language—are remarkably accurate.

Writing, like speaking, requires you to choose from among a number of language varieties. Often the same instinct that guides you as you speak will help you as you write—but not always, because writing and speaking are not quite the same.

When you write, your judgment may trip you up more often than when you speak. You are more likely to adopt a formal tone when an informal one would be more suitable; to use slang or jargon in situations where they're not appropriate; or to mix styles in odd ways. The question to ask yourself as you write is "What language is *appropriate* to the situation in which I am writing?" This chapter offers guidelines to help you answer that question for many writing situations in which you may find yourself.

FORMAL OR INFORMAL?

Sometimes you will want to write with a rather formal voice; other times, with a more informal one. Your writing situation determines the degree of formality. For example, you'll choose a relatively formal voice when writing a résumé to apply for a job, or when explaining your religious beliefs in a philosophy paper, or when arguing in a letter to the editor that a traffic light should be installed at a dangerous intersection. In such writing situations an informal voice would be inappropriate.

But there are also situations in which a formal voice would be inappropriate. In a letter to a friend or in a memo to a co-worker, a formal voice might sound too distant, too unfriendly. Or if you were describing your first blind date, or the absurdities of a soap opera, or the recent pranks of your six-year-old, a formal voice might sound pretentious.

To illustrate some of the differences between a formal and an informal voice, we'd like to share with you two items that appeared in the *Washington Post* just after Smokey the Bear died at the National Zoo. First read this excerpt from an informal article:

> Like many greats, Smokey [the] Bear had to pass on to get the attention he lacked in the declining years of his life.

Now, nothing is too good for the only animal in America with his own private zip code (20232). He was jetted out to Albuquerque yesterday in a specially made box painted forest green with handles on both sides, and a boulder in Smokey Bear Historical State Park will commemorate his passing.

· · · · ·

Even his wife, Goldie, was reconciled to him at the end. They had a pro forma marriage that even Ann Landers couldn't have saved, but Goldie alone was with him at the end. "She didn't want to leave, she had to be coaxed out," a zoo spokeswoman said. "It was very heartbreaking."

· · · · ·

He [Smokey] was discovered in June, 1950, a 5-pound cub clinging to a burnt tree in New Mexico's Capitan Mountains. A forest ranger's daughter nursed him back to health, fed him pablum, and catered to his penchant for sleeping in washing machines. As soon as he was healthy, he was flown to Washington in a plane with his picture painted on the fuselage and slotted to be the living symbol of a cartoon character a California agency had dreamed up five years earlier.

Smokey's popularity has been phenomenal. . . . his mail ran as high as 13,000 letters per week, enough to keep three people working full time dashing off answers over his pawprint.

Now read Smokey's obituary, written in the formal voice considered appropriate for an obituary:

Smokey Bear, an employee of the National Park Service from shortly after his birth until retirement last year, died in his sleep Monday night at his home in the National Zoo. He was 26.

"It was just old age," a Park Service spokeswoman said simply of Mr. Bear's demise. "When they went to check him this morning, they found he had died."

Mr. Bear was the zoo's best known resident, and was familiar to millions of Americans as the symbol of the national campaign to prevent forest fires. His deep but kindly bass voice was often heard over radio and television as he declaimed, "Remember, only you can prevent forest fires!" [He] was perhaps better known to Americans than any personality other than the president. A 1968 survey revealed that nine out of 10 citizens knew who Smokey Bear was.

A native of New Mexico, he was himself intimately familiar with the horrors of blazes in the woodlands of the nation. He was less than a year old when a park ranger found him in the smoking ruins of what had been a forest in New Mexico, and rescued Mr. Bear, who was suffering from a burned paw. Mr. Bear was flown to Santa Fe, New Mexico, and from there to Washington where he took up residence at the National Zoo.

Although he had no formal schooling, Mr. Bear was accepted into the Park Service shortly after his arrival in Washington, and remained with that agency until his retirement a year ago this month. . . . When he retired Mr. Bear was made a member of National Association of Retired Federal Employees and was given a membership card by that organization.

. . . . .

Mr. Bear was married in 1962 to the former Goldie Bear, who was not a blood relation, despite the similarity of last names. In 1971 the still childless couple adopted a youngster from New Mexico, whom they named Young Smokey. Last April, Young Smokey, who is now about 6 years old, took over for his father following Mr. Bear's retirement.

Mr. Bear is survived by his wife of the home in Washington; and the son, Young Smokey, also of the city.

Mr. Bear's body is being flown to New Mexico for burial.

These two pieces of writing, dealing with essentially the same subject matter, illustrate some differences between informal and formal English. The first article reads like many other newspaper stories: It is written in informal, easy-to-read "journalese"; it refers to its subject throughout by the name he was generally known by; it reports facts, but it also attempts to involve the reader by including some "human interest" details—rather than holding off the reader as an obituary would be expected to do.

The obituary, on the other hand, is written in a more formal and "distanced" manner. The sentences are short and direct; the deceased is referred to formally as "Mr. Bear"; and no extraneous information is allowed to creep in. The obituary merely informs the reader of facts about the life and death of Smokey the Bear, as obituaries are supposed to do.

Even the headlines for these two items prepare the reader for their intended effects; the article is entitled "Smokey's Enduring Appeal," while the obituary is headed "S. Bear, Fire Fighter," citing the occupation of the deceased, as is often done in obituary headlines.

When you write, you'll want to adjust your writing voice to fit what you are trying to accomplish. This means that you'll probably write formally in some situations, informally in others. One student, for example, chose formal language for the paper in which this paragraph appeared:

Black women, for the most part, have been forced into roles of strength in the man-woman relationship, while many white women have been forced into a more passive role; I see our struggles as women, therefore, as separate. Each group seems to be struggling toward the other's position. She, the white woman, strives to come out of her shelter; I, the black woman, seek sanctuary in the shelter she has had.

Because this paper presents an argument, the writer's sentences are complex and carefully structured; her language is precisely chosen. Her writing voice matches her purpose in writing.

In another paper, this same student writes more informally, in a simpler, more direct style appropriate for a personal remembrance. She uses plain, everyday vocabulary and writes almost conversational sentences:

> I know what it is to be denied a childhood. For me it begins at age
> ten. My mother, who has been reunited with my father for approximately
> two years, leaves him again. She now has two girls to support alone, one
> ten years old and another nine months. She is uneducated and unskilled.
> She works—sick or well—long, laborious hours doing day-work for little pay.
> The pittance she makes each day is budgeted into many portions—milk
> for the baby, food for dinner, payment for the babysitter, carfare for
> work the next day, lunch money for me, "savings" toward the weekly
> rent. There is absolutely no money for entertainment, clothes or extras.
> We cook, eat and sleep in rented rooms, moving often.
>
> Each day when Mother leaves for work I am afraid I will never see her
> again, for it seems that every day someone is either raped or murdered
> on the tenement rooftops, hit and killed by a bus, or dragged from the
> river. I am never sure where she works because more than half the time
> she doesn't know beforehand herself. She first goes to the Employment
> Agency to be "sent out."
>
> I reach the ugly stage. Baby beauty becomes the adolescent uglies. My
> sister Marie replaces me as the lovely new baby-doll. And I become mother
> to her, cheated now of my adolescence, as well as having missed my
> childhood.

"IN-GROUP" OR STANDARD?

Years ago students were taught to avoid all "in-group" language in their
writing. "Never use slang," preached English teachers, "and never write
in an ethnic or a regional dialect. Always use standard English." But
today most English instructors agree that in-group language is sometimes appropriate, even though in most writing situations it is not.

When are slang and dialect likely to be appropriate? They are clearly
acceptable when you are quoting the words of people who actually
speak in slang or dialect. If you are quoting Sojourner Truth's famous
"And Ain't I a Woman?" speech, you wouldn't "correct" Truth's dialect as some misguided English teachers once did. You would let ex-
slave Sojourner Truth speak with the ringing authority of her own
voice:

> That man over there. He says women need to be helped into carriages
> and lifted over ditches and to have the best everywhere. Nobody ever
> helps me into carriages, over mud puddles, or gets me any best place.
> *Ain't I a woman?* Look at me! Look at my arm. I have ploughed. And
> I have planted. And I have gathered into barns. And no man could head
> me. *And ain't I a woman?*

I could work as much, and eat as much as any man—when I could get it—and bear the lash as well. *And ain't I a woman?* I have borne thirteen children and seen them sold into slavery, and when I cried out with a mother's grief, none but Jesus heard me. *And ain't I a woman?*

It is appropriate, then, to quote the special language of others. No one is likely to disagree with this. But when is it appropriate for you to put your own slang or dialect into your writing? Here we are on more dangerous ground; any guidelines are likely to be controversial.

In general, dialect and slang are more appropriate in creative, "expressive" writing than in practical or intellectual writing. If your purpose in writing is to express your personality or your ethnic or regional identity, then it's appropriate to write in your own speaking voice, as this student did:

Look, white brother, ya got no soul. No brother, I am not referring to your heart. I mean real down-to-earth soul. Nah man, I am not talking about soul food, like chittlings, hamhocks or pigs feet. I am talking 'bout soul, ya know? Rockin', grindin', windin', bindin', bumpin' soul. No, Lester, I do not mean to exercise. Brother, I am talking about something hip, mean, bad, out-a-sight. Lester, I did not say anything about a hippopotamus who can not see. Lester, you must be some type of nut. Lester, you are impossible. For heaven's sake, let's forget the whole thing.

As black poet Imamu Amiri Baraka (LeRoi Jones) points out, the spoken dialect carries an expressive meaning that can't be translated:

I heard an old Negro street singer last week, Reverend Pearly Brown, singing, "God don't never change!" This is a precise thing he is singing. He does not mean "God does not ever change!" He means "God don't never change."

Slang and dialect, since they are spoken by "in-groups," can be very effective when you're appealing to an in-group audience. The common language is a way of expressing your solidarity with the group. A union leader, for example, might write campaign literature in the language of the steelworkers who will be voting in the election. Or a Chicano community leader will write to his or her constituents in the language they all share. Here, for example, are the words of José Ángel Gutiérrez, addressed to fellow Chicanos:

You've got a handful of gringos controlling the lives of *muchos mexicanos.* And it's been that way for a long time. . . . In 1960 there were twenty-six Texas counties in which Chicanos were a majority, yet not one of those counties was in the control of Chicanos. If you want to take that you can. You can be perfectly content just like your father and your grandfather were, *con el sombrero en la mano.*

In-group language is often appropriate for informal writing. For example, here are some sentences from a student paper about the after-hours pranks of a cross-country track team:

> Tires could be heard squealing in the night as my car pulled away, with the town-and-country wagon following. I turned off the main drag down a side street, with a pair of headlights still trailing some distance behind. While I was concentrating all my efforts on controlling my swaying mobile, my backseat buddies thought it would be fun to lob a firecracker at our trailing team members. Simultaneous with the firecracker's disposal came the word "Cop!"

Sometimes, then, in-group language is appropriate in writing. You'll find, however, that most writing situations require that you tone down your natural speaking voice and write in standard English. Slang and dialect attract a reader's attention to the writer's *way* of speaking, and in most situations this is distracting. If you want readers to focus on *what* you're saying, you won't make them too conscious of *how* you're saying it. Also, in most writing situations slang or dialect is simply out of place—as a matter of courtesy. It's bad manners to assert your uniqueness too strongly in a business letter or a college term paper, especially when your readers don't share your in-group language. So unless you have a special reason for choosing an in-group language, you should write in standard English.

TECHNICAL OR PLAIN ENGLISH?

Sometimes you'll need to choose between technical English, understandable only to specialists, and plain English that everyone can understand. Usually your audience will determine your choice. A lawyer, for example, will use legal language when writing a brief to other lawyers, but when summarizing that same brief for a client, he or she will shift to nontechnical English. Someone we know who supervises computer technologists finds that she must write technically accurate directives for her staff and simplified memos in plain English for her own supervisors. If she writes the directives in ordinary English, her staff will make mistakes. If she writes technical memos for her supervisors, who are not specialists, they won't understand her—and they'll be annoyed with her for wasting their time.

A sociologist will use a great deal of technical language when writing for other specialists, but will shift to ordinary language when writing a textbook for beginners. He or she may introduce technical terminology in the textbook, but will be careful not to overwhelm the beginner with too much of it, even at the risk of sacrificing complete accuracy. Of course we have all been victims at one time or another of a textbook writer who forgot his or her audience. But the really good textbook writers are those who suit their language to their audience. They write in plain English, so their readers can understand them.

Writers often use technical English when nontechnical would be more appropriate. Doctors, lawyers, scholars, and government or military officials are sometimes so impressed with themselves for having mastered a technical vocabulary that they use it whenever they get a chance—even when it's clearly inappropriate. A scholar, for example, once asked a farmer if he was "excavating a subterranean channel." The farmer replied, "No, sir, I am only digging a ditch."

Supreme Court Justice Oliver Wendell Holmes, himself a highly educated man, once complained about such misuse of technical language. Said Holmes, "I know there are professors in this country who 'ligate' arteries. Other surgeons only tie them, and it stops bleeding just as well." Like Holmes, we think it's best to avoid technical language when ordinary English will do as well. Don't write "This semiautomatic, small-caliber, shoulder-fired weapon, because of mechanical derangement, ceased to function." Just tell your readers that the rifle jammed.

Let's conclude with a useful guideline. In general, choose plain English. Use technical English only when 1) you are knowledgeable enough to use it correctly; 2) your readers are knowledgeable enough to understand it; and 3) your purpose in writing truly requires it.

NONSEXIST LANGUAGE

Sexist language is fast becoming inappropriate in our society because it demeans women and girls by simply not recognizing them. Such language emphasizes maleness as the human norm, with the inevitable consequence that femaleness becomes less than quite human. The language we hear and read is a major influence on how we perceive the world. Sexist language encourages us, from childhood forward, to live our lives according to gender-linked stereotypes—beginning with the apparently harmless nursery rhyme that goes:

Snakes and snails
And puppy dogs' tails,
That's what little boys are made of.
Sugar and spice
And everything nice,
That's what little girls are made of.

Sexist language also conditions us to look at and behave toward others in prescribed ways. As Mary Orovan states in her language pamphlet "Humanizing English," "Words tend to 'freeze' our thinking patterns." The well-known linguist Benjamin Whorf puts it this way: "The limits of my language are the limits of my thought." What we need to do, then, is to break the sexist mold that has limited our language—and therefore our thoughts and expectations. We know that language changes constantly, as human beings need new forms to express new perceptions of themselves. With the rising awareness of sexism and its threat to human dignity, language is being closely examined for sexism.

As our language phases out its sex bias, the nonsexist replacements will in turn help to reduce the sexism in our society. That cannot fail to happen. We think in language, and nonsexist language will produce a different kind of thinking. Once we think differently, we can begin to act differently; eliminating sexism from language will inevitably help to eliminate sexism in human behavior.

Let's assume that you want to show equal respect to both sexes of the human race. How can you do so? You might begin by being careful as you write not to leave women out of the human race. With *man* having meant *human* for so long, women have been left out. Think of how often you encounter such expressions as "mankind," "the brotherhood of man," "man and his universe," "man and his God," "All men are created equal," "The Norsemen settled along the coast of . . . ," "Anthropology is the study of man and . . . ," "manmade," and "man's achievements." None of these common expressions recognizes that at least one-half of the human beings in the world are female.

You might argue, of course, "Oh, *everybody* knows those uses of *man* mean *all* people." But even if that were absolutely true, there is a wide gap between perhaps being included and clearly being equally recognized. Because women remain invisible in such "man-words," there is at least a fifty-fifty chance that they will not be equally recognized in the consciousness of the writer—or the reader.

You can be sure that your reader will know you mean everybody when you substitute for these man-words such words as *human, humanity, person, people,* and *individuals.* Some of these substitutions may feel awkward to you at first, but just remember that every expression in our language was new and awkward at some time. The more frequently we all use these inclusive words, the sooner they will sound natural to our ears.

In addition to avoiding the man-words, you will also want to watch your pronouns. Just as *mankind* does not clearly include everybody, neither do *he, his,* and *him* when used in a general sense. A sentence like the following would seldom recognize everyone in a class: "The student who hands in his final paper even an hour late will risk a grade of Incomplete for the course." Restricting yourself to the masculine pronoun can indeed lead to some strange sentences—like this one uttered by a New York state legislator: "When we get abortion law repeal, everyone will be able to decide for himself whether or not to have an abortion."

The two most common singular pronoun forms now used to indicate everybody are *he and she* (sometimes *he or she*) and *he/she*. These can become *his and her* or *his/her*, and *him and her* or *him/her*, as needed. Using either of these you could write: "The student who hands in his or her (his/her) final paper even an hour late will risk a grade of Incomplete for the course."

You may find yourself puzzling over how to eliminate the sexism in sentences containing pronouns such as *each, one, none, either, neither, any, every, somebody*, and *whoever*. No doubt you have been taught that all such pronouns must be singular: "Everyone wore his oldest jeans to the senior hayride." Like all rules, this was invented. This particular one originated back in the 1700s, and like all rules, it can be rewritten.

Actually, everyday usage—language evolving on its own, as it so often does despite our made-up rules—is not waiting for us to decide to change this rule. As William H. Green acknowledges in a May 1977 article entitled "Singular Pronouns and Sexual Politics," everyday usage seems to be moving toward *they, their*, and *them* to follow such singular pronouns. For example: "Every student in turn added their books to the growing pile as they rushed out to the game, taking their flags and their cheering cards with them."

If usage continues to follow this trend, it will merely be repeating pronoun history. The singular of the pronoun *you* was once *thou*; today we use one form, *you*, for both the singular and the plural. So we already have a precedent for *they, their, them* as singular general to replace the limiting *he, his, him*.

While we wait for formal written usage to catch up with more informal usage, you may want to recast your singular sentences into the plural, to include everybody: "Students who hand in their final papers even an hour late will risk a grade of Incomplete for the course." "All the students in turn added their books to the growing pile as they rushed out to the game, taking their flags and their cheering cards with them."

You will find more examples of sentences that resolve the gender-linked pronoun problem under "Match Your Nouns and Pronouns" in "Revising Problem Sentences" in the handbook section.

Another way to remove sexism from your language is to avoid sex-linked occupational and organizational terms. As more careers attract both men and women, our former occupational terms are gradually becoming false designations. You will be more accurate if you say *police officer* instead of *policeman*, *flight attendant* instead of *stewardess, firefighter* instead of *fireman*, and so on. And if you listen, you will notice that in many organizations *chairperson* is replacing *chairman*.

As you work on eliminating sexism from your language, you will want to be alert to how language is sometimes used to diminish the dignity of both women and men. Can you sense a possible difference between the meanings intended by *housewife* and *homemaker*, for example? Or between *handsome hulk* and *attractive man*? You will want to take care not to write *woman doctor* or *woman executive*, just as you will want to avoid *male nurse* and *male secretary*. And there is no reason to distinguish between the sexes by using *sculptress* or *poetess* or *aviatrix*. Nor do feminists like being called *women's libbers* any more than male athletes want to be referred to as *jocks*. You can think of other such diminishing expressions that trivialize human beings.

Finally, there are words, often verbs or adjectives, that seem to be assigned exclusively to either maleness or femaleness in our cultures. Choosing these instead of more neutral designations can make your writing sound sexist. For example, women have been too long described by such adjectives as *dainty, flighty, shapely, sweet, cute, petite, catty, glamorous*—even *womanly!* And through such verbs as *chatter, fret, squeal, sob, gossip, giggle,* and *glide* (to walk). Men, on the other hand, have been assigned such adjectives as *strong, brave, sturdy, daring*— even *manly*. And verbs like *stride, bark, swear, bellow,* and *roar*.

All gender-linked usage restricts the ways in which both men and women can imagine themselves and therefore how fully *human* they can become. By getting rid of the sexism in your language, you can help to remove some of the restrictions from both your own imagination and the imaginations of your readers.

EXERCISE 1   FOR READING AND DISCUSSION

Bring in, from your own reading, two selections written in contrasting voices —one formal and one informal. Be prepared to explain how the distinctive voice of each one has been achieved—through word choice, sentence structure, and so on. Consider whether the voice of each piece is appropriate for its apparent purpose.

EXERCISE 2   WRITTEN

Write a paper in which you show vividly, through many examples, that whites have borrowed language from blacks.

EXERCISE 3 FOR DISCUSSION

Look at the following student papers in part 8 and comment on how either formal or informal language contributes to the effect of each paper. Is the language appropriately chosen?.

Irish vs. American Education (#1)
A Suicide (#8)
Charlie's Carry-Out (#5)
Re-entry (#12)
Better to Die at Home (#18)
Water-skiing to Signals (#10)

EXERCISE 4 FOR READING AND LISTENING

For at least a week, look and listen for examples of sexism in language in your day-to-day life—at work, at school, in advertisements, at home, in stores, on radio and television, at social events, wherever you go. Try to be alert to all the sexist language problems pointed out in this section: man-words, pronouns, occupational and organizational terms, trivializing expressions, "male" and "female" words, and so on. Perhaps you can even find some absurdities, like this one from a children's book: "Man, like the other mammals, breast-feeds his young." Bring your five most choice items to class.

EXERCISE 5 CLASSROOM ACTIVITY

Remove the sexism from the sexist language collected for exercise 4 above.

EXERCISE 6 JUST FOR FUN

One of our students wrote the following poem about language:

NOSTALGIA
(or, Getting with It)

I remember
    when a chick was the offspring of a hen,
    when a dude was a ranch vacationer,
    when a greaser was a garage mechanic,
    when a square was a geometric figure,
    when a freak was a side-show performer,
    when a sucker was a lollypop,
    when a shrink was a dry-clean-only dress,
    when a pig was a farm animal,
    when cool was the opposite of warm,
    when making out was being successful (at anything),
    when flipping out was missing the mat in tumbling,
    when to dig had to do with ditches,
    when a hangup was Monday's wash on the line,
    when my bag was the grocery sack,

when a bug was an insect,
when pintos, mustangs and cougars had legs,
when uptight was how a corset was laced,
when grass was something you mowed,
when tea was something you drank,
when pot described grandpa's belly,
when a weed was a nuisance (to anyone),
when high was the sky,
when a joint was a hangout,
when hash was mashed corned beef,
when upper referred to a department store level,
when a trip involved packing a suitcase,
when rock had to do with geology,
when acid had to do with chemistry,
when a bust was part of the anatomy,
when bread was something to butter,
when a head-shop was a beauty parlor,
when long-haired described classical music,
when a turn-on involved a light switch,
when a ripoff meant getting out the sewing basket,
when a pad was something you wore, periodically.

PART III
Writing to Support a Point

Your thesis is a promise.
—Diana Hacker

CHAPTER 6
FOCUSING ON A POINT

Try this reading test. Read the paragraph *once* only:

> Suppose an elevator starts at the first floor with six passengers, and stops at the next floor where four people get out and two get on; it continues upward to the next floor where three get on and no one gets off, but at the following floor two get off; at the next floor two get on and three get off.

And now the question: How many times did the elevator stop? Chances are you did not "pass" this reading test, even if you are a very good reader, because the test was rigged against you from the start. It didn't tell you what the point was, so you probably supplied a purpose or point to the paragraph and then read for the details that related to that point. Most readers think they're supposed to be watching for the number of people on the elevator, so they focus their attention on the people getting on and off the elevator, not on the elevator stops.

If you "flunked" this test, it was the writer's fault, not yours. Suppose for a moment that you were the writer giving the test. If you really wanted your readers to watch out for the number of times the elevator stopped, you (being a sensible person) would probably ask the question *before* the test. You would let your readers know, in one way or another, what the point was.

As you write papers this semester, what can you do to make sure readers won't miss *your* point? The answer is surprisingly simple. State your main point clearly and concisely—preferably in one sentence—and put that sentence early in your paper, either at the beginning or at the end of an introductory paragraph. This one-sentence declaration of the main point of a paper is called a *thesis statement*. The thesis statement is the most important sentence in your entire paper. It tells readers the point of the whole paper so that they can spot the most important ideas as they read on. In essence, your thesis statement maps out the territory into which you are taking your readers.

Let us show you a few examples, so you can see how a thesis statement focuses the reader's attention on the main point of a paper. This student writer has placed his thesis statement at the end of his introductory paragraph:

> During my childhood I had to pass the city jail to get to town. The barred windows of the jail were easily visible from the street. Of the many times I passed that jail I recall seeing only black faces behind those bars. It was many years later before I knew why that was so. *The primary reason for the disproportionate number of blacks in our jails and prisons is their low economic status.*

The thesis statement (italicized) clearly announces the writer's main point: that blacks populate our jails and prisons in disproportionate numbers because they are poor. Readers know what to expect in the rest of the paper; as they read they will look for evidence that poverty is the main reason so many blacks are behind bars.

Another student writer begins his introductory paragraph with a thesis:

> *Supermarkets are not designed for the quantity family buyer.* To see what I mean, come with me on a typical weekly grocery-buying trip for my family of eight. We will shop at an average supermarket, my neighborhood A & P.

Readers learn the point immediately: that supermarkets are not set up for customers who buy in quantity. The rest of this student's paper will show readers just how true this statement is.

One last example, written by the mother of a first-grader. She places her thesis at the end of her opening paragraph:

> Without a doubt my daughter Nicole suffered academically from not entering Forestville at the beginning of her kindergarten year. Instead she was computerized, zoned, and bused to Brookline Elementary. *Though by all outward appearances our community's two elementary schools are comparable, Forestville is academically superior to Brookline.*

The thesis prepares readers for a paper that contrasts the merits of Forestville with the shortcomings of Brookline. Readers know exactly what the writer intends to show them: that Forestville is academically superior to Brookline.

WRITING A THESIS

Now that you have seen some thesis statements in context, let us take a closer look at these important sentences. A thesis statement, as we said before, is *a one-sentence declaration of the main point of a piece of writing*. A successful thesis statement has three characteristics.

First, a thesis statement must be a *generalization;* it cannot be merely a fact. A flat statement of fact, such as "Edgar Allan Poe was born in 1809," doesn't communicate a main point, so it just won't do as a thesis. It takes a generalization to state a main point. "Edgar Allan Poe's life was filled with bitter disappointments"—a general statement requiring specific development later in the paper—would make a good thesis. So would "Poe, according to his biographers, had difficulty relating to women sexually." That's a generalization about Poe's life, not just a fact about it. You could develop it into a paper filled with facts about Poe's relationships with women.

Your thesis must communicate a generalization that you can develop in the rest of the paper. Let's say you want to share with readers your enthusiasm for Professor Baldwin's History 157. You wouldn't choose as your thesis "History 157, taught by Professor Baldwin, is offered at 10:00 on Tuesdays and Thursdays." You might include that fact in your paper, to be sure, but you wouldn't use it as your thesis. You'd choose a generalization, perhaps one like this: "Whoever said that history is nothing but polishing tombstones must have missed History 157, because in Professor Baldwin's class history is very much alive." That's an idea that you could develop further. It's a good focal point for a whole paper.

Or, imagine that you want to write a paper showing the dangers of the "55," a helicopter in which you nearly died. You are tempted to use "I nearly crashed to my death in a '55' helicopter" as your thesis, until you notice that it is too factual. So you choose a generalization instead, one that sums up your main point: "Though it looks innocent enough, the '55' is an extremely dangerous helicopter."

One last example. If you wanted to show readers that golf is an expensive sport, you wouldn't use "A good set of golf clubs costs at least $150" as your thesis. That's too factual. You'd state your main point in a generalization, maybe one like this: "If you've never played golf before but are thinking of trying it, I'd advise against it—unless you have the funds to support this expensive hobby."

So a thesis statement is a generalization. But—and this brings us to the second characteristic of a successful thesis—it should not be too general. It should be a *limited* generalization, one that can be developed within your word limit. If your generalization is too broad, you're promising readers too much, unless you happen to be writing a book. In freshman English you will normally be writing papers of 300 to 1000 words, so you'll need to be especially careful to limit your thesis statements. You should not choose a thesis like "Marriages are breaking up at an accelerating rate for a complex variety of reasons," because you can't develop this statement convincingly in a short paper. You'd be better off limiting the generalization radically, perhaps to "My first marriage ended in divorce because I married for the wrong reasons." This you could probably develop in a 500- to 1000-word paper—unless, of course, you get carried away.

It takes common sense to decide when a thesis statement is too broad. If you love Italian food, you might be tempted to work with a thesis like "San Francisco has more first-rate Italian restaurants than any other major American city." But common sense warns you against such a thesis, which is much too broad to develop in a short paper. Common sense leads you to a more limited generalization, such as: "At the top of my list for good food, good service, and a charming atmosphere is a little Italian restaurant called Luigi's."

Or, imagine you want to show parents how to provide outlets for their children's aggression. You begin with the thesis "There are many ways to provide your children with outlets for their aggressive feelings," but then you realize you can't do justice to such a statement in one short paper. So you limit your thesis: "A number of toys on the market provide safe and effective outlets for your child's aggressive feelings."

So far we have said that a successful thesis is 1) *a generalization,* and 2) a *limited* generalization. The third characteristic of a successful thesis is that it is *sharply focused.* It is not too vague. A thesis like "Edgar Allan Poe is an interesting writer," for example, is too vague. You could write about Poe's life, about his theory of poetry, about his horror stories, about almost anything connected with Poe—and still be more or less sticking to your thesis that Poe is an "interesting writer." So the thesis is poorly focused.

A vague thesis is not quite the same as an overly broad one, though a vague one may also be too broad. Consider "Most P.E. instructors are incompetent," for example. The first problem with this thesis is that it is too broad. "Most P.E. instructors" includes those from Bogotá, from Chicago, from Kyoto, from London, from anywhere. It would take a very long book to prove that P.E. instructors all over the world are incompetent. Obviously, the thesis needs limiting. It might be limited, for example, to "The majority of P.E. instructors at City College are incompetent."

This limited thesis is much better, but it is still too vague. The key word "incompetent" could mean too many different things. Do the instructors skip classes or show up drunk, are they so overweight they can't participate in sports, are they unskilled in sports, are they poor teachers of sports—or what? The thesis needs a more precise focus. We might sharpen its focus like this: "The P.E. department at City College is more interested in promoting winning teams than in teaching lifetime sports to average students." That's a thesis a writer could probably work with. It is limited, and it is sharply focused.

Usually the vagueness of a thesis can be traced to a word that could mean too many different things—a word like *interesting* or *enjoyable* or *lousy*. Where precisely is a paper going when it promises to show us that Poe's life is "interesting" or that swimming is "enjoyable" or that *Citizen Kane* is a "lousy" movie? Your guess is as good as ours.

As you scribble on scratch paper in search of a thesis, it's common to begin with one that's too vague, because your ideas may not yet be clearly focused. Sharpening a too-vague thesis is part of the process of discovering what you really want to say. Each of these students, for example, began with a blurred focus and ended with a sharp one:

too vague	*sharpened focus*
Alimony is a rip-off.	Alimony is an injustice to men and an insult to the dignity of women.
The Parkdale Community College cafeteria serves bad food.	At the Parkdale Community College cafeteria you will search in vain for a nutritious meal.
Conquering a weight problem can be rewarding.	After trying every diet that's been popularized in the past five years, I finally found one that worked: old-fashioned calorie counting.
The Moto-guzzi is a better bike than the BMW.	The Moto-guzzi is a better all-round touring bike than the BMW.

A more precise thesis, though it may be harder to write than a vague one, gives you control over the rest of your paper. So it is worth the extra effort.

To sum up, a thesis statement is a one-sentence declaration of the main point of your paper. A good thesis statement has three characteristics: it is a generalization, not a specific fact; it is limited, not too broad; and it is sharply focused (not too vague).

We have devoted much of this chapter to just one sentence in your introduction, because it is so important. But now we would like to consider your introductory paragraph as a whole.

WRITING AN INTRODUCTORY PARAGRAPH

Your introductory paragraph should *introduce* readers to your paper. Remember that readers come to your paper cold, not knowing what to expect. They have no idea what your point is. So your job, in your very first paragraph, is to announce the main point of your paper.

Your thesis statement—the one sentence that most clearly announces your main point—should nearly always appear either at the beginning or at the end of your introductory paragraph. Whether you place it at the beginning or the end depends on the effect you want to achieve. For a slow-paced effect, put the thesis at the end; for a blunter, more straightforward effect, put it at the beginning.

For a slow-paced effect, you begin a few steps back from your thesis, orienting readers, giving them a feel for the subject area into which you are taking them. Then you zoom in on your thesis, the last sentence of the paragraph. If you think of a zoom-lens movie camera, you'll have some notion of how this kind of paragraph works. With a zoom lens you can film a broad panorama as background for your actual subject, then zoom quickly to the subject itself. Here is an example of what we might call a "zoom" paragraph:

> Little League sports were developed many years ago as amateur sports for young people. Little League's primary purpose was physical development, sportsmanship, and the advancement of peace and goodwill through athletic competition. However, if our local organization is a good example, Little League sports have strayed far from these goals. *The Palmer Park Little League is clearly run for the benefit of the adult coaches and parents.*

The writer begins broadly, speaking of Little League sports in general, and then zooms in on the message of his paper: that one specific Little League organization (the one the writer is familiar with) is run for the benefit of adults, not children.

Here is another zoom paragraph:

> During my junior year of high school my family moved from a suburban American community to a small village in rural Ireland. The change was a very pleasant one once we got over the initial cultural shock; and we learned a great deal from the visit. My biggest discoveries came from being enrolled in the local convent, a school that was very different from my old high school. *The difference lay not in the subjects that were taught, but rather in the way they were taught and the surroundings they were taught in.*

The first three sentences of this introductory paragraph are designed to orient readers. They let readers in the door, gradually making them feel at home. If the writer had hit her readers with her thesis right away, they'd have felt she was pushing them into her paper too quickly, without giving them a chance to catch their breath.

The zoom paragraph allows you to chat awhile with readers before getting to your main point. The effect is polite and friendly, as if you were inviting readers into your paper. Notice, for example, how smoothly this student writer eases us into her paper on the violence in Grimms' fairy tales:

> The Brothers Grimm have always seemed a friend to parents at bedtime. They have helped get the kids into bed without too much trouble, and they've sent them quickly off to dreamland. But little do parents realize, when they leave the room and turn out the lights, that their children dream of wicked witches in gingerbread houses, trolls under bridges, and poisonous apples. *In their own way, the Brothers Grimm have been teaching children that life is no fairy tale.*

As you have seen, the zoom paragraph builds toward the thesis. For much of the writing that you will do this semester, the zoom paragraph will serve very well. Sometimes, though, you may decide to get to your point faster—with what we'll call a "pointed" paragraph. A pointed paragraph begins with the thesis:

> *Fresh foods are more economical than commercially prepared frozen foods or prepared mixes.* Let's do some comparison shopping to see just how true this is.

Pointed paragraphs are often appropriate in practical writing situations, when readers expect you to get right to the point. This kind of introductory paragraph can be short, sometimes as short as the thesis statement alone. Though it often lacks the graceful flow of the zoom paragraph, the pointed paragraph has the advantage of being straightforward. Notice, for example, how quickly this writer gets to her point:

> *Tippy's Taco House, on Route 1 in College Park, is a good place to stop when you are craving Mexican food.* Both the food and the service are better than you can usually expect from a small, inexpensive fast-food restaurant.

The effect is straightforward, almost blunt, but quite appropriate for a paper with an obviously practical purpose, to entice lovers of Mexican food to Tippy's Taco House.

Though usually short, a pointed paragraph can be several sentences long, like this one:

> *I have experienced something that let me know more about death than a lifetime of reading and theorizing could.* One morning, quite unintentionally, I became dissociated from my body. It happened shortly after I finished reading Robert Monroe's *Journeys Out of the Body.*

Sometimes, though, you can get by with a one-sentence introductory paragraph such as this one, which consists of the thesis alone:

Majoring in P.E. demands more intelligence than most people think.

A one-sentence introduction can be set off in a paragraph by itself to help the reader see that its function is to introduce the paper.

Whether you begin with a zoom or a pointed paragraph, your readers should understand immediately, without even consciously thinking about it, that your introduction is an introduction. And they should understand, again without effort, just what your thesis is. When you're writing to support a point, the primary function of your introduction is to let readers know your point. It's as simple as that.

WHEN TO WRITE YOUR INTRODUCTION

When should you write your introduction? The answer to this question is not as obvious or as simple as you might think. Yes, of course it makes sense to write the introduction first, before you write the body or the conclusion of the paper. For the introduction not only tells readers what to expect; it tells you, the writer, what to put in the body of the paper.

Yes, you should write the introduction first. But don't be surprised if you go through several false starts before coming up with an introductory paragraph that's workable. It would be helpful if you always knew before putting pen to paper (or fingers to typewriter) just what your main idea would be. Then, as you wrote your opening paragraph, you could confidently introduce readers to your paper—before you'd even written the paper. But you won't always have that kind of control over your material right from the start.

Often you'll need to write your introductory paragraph not to reveal your focus, but to discover it. And discovery is not a neat and tidy process; it almost always involves false starts. Here, for example, is one student writer's false start:

The women's liberation movement which started its big push in the United States back in the 1960s is a well-intentioned movement. And I agree with its basic goals. *At the same time I do have some disagreements with its goals.*

Not bad for a false start, but the focus is pretty foggy. The student's next try was better:

I agree with the economic goals of the women's liberation movement, such as equal pay for equal work and the right to credit. *However, the women's movement goes too far in challenging two traditional roles for women: the role of wife, and the role of mother.*

It's a good idea to experiment awhile, as this student did, before settling on an introductory paragraph. Keep writing introductory paragraphs until you think you've got the focus you want, then turn to the business of writing the paper. Don't worry too much at this point about how your introduction "sounds." Why not? Because you may need to rewrite the introduction later, after you've written the paper.

Papers have a way of changing as they are being written, and this is not necessarily a bad thing, as long as you are aware of the changes— and as long as you are prepared to rewrite your introduction later. Sometimes a paper becomes more clearly focused as it is being written. Other times the focus changes as you discover, through writing, what you really wanted to say.

For example, the student who wrote the introductory paragraph criticizing the women's movement discovered, once he began drafting the body of his paper, that he couldn't write a convincing argument in support of his main point. He had said that he was in favor of the *economic* goals of the women's movement, but that he did not support its challenges to the roles of wife and mother. Once into the paper he realized that the roles of wife and mother were more tied to economics than he had thought, because these traditional unpaid roles, in a society where divorce is common, leave women economically vulnerable. As soon as our writer saw this problem, he scanned his rough draft in search of a main point that he would be able to develop convincingly.

As it turned out, the strongest section of this student's rough draft was a description of his wife's job as mother of their six children. The women's movement, at the time his paper was written, seemed to be saying that women like his wife weren't leading meaningful lives. It didn't give full-time mothers the recognition he felt they deserved. So he revised the paper, focusing on his new point: that motherhood, though unpaid, can be a full-time job that deserves our respect. Here is the student's revised introductory paragraph. Notice how much his introduction has changed since his first effort:

> The women's movement should be applauded for helping women make economic gains. But the movement should be careful, in its push for economic goals, not to lessen our respect for women's traditional unpaid roles—particularly the role of mother. *If you think motherhood is not as challenging, meaningful, and rewarding as other full-time jobs, let me show you a day in the life of my wife, Lurleen, mother of six.*

You may be surprised to hear that a student writer spent so much effort rewriting his introduction. But successful student writers, like professionals, often spend more time on the introduction than on any other section of the paper—and for good reasons. The introduction establishes the focus of the whole paper, and it's not always easy to settle on a good focus. Also, the introduction must be logically related to the body of the paper, and in a rough draft the body of the paper doesn't always support the introduction as well as it might. Sometimes, when the body and the introduction don't fit together properly, you'll choose to rewrite the body. But more often you'll probably decide to rewrite the introduction, because that is easier to do. And, finally, your introduction needs more work than the rest of the paper simply because it is so important. It determines how readers will approach the paper. If you head them in the wrong direction, their reading of the whole paper will be confused or distorted. So introductions are important enough to deserve your special attention. One professional writer claims he puts 85 percent of his effort into his introductory paragraph. That's pretty extreme, but not as extreme as you may be tempted to think.

YOUR THESIS IS A PROMISE

When you write a clear, focused introduction, you are showing respect for your readers. It is as if you were saying to them, "I understand your time is valuable, so I'm going to let you know right away what I'm up to." If all writers were this straightforward, readers would waste much less of their time trying to figure out just what the writer had to offer them.

You can think of your introduction, particularly your thesis statement, as a contract between you and your readers. You are contracting with readers for a bit of their time. In return, you promise to show, to the reader's satisfaction, that your thesis is true. Readers who don't care whether the thesis is true probably won't read past the introduction unless they have to. But readers who do care will expect solid, respectable evidence in return for their investment of time.

So your thesis statement is a commitment, a promise. Your job as a writer once you've stated your thesis is to meet your commitment, to honor your promise. But that is the subject of the next chapter.

EXERCISE 1 FOR CLASS DISCUSSION

Below are a number of paired thesis statements. In each pair, one would probably work better than the other. Choose the one you think is better and be prepared to explain why in class discussion.

1a. Though I grumbled about it as a child, today I thank my parents for their strict discipline.

1b. Too many children today are running about undisciplined.

2a. Women often fall into the trap of sacrificing themselves for others.

2b. My mother made the mistake of sacrificing a decade of her life to the care of her demanding, tyrannical, bedridden mother-in-law.

3a. In this world of today, television is too violent.

3b. If you don't believe that television programming is violent, you should have tuned in to channel 4, between 7 and 9 on Tuesday night; here's a blow-by-blow description of what you would have seen.

4a. Psychological studies show us that the ideal parent has a number of important characteristics.

4b. My wife, Michele, comes closer to my idea of an ideal mother than anyone else I know.

5a. The Japanese custom of arranged marriages has some remarkable advantages over our traditional dating/courtship method.

5b. In Japan parents of an engaged couple check horoscopes to see if the match is likely to work out.

EXERCISE 2 FOR CLASS DISCUSSION

Let's say you are an experienced mountain climber. Because you know quite a bit about this subject, you decide to write a 500- to 1000-word paper on it for your freshman English course. You scribble on scratch paper awhile, trying to come up with a good thesis. Which of these thesis statements would you reject as too factual, too broad, or too vague? Which ones do you think might work as your thesis statement?

1. Of the many unsuccessful attempts to climb Mt. Everest, each one failed for a variety of reasons.
2. Mountain climbing, as dangerous as it may seem, is actually a very safe sport.
3. Mountain climbing is an extremely dangerous sport, regardless of the climber's ability.
4. On the last attempt to conquer Mt. Everest, two climbers lost toes to frostbite.
5. Mountain climbing is an exciting sport.
6. As hard as it is to believe, the sport of mountain climbing depends less on physical preparedness than on mental discipline.
7. Planning an expedition to climb Mt. McKinley takes years.
8. For me climbing is an ego trip.
9. A mountain climber must be able to put his or her life in other people's hands.
10. Many mountain-climbing expeditions fail not because of the mountain, but because the climbers' personalities keep getting in the way.

11. Being able to give entirely of oneself is the most important part of being a successful mountain climber.
12. Tying knots is an important skill in mountain climbing.

EXERCISE 3   SMALL-GROUP ACTIVITY

Look through the topics in part 7. Choose three topics on which you think you could write papers, then scribble on scratch paper awhile, trying to come up with a good thesis statement for each of your three topics. Circle your best thesis statement for each topic, then bring your thesis statements—still on scratch paper—to class.

In class, working in small groups, ask your classmates to evaluate each of your thesis statements, using these questions as guidelines: (1) Is it a generalization (not a specific fact)? (2) Is it limited (not too broad)? and (3) Is it precisely focused (not too vague)?

If the thesis statements of some of your group's members are weak, help each other out. Make sure each member of the group ends up with at least one successful thesis statement that could lead to a paper the other group members would be interested in reading.

EXERCISE 4   FOR CLASS DISCUSSION

How well does each of the following introductory paragraphs serve to orient you, then focus your attention on the writer's main point?

1. So he's driving you crazy! That soft, rosy bundle of joy you welcomed into your life just a short time ago has, seemingly overnight, become an iron-willed perpetual motion machine. He has the curiosity of a cat, the agility of a mountain goat and more energy than most power plants are capable of producing. He's faster than a speeding bullet, more powerful than a locomotive and today he learned to climb the shiny new fence that just set you back $800. Take heart, dear friend. Do not despair. Save your strength, because things are definitely going to get worse. The "terrible twos" can't hold a candle to the traumatic teens.
2. Child abuse is physical or emotional harm to children by parents or guardians. Physical abuse includes intentionally inflicted bruises, fractures, burns or other wounds, attempts to drown, and so forth. Emotional abuse is battering with words that reject or ignore a child.
3. Traditional Japanese architecture and furnishings are so different from those of the West that it is virtually impossible to reproduce the style of a formal Japanese dinner party outside Japan. Nevertheless, I would like to venture a simple account of the basic essentials which a Western hostess can adapt.
4. Today people are more conscious than ever of health, and exercise seems to have become the most important ingredient for good health. Never before has one seen so many joggers and bicyclists out on our streets. For the over-30 gang who are overweight, out of shape, non-athletic, but healthy, I recommend rope jumping as a convenient form of exercise.

5. So often we make the mistake of thinking of jails as prisons. They need to be distinguished. I had the misfortune of spending several months incarcerated in both of these dreadful institutions.

6. Many schools, institutions, and hospitals serve food which has little nutritional value. Montgomery Community College is one of these.

7. After spending about a month in the hospital I believe that it is safe for me to say that the hospital is not a very nice place to be. When I was injured I weighed about one hundred and sixty pounds and was in very good condition. But by the time I was released I was down to about one hundred and thirty pounds, had a bad case of jittery nerves, and I had broken out in pimples again. Most of the weight was lost because the first week I was on a liquid diet. Then when I was able to eat, I found the food was so bad that I didn't want to eat. Then there were the damn holes in the roof. There were millions of them and after staring at them for a short time I would look away and every- thing would have holes in it.

8. Washington is a unique city for art lovers. There is something for everyone, and it is all free. On the Mall, the Freer offers its Oriental treasures; the pristine marble of the National Gallery houses the old masters of the Kress and Mellon collections; and the dynamic new Hirshorn contains the work of artists of this century. Not far away, one can browse in the National Portrait Gallery, or experience the Corcoran, where something new is always happening. Georgetown and Capitol Hill boast clusters of small commercial galleries, abound- ing with contemporary efforts for those of more adventurous tastes. My favorite Washington gallery, however, is located in the once elegant and still interesting neighborhood surrounding Dupont Circle. There, on 21st Street, just above Massachusetts Avenue, you will find the Phillips Collection, the most delightful gallery in town.

9. The basic principle of a parochial school mainly involves that of receiving a good education along with discipline. I attended a parochial school for eight years, from 1964–1972. Since that time, I have been involved with programs in public elementary schools, and I have come to the conclusion that the principles of a parochial school should be incorporated into the public school system.

EXERCISE 5 SMALL-GROUP ACTIVITY

Turn to the topics in part 7 and scan them until you find three topics you think you might be able to write a paper on. Write introductory paragraphs for papers on each of these three topics, but don't write the papers. Bring your introductory paragraphs to class to test them out on sample readers.

In class, working in small groups with other students, test each introduction on them as sample readers. (1) Does each introduction orient them, make them feel at home? (2) Does it let them know the main idea in a clear thesis statement? (3) Does it get them interested in reading further?

As you work in groups, be on the lookout for your classmates' successful efforts. You can learn much about writing by seeing what works for others.

It is easy to write a check if you have enough money in the bank, and writing comes more easily if you have something to say.

—Sholem Asch

CHAPTER 7

SUPPORTING YOUR POINT

Your thesis statement is a promise. It promises readers that your paper will be filled with convincing evidence in support of its thesis. For example, if your thesis is that your city's baseball team is a top contender for next year's pennant, you have promised readers enough evidence (probably in the form of statistics) to prove your point. Or, if your thesis is "Alimony should not be awarded except in rare, justifiable cases," you have promised substantial evidence to support that point of view.

Think, for a moment, about the writing that will be required of you after this course is over, in other college courses and on the job. Most of you are already familiar enough with school writing to know that professors are impressed with fact-filled presentations. You know very well that an essay exam filled with unsupported generalizations gets a lower grade than one packed with relevant details and solid information in support of a point. And work-related writing requires as much substance as school writing, sometimes even more. Most supervisors are very busy people who do not appreciate having their time wasted. So they request substantive writing, writing filled with relevant and necessary information.

In your other college courses and in on-the-job writing, you probably won't have too much trouble coming up with appropriate material with which to fill out your writing. Usually the material is almost given to you, or you know where to find it. For example, let's say you are writing a paper for Ancient History 103. Your instructor has asked you to compare two culture heroes, Gilgamesh and Job, to show the difference between Babylonian and Hebrew values. Because your material comes from the reading you have done in the course, you won't have much trouble filling out your paper; as a matter of fact, you'll have trouble trimming down such a wealth of material. The same is true of on-the-job writing. If your writing task, for example, is to summarize for your supervisor the important decisions made in a meeting that he or she was unable to attend, you'll have no problem coming up with material for your summary. Your problem will be deciding what is important enough to mention, and what to highlight. You'll have more information than you'll need.

But freshman English may present you with a unique writing situation. It is a course in *how* to write, so it doesn't necessarily provide you with material to write about. So, while you have material almost given to you in other college courses and in on-the-job writing, in freshman English you may have to come up with material on your own. And let's face it, this is not always easy.

CHOOSING A THESIS YOU CAN SUPPORT

In writing for freshman English, be careful to choose a thesis you will be able to support. Unless you are writing a research paper (in which case you will get your supporting material from written sources), we advise you to write about what you already know. To help you discover how much you already know, we have printed more than two hundred writing topics in part 7 in the back of this book. These topics cover a wide range of subjects: sports, religion, race, men and women, violence, and so on. At least some of them will touch on your areas of expertise.

You may be a police officer, a government worker, a basketball player, an amateur actress, a mountain climber, a vegetarian, a nurse's aide, a sports car enthusiast. Such people have special knowledge worth sharing with readers. If you think you know nothing worth sharing, we think that you, like the students we've taught, will find that you have a great deal to say once you look through our topics.

To illustrate how you can use your own knowledge to support a thesis, here is a list describing other students' successes.

1. Trained as a helicopter pilot at Ft. Walter, Bob experienced first-hand the dangers of helicopter school. He was especially aware of the dangers of the "55," a helicopter in which he nearly died. He had more than enough knowledge to write a convincing essay on the dangers of the "55."

2. Brenda, a mother concerned about the quality of her neighborhood high schools, had done some investigating. She had talked to school officials, to teachers and counselors, to other parents, and to students. Finding that the schools were just barely adequate to prepare a student for college, she wanted to share her discovery—and her alarm— with other residents of her community.

3. Sue, a lover of art galleries, took her readers on an appetite-whetting tour of her favorite gallery, the Phillips, in Washington, D.C. She visited the gallery again right before writing the paper, so the details would be fresh in her mind.

4. An avid ice-hockey fan, Lloyd was disturbed by the violence of the game—not because he was squeamish, but because the violence was making the skills of the players almost beside the point. He wrote a paper arguing that if the violence were reduced, the players would be better able to display the true skills of the game.

5. Steve had gone to most of the Italian restaurants in town, in search of the perfect pizza. Having finally discovered it at Geppetto's, he shared his discovery with fellow pizza-lovers in a glowing review of the restaurant.

6. Tom had been hearing a number of arguments against allowing girls into Little League baseball, and he was struck by the absurdity of the arguments. So he wrote a paper which simply displayed these arguments in all of their absurdity, leaving his readers to conclude that girls should be allowed to participate in Little League.

7. Lurleen, a young woman whose father had recently died of cancer, was bothered because everyone, herself included, had pretended to her father that he wasn't dying. She had read a book, *On Death and Dying*, which made her wish even more that she had spoken honestly with her father. So she wrote a paper, based primarily on her own experience, to share her insights with readers.

8. Ken, a career Air Force person, had spent several years in Japan. He was fascinated by Japanese sports, especially Sumo wrestling. Because most westerners know very little about this unusual sport, he put his readers on the scene, with ringside seats, in an action-packed essay.

GETTING CLOSE TO YOUR SUBJECT

But . . . some of you may be thinking . . . I haven't gone to helicopter school or to Japan or even to local art galleries; I have not discovered the perfect pizza, never attended ice hockey games, and couldn't care less about my neighborhood schools. *I don't have anything to write about.*

We doubt that's true, but if you think it is, here's some practical advice. If you are having trouble developing your papers because you lack material with which to fill them out, you can always choose a topic that requires you to look for material. Select topics that ask you to seek

out material in the world you live in. Some of our topics in part 7 encourage you to do just that. Here are a few examples:

1. Write an article about a natural foods store in your community.
2. Be alert to how older people (65 or older) are portrayed on television. Does stereotyping occur? Watch enough situation comedies
   and similar programs to be able to describe two or three stereotypes.
3. If one of your instructors gave a lecture this week, summarize it for
   a friend who missed class.
4. Find out about family life in another culture, preferably by talking
   to someone who has experienced it firsthand. Report on your findings in an interesting, readable style.
5. A problem for working mothers is adequate child care. Investigate
   what, if anything, your community is doing about child care and
   report what you learn. Include suggestions for further action in
   your paper if you wish.
6. What picture of American Indians, Afro-Americans, Italian-Ameri-
   cans, Southern whites, Chinese, or other minority group is presented in movies and/or television dramas? Limit this topic
   radically, perhaps by discussing the image of one of these groups as
   presented in one film or TV series.
7. Talk with a person who has worked on a hot line. Ask him or her
   about the reasons people seem to have for considering suicide.
8. Interview someone who lived through the Great Depression. Shape
   this topic as you see fit.
9. If you know a gay couple who will talk freely with you, describe
   their day-to-day life together in a paper.
10. Write a 50- to 100-word summary of last week's sermon, comment-
    ing on it if you wish.

To do a good job with any of these topics, you would need to get close
to your subject. Then the necessary details, the material for your writing, would be right there in front of you. Literally getting close to your
subject is a good method for writing, even if you already know something about your subject. As Stuart Chase put it, "It is much easier to
sit at a desk and read plans for a billion gallons of water a day, and look
at maps and photographs; but you will write a better article if you
heave yourself out of a comfortable chair and go down in tunnel 3 and
get soaked."

Your instructor may have his or her own way of helping you get close
to a subject. Some instructors, for example, use a collection of essays to
provide material for writing. Others ask students to write about litera-

ture or "great books." When you write about a particular essay, story, or book, your material is right at hand. With a careful reading, you'll be close enough to your subject to write a paper filled with detail. Here are a few of our own topics from part 7, based on such reading:

1. Read Herman Hesse's *Siddhartha*, a short novel about a young Indian searching for spiritual understanding. Write a character study of the young Siddhartha.
2. Write a humorous essay in which you show that certain fairy tales, or some other stories intended for children, are perversely violent.
3. Read some of *Small Is Beautiful*, by E. F. Schumacher, about appropriate technology, and apply his theory to a specific instance, arguing either in support of or against Schumacher. The theory might be phrased: What is needed is not mindless growth, but programs that are tailored to the culture, resources, and aspirations of a particular region.
4. Read enough in *The Crime of Punishment* by Karl Menninger to be able to explain in a paper Menninger's concept of scapegoating in our crime-and-punishment system.
5. *The Coming of Age*, a book by Simone de Beauvoir, contains an interesting chapter on "old age in historical societies." Read this chapter and summarize it for someone who hasn't the time to read it.

BRAINSTORMING ON SCRATCH PAPER

Let's say you've selected a thesis you think you can support. And let's say you've written a first-draft introductory paragraph that either begins or ends with a thesis statement. Your next step is to decide just how you will support that thesis statement. What you're really deciding, of course, is how to write the rest of the paper.

Unless you have a very clear idea of how to support your thesis in the rest of the paper, it's a good idea to stop at this point and brainstorm on scratch paper. Put your thesis statement at the top of the sheet, then jot down as many details, facts, or examples as you can think of to back up or support the thesis.

One student brainstormed this list before writing a paper showing the difficulties of enduring a five-day Navy "survival" school:

Thesis: If you think it's easy to survive off the land, let me set you straight. Here's how I managed to get through a five-day Navy "survival" school.

found 50 crabs—for 105 hungry men

captured a dozen limpets (tasted like art gum erasers)

followed a recipe for grass soup—tasted like weeds!

chased a tiny ground squirrel, not really enough to serve one person—and didn't catch it anyway

discovered the yucca plant, very tasty—but had the effect of a bushel of dried prunes

raunchy-looking grubs and lizards—not so bad when you're desperate

With this "brainstormed" list as a guide, the student wrote a fact-filled paper showing readers just how hard it is to survive off the land.

Another student brainstormed the following list on scratch paper before writing about a community college program for handicapped children:

Thesis: The Children's Developmental Clinic at Prairie Community College offers a wide range of developmental activities for physically and mentally disabled children.

—for physically handicapped children:

jumping on trampolines

swinging on a 50-foot rope hanging from the ceiling

riding big-wheels and two-wheeler bikes

playing basketball on a miniature court

walking on balance beams

standing on a gymnastic horse

tossing beanbags

tumbling on mats and cushions

rocking on old-fashioned rocking horses

—for children with learning problems:

numbers games, sometimes integrated into sports activities

spelling games

reading games, such as "Animal Habitat," created by a sophomore at Prairie Community College

With this list to work with, the writer had little trouble filling out a 500-word paper in support of her thesis. As she wrote, she expanded the items on her list, describing in detail the learning games such as "Animal Habitat" and explaining how the physical activities help improve motor skills. When she finished with the paper, it contained more than enough evidence to convince readers that her thesis was true: that the clinic indeed "offers a wide range of developmental activities for physically and mentally disabled children."

The main purpose of brainstorming is to get enough details down on paper so you won't have to stop to think them up as you're writing. But brainstorming sometimes has a side benefit. Occasionally brainstorming will show you—before you even attempt to write a paper—that you don't have enough evidence to support your thesis. For example, one student began with the thesis, "Single people are often discriminated against in job interviews." Once he began brainstorming on scratch paper, it became clear that he had too little evidence to support his point. As it turned out, his only evidence was that he suspected he had once been discriminated against in a job interview because he was single. Since this one example was not enough to prove his point—and since this student saw no way in the time available to get the evidence he needed—he decided to give up on the topic. He found another thesis instead, one he could support more convincingly.

REVISING WITH ATTENTION TO LOGIC

If you've selected a good thesis statement and if you've brainstormed enough supporting details on scratch paper, you may write a rough draft in which the supporting material logically supports the thesis. But this does not always happen.

As a paper is being written, it can begin to have a life of its own. You probably know from experience what we mean. Maybe you once wrote a thesis in favor of capital punishment, but found that your paper slanted in the opposite direction. Or perhaps you intended to prove that the Ten Commandments are important rules for twentieth-century Americans to live by, yet were unable to justify more than six of them. Or maybe, as you were writing, you just went off on a tangent. These things do happen sometimes.

For one reason or another, then, your rough draft won't always turn out the way you've planned. So, once you've finished a rough draft, it's a good idea to read it over with a critical eye. Ask yourself: Does the body of this paper *logically support* its thesis statement?

It may take several readings of a rough draft before you begin to see how logical (or illogical) it is. Getting distance from your own writing to check it for logic can be difficult, especially if you feel strongly about your subject. A good technique is to read the rough draft as if you were someone who *disagreed* with your thesis. If you find it impossible to pretend that you disagree with your thesis, find a test reader, preferably one who *does* disagree with your thesis. Or ask your instructor to read the paper, or someone else who has been trained to read for logic.

Though formal training in logical thinking might improve your ability to test for logic, common sense will take you a long way. Just ask yourself some tough questions. If you're arguing that prayer should be allowed in public schools, ask yourself: Is my supporting material strong enough to persuade readers who don't already agree with me? Or, if you're trying to show that fresh foods are less expensive than canned, frozen, or ready-mix foods, ask yourself: Does my paper contain enough facts to convince even skeptical readers? Or, if your point is that suicide is immoral, ask yourself: Is my paper persuasive enough to change the minds of readers who believe the opposite?

If your answer is *yes*, fine. If it's *no*, you have some more work to do. You'll need to strengthen your supporting material so that readers who do not already agree with your thesis will at least be forced to take it seriously—even if they do not end up completely in agreement with you.

EXERCISE 1   FOR CLASS DISCUSSION

Consider what evidence a writer could use to support each of these thesis statements, which were mentioned in chapter 6:

1. Supermarkets are not designed for the quantity family buyer.
2. Though by all outward appearances our community's two elementary schools are comparable, Forestville is academically superior to Brookline.
3. Poe, according to his biographers, had difficulty relating to women sexually.
4. Whoever said that history is nothing but polishing tombstones must have missed History 157, because in Professor Baldwin's class history is very much alive.
5. Though it looks innocent enough, the "55" is an extremely dangerous helicopter.
6. If you've never played golf before but are thinking of trying it, I'd advise against it—unless you have the funds to support this expensive hobby.
7. At the top of my list for good food, good service, and a charming atmosphere is a little Italian restaurant called Luigi's.
8. A number of toys on the market provide a safe and effective outlet for your child's aggressive feelings.
9. The Palmer Park Little League is clearly run for the benefit of the adult coaches and parents.
10. Majoring in P.E. demands more intelligence than most people think.

EXERCISE 2   FOR CLASS DISCUSSION

In each of the following student papers in part 8, discuss how the writer has supported his or her point.

Time Out (#19)

Who Goes to the Races? (#16)

A Dangerous State of Mind (#13)

Borrowings from Black Culture (#7)

So He's Driving You Crazy (#9)

EXERCISE 3 FOR CLASS DISCUSSION

Comment freely on the following quotations:

a. There is no need for the writer to eat a whole sheep to be able to tell what mutton tastes like. It is enough if he eats a cutlet. But he should do that.
—W. Somerset Maugham, *British writer*

b. If I had sat down to read everything that had been written—I'm a slow reader—I would never have written anything.
—E. B. White, *American essayist*

c. Do not be grand. Try to get the ordinary world into your writing— breakfast tables rather than the solar system; Middletown today, not Mankind through the ages.
—Darcy O'Brien

d. To tell about a drunken muzhik's beating his wife is incomparably harder than to compose a whole tract about the "woman question."
—Ivan Turgenev, *Russian novelist*

e. An abstract style is always bad. Your sentences should be full of stones, metals, chairs, tables, animals, men, and women.
—Alain, *French philosopher*

f. I'm a bit like a sponge. When I'm not writing I absorb life like water. When I write I squeeze the sponge a little—and out it comes, not water but ink.
—Georges Simenon, *French mystery writer*

g. A writer who does not speak out of a full experience uses torpid words, wooden or lifeless words, such words as "humanitary," which have a paralysis in their tails.
—Henry David Thoreau, *American writer*

h. Writers get ideas . . . from real life. It's OK to lock yourself in the broom closet to write, if you have spent 95% of your time involved in life.
—a student

EXERCISE 4 FOR THOUGHT

In recent years there has been a trend in the Western world to pay more attention to the wisdom of the East. Could the following Zen story help you in any way in your search for material for your writing?

Daiju visited the master Basō in China. Basō asked: "What do you seek?"

"Enlightenment," replied Daiju.

"You have your own treasure house. Why do you search outside?" Basō asked.

Daiju inquired: "Where is my treasure house?"

Basō answered: "What you are asking is your treasure house."

Daiju was enlightened. Ever after he urged his friends: "Open your own treasure house and use those treasures."

EXERCISE 5   JUST FOR FUN

I always start writing with a clean sheet of paper and a dirty mind.
—Patrick Dennis, *creator of Auntie Mame*

. . . writing is not the dainty arranging of superficialities, it is the solid
construction of thoughts.

—Donald Murray

CHAPTER 8
SHAPING YOUR PAPER

Let us admit from the start that we do not have any easy-to-follow, step-
by-step method that will always work for organizing your writing. A
paper will probably start to take shape in your head; its shape will become clearer as you scribble on scratch paper and perhaps sketch an
outline; then, after you've written the rough draft, you may find yourself reshaping it with scissors and tape.

It's safest to shape your paper before you begin your rough draft. If
you just plunge in, hoping to get your bearings as you write, you may
write a well-organized paper, but the odds are against it. So plan the
shape of your paper, at least sketchily, *before* you begin to write.

Organize before you write. This sounds like simple enough advice to
follow, but you probably know from experience how tempting it is *not*
to do so—particularly if you haven't had much practice organizing in
your head, or on scratch paper, or with outlines. Maybe you've tried
organizing in your head, but found that one thought led to another
which led to another and so on, leaving you with a string of loosely
related ideas. Or maybe you've turned to formal outlining in hopes of
pinning down your ideas, but found outlines more trouble than they
seemed to be worth. When students are required to submit formal outlines with their college papers, many of them write the outline after
they've written the paper. Some of these students are probably just lazy,
but we think many of them believe that formal outlining won't help
them write a better paper.

SCRIBBLING ON SCRATCH PAPER

Organizing in your head and formal outlining are two ways of shaping
a paper before you write, but they are not the only ways. Somewhere

between the extremes of "just thinking" and Roman-numeraled out-lining there is a middle ground: scribbling on scratch paper. As you become a practiced writer, you'll discover that thinking informally on scratch paper has advantages over both the extremes.

Scribbling on scratch paper is a better way to organize a paper than just thinking, because it helps you pin down your ideas. It gets them out where you can see them, so you can have some control over them. But unlike formal outlining, which can pin down your ideas too soon, scribbling doesn't commit you prematurely. If your scribbling doesn't lead you to a good idea for organizing your paper, you can always throw it out and then scribble some more until you do hit on a bright idea.

Let us show you how several students organized their thoughts on scratch paper. As you will see, in each case the jottings on scratch paper grew out of the writer's purpose. For example, one student's purpose was to convince readers to try a local Italian restaurant. He decided that readers would be tempted by the restaurant's atmosphere, its menu selection, the quality of its food, its friendly service, and its low prices. This list of items, jotted down on a piece of scratch paper, became the blueprint for his paper:

Luigi's -- first-rate Italian restaurant
charming atmosphere
wide menu selection
excellent food and wine
efficient, friendly service
moderate prices

Once this much was jotted down, the writer might have decided to arrange these items in a different order, perhaps stressing the prices first and the atmosphere last, or he might have decided to delete one or two of the items. But with this simple list he was able to control the shape of his paper.

Another student wanted to show readers that divorce rulings often treat men unfairly. Although this student wasn't well enough informed to give an accurate summary of the ways in which his state's divorce laws treated men unfairly, he did have three friends whom he felt had been treated unfairly by divorce rulings. Because his friends' experiences were the only material the student had to work with, he decided to or-

ganize his paper around these real-life examples. His scribblings on
scratch paper were very simple:

*Fred -- unfair allotment of
finances*

*Joe -- lost custody of
children, unfairly*

*Larry -- financial losses and
the loss of his only
child*

As it turned out, these were the only jottings on scratch paper that this
student needed. He was able to organize each of the three sections of
the paper in his head. But if he'd had any trouble organizing the material within a section of the paper, he could have turned once again to
scratch paper. These new jottings might have looked like this:

Joe -- lost custody unfairly

*Joe's wife is barely
competent as a
mother.
-- yells at the
kids
-- beats them
-- lets them stay
out late, eat
junk food,
watch whatever
they want on TV*

*Joe is a devoted
father.
-- reasons with
the children,
rarely resorting
to physical
punishment
-- sets limits
on the
children*

*-- shows no
interest in
doing things
with the
children*

*--takes them to
ball games
and on
camping trips,
helps with
homework, goes
to PTA meetings*

Our third student, who had recently visited her city's art museum, planned to show readers what a wealth of art was hiding in a converted townhouse in an out-of-the-way neighborhood. To whet her readers' appetite for this museum, the writer decided to take readers along with her on a visit. She took them down the street, in the door, and through the various rooms, pointing out the noteworthy paintings as she went along. The shape of the museum almost shaped her paper for her. These few notes were the blueprint for her paper:

*describe where the gallery is --
in a once-elegant neighborhood*

*the old wing
of the building* — *Van Gogh
Degas
Cezanne
Renoir*

the new wing — *Picasso
Braque
Rothko*

A last example. One student, a police officer who regularly watched two police programs on television, intended to show that TV has glamorized the police profession. Here is his scratch-paper sketch of the paper:

"Police Story" -- Contrast the
    <u>exciting</u> events in one
    episode with the <u>dull</u>
    <u>routine</u> of one evening
    on the job.

"The Rookies" -- Contrast the
    <u>illegal</u> procedures of
    the rookies with the
    <u>strict</u> <u>rules</u> police
    officers must be
    careful to follow

As you can see, he organized his paper around two TV programs he knew something about: "Police Story" and "The Rookies." For each program he contrasted the televised fantasy with the reality he had experienced as a police officer.

There are any number of ways to sketch the shape of your paper on scratch paper, and your own jottings, which need be understandable only to you, are likely to look messier than the examples we've shown you. You might write lists in random order, then number the items; you might scatter ideas all over a page, then draw lines between related ideas; you might use circles or boxes or arrows or even a second color of ink. Do whatever helps you visualize the shape of the paper you are about to write.

OUTLINING

Sometimes, especially when you're writing long papers, you'll find that outlining gives you greater control over your rough draft than informal scribbling on scratch paper. You might doodle a bit on scratch paper first, since that keeps you flexible as your ideas are taking shape. But once your ideas have begun to take shape, you may want to write a sentence outline.

A sentence outline with the thesis statement placed at the top pictures the logical relationships among your ideas. The thesis statement is the "point" you are going to support in your paper. The rest of the sentences in the outline are layered to picture their relationship to the thesis:

Thesis Statement: _____.
    A. _____.
       1. _____.
       2. _____.
       3. _____.
    B. _____.
       1. _____.
       2. _____.
    C. _____.
       1. _____.
       2. _____.
       3. _____.
       4. _____.

First-layer supports (the A's and B's and C's) are direct proofs of the thesis statement. They are indented and listed under the thesis statement to show that they support it. You can think of them as propping up your thesis, which would collapse without them. Second-layer supports (the 1's and 2's and 3's) prove the first-layer supports. Again, each one is indented and listed under the statement it supports, to picture that "support" relationship. You could of course have third- and fourth-layer supports, but unless you are writing very long papers, your outline should not be so detailed. Your outline is merely an overall picture of your paper. You fill in the details as you write the rough draft.

Your main purpose in writing a sentence outline is to picture the relation between your thesis statement and the major sections of your paper. To picture that relation as clearly as possible, you should keep your outline simple. An outline for a 500- to 1000-word paper can and probably should be as simple as this student's was:

Thesis Statement: Concentration is the key to becoming a consistent winner in tennis.
   A. Chris Evert wins consistently because she is a master of the art of concentration.
   B. Ilie Nastase improved his game after he learned to concentrate.
   C. Jimmy Connors plays erratically because he has not yet learned to concentrate.

Notice that the most important word in the thesis—"concentration"—is echoed in each of the supports. This keeps the focus on the main point of the paper. Notice also that the three supporting sentences are structured very similarly: "Chris Evert wins consistently . . ."; "Ilie Nastase improved his game . . ."; "Jimmy Connors plays erratically. . . ." Each of the three sections of the paper will support the thesis in exactly the same way, through an example, and this parallel sentence structure helps to picture that similarity.

When you are outlining, don't be afraid to repeat words and sentence structures, even to the point of monotony, as this student has done:

Thesis Statement: Scientists tell us that our nuclear weapons testing, supersonic aircraft, and aerosol sprays are gradually destroying the protective ozone layer that surrounds our planet.
   A. Nuclear weapons testing is destroying the ozone layer.
   B. Supersonic aircraft are destroying the ozone layer.
   C. Aerosol sprays are destroying the ozone layer.

This very simple sentence outline helped its writer to keep focused on her main point as she wrote her rough draft. It helped her remember just *exactly* what she was trying to show her readers. As a matter of fact, as she got into her rough draft, she was tempted to discuss the politics connected with nuclear weapons testing and the controversies surrounding the supersonic Concorde airplane. But her outline showed her that she'd be straying from her points: that nuclear weapons-testing *is destroying* the ozone layer; that supersonic aircraft *are destroying* the ozone layer. Her outline told her to stick to scientific evidence of this destruction.

So keep your outlines simple. A complicated outline might sound better than a streamlined one, but it won't be nearly as useful. After all, the purpose of an outline is to picture the relation among your ideas as clearly as possible, to help you as you write your rough draft. When you do write your rough draft, you'll probably want to vary your wording and sentence structures to avoid monotony. But while outlining, don't let yourself get too fancy.

If you feel the need to write a two-layer outline, we suggest that you work on it a layer at a time. First block out the overall structure of the paper with a simple, one-layer outline. Then go back and work on the second layer. This way you won't get too bogged down in the details of the outline while you're still struggling with your paper's overall design.

We have kept our treatment of outlining simple because we believe that outlines should be simple if they are to serve as blueprints for your papers. We have learned, through our own experience and the experiences of our students, that complex outlines can paralyze writers. They force the writer to decide too much too soon. Simpler outlines will keep you flexible for the creative process of writing a rough draft. Because they are just sketches of the overall design of your paper, simple outlines leave room for new insights that may occur to you as you write.

CUTTING AND TAPING

Even though it's safest to organize before you write, we're aware that writers—both students and professionals—don't always choose this method. A writer sometimes begins with just a hint of a plan, then writes awhile in hopes that the paper will take shape as it is being written. This is a perfectly acceptable, if risky, way to organize a paper. Your rough draft may turn out so tangled that your only hope is to begin all over again. But if the rough draft at least begins to take shape as you're writing it, you'll probably be able to cut and tape it into shape later. Even when you begin with a clear blueprint, sometimes your rough draft won't turn out quite the way you'd planned. Then, too, cutting and taping is your answer.

In chapter 2 you will find a general discussion of the cutting and taping process. This process includes deleting unnecessary material, possibly moving paragraphs and sentences about, and writing any new material that seems needed. For an example of cutting and taping, you can turn back to chapter 2.

In this chapter we will focus on cutting and taping to improve the organization of a paper. Let's begin by looking at a paper's organization from the point of view of a reader.

Reading expert Mortimer J. Adler tells us that good readers X-ray their reading material. They make every effort to see the skeleton that lies beneath what they are reading. The skeleton shows them how the parts of the paper are connected to each other and how they contribute to the main point of the whole paper. "The reader tries to *uncover* the skeleton," says Adler, and "the author starts with the skeleton and tries *to cover it up* . . . to put flesh on the bare bones."

Readers will look for the bones of your paper in certain *key sentences,* and in general you should make sure you've put these key sentences in places where readers will be looking for them. The thesis statement is of course the key sentence for the whole paper, and readers tend to look for it in the first or last sentence of the opening paragraph. Within a paper readers will look for other key sentences that help them see how the parts of the paper are related to each other and to the whole. These key sentences are most often found at the beginnings of paragraphs, and that's where readers tend to expect them. As you probably know, these key sentences are known as *topic sentences*.

As a general rule, your thesis statement and topic sentences should interlock. Just by reading these key sentences, readers should be able to see the shape of the paper. Let us give you a couple of examples to show you what we mean.

The young woman whose outline for a paper on tennis you saw earlier, began her paper with this paragraph, opening with her thesis statement:

> *Concentration is the key to becoming a consistent winner in tennis.*
> And to achieve concentration you must learn to control your emotions.
> A look at three professional tennis players will make this point clear.

Here are the topic sentences of the student's next three paragraphs. Notice that each one clearly connects with the writer's thesis:

> Few women players today can even compare with Chris Evert, for she is a master of the art of concentration.
>
> Ilie Nastase, better known as "Nasty," probably the rudest player ever to come on the tour, improved his game once he learned to concentrate.
>
> Jimmy Connors is an erratic player because he has not yet learned to concentrate.

These topic sentences have been lifted straight out of the student's paper, and if they resemble an outline, when connected with the thesis, that's no accident. Take the key sentences out of a well-organized paper, and you have a sentence outline.

Here is the skeleton of another student paper. The thesis appears at the end of the introductory paragraph:

> Locating an ideal camp site requires a great deal more than a desire to nestle down by a camp fire near a quiet stream. The place which offers the greatest eye-appeal can quickly lose its charm when night comes, the fog rolls in and the mosquitoes infest your camp. So resist choosing your camp site just for its beauty. *Instead, look for natural protection, the right soil conditions, and easy access to running water.*

The topic sentences interlock with this thesis; we've italicized the part of each topic sentence that most clearly points back to the thesis:

> Nature provides many *natural sources of protection* against the elements if you are resourceful enough to use them.
>
> The *soil condition* is of vital importance no matter where you are camping.

Although water-logged soil can turn out to be a real source of trouble, your camp should be located *close to a spring of running water.*

As you can see, the skeleton of this student's paper resembles an outline. Just by reading the key sentences of the paper, readers can see how the parts all add up to the whole.

When you are trying to improve the organization of a rough draft, begin with the skeleton of the paper. Can a reader, just by scanning your thesis and topic sentences, tell how your paper is organized? If not, strengthen that skeleton.

As you work to strengthen the skeleton, you may find yourself making other changes—deleting material, moving sentences or even whole paragraphs about, even adding new material. With the help of scissors and tape you can take apart and reassemble your paper, experimenting with new arrangements of your material. Don't worry if your pages start looking messy—this is your rough draft, after all.

If you're having a hard time deciding whether a rough draft needs reorganizing, or if you can't think of a way to reorganize it, ask someone for help. A friend, instructor, or parent—anyone with a fresh perspective—may have insights that will lead you in the right direction.

Sometimes just talking about the shape of your rough draft or trying to draw a picture of its shape on scratch paper will lead you to a new insight. Keep yourself flexible, experimenting with different possibilities, and sooner or later you will discover the right shape for your paper.

In this chapter we have given you three practical strategies for organizing a paper: scribbling on scratch paper, outlining, and reorganizing with scissors and tape. If you're not in the habit of using these techniques—and many students aren't—give them all a try. This semester. See for yourself the difference they can make.

EXERCISE 1   FOR CLASS DISCUSSION

To outline or not to outline is often a question for novice writers. And whether to require an outline is a question for composition instructors. Some discussion in class of both the advantages and disadvantages of outlines could well be worthwhile. Here are some professional writers' observations that might help get such a discussion going:

    a. [Outlining] too often becomes an artificial framework that a student has to justify. If writing is a learning process, then you will discover better ways of doing things as you go along.
                                               —Cyril H. Knoblauch

    b. How can you tell what your house will look like or keep up with the building of it if you don't start with a blueprint?
                                               —Anonymous

c. If you are used to starting every writing job with an outline, don't. Wait until you have felt the click. Before that, any outline will tie you down.

—Rudolf Flesch

d. [The] writer may create a formal "Harvard" outline in which each point is in a complete sentence. It is more likely, however, that he doesn't follow the rules of Roman numerals and Arabic numbers, of capital letters and small letters, but draws what he has to say in a circle or a square, develops it in chart form, or scribbles it very informally, putting ideas down in random patterns and then drawing lines between ideas.

—Donald M. Murray

e. If you are the kind of person who loves card files, try dropping all your cards on the floor some time. It will do you no end of good.

—Rudolf Flesch

f. Complicated outlines tempt you to think too much about the fine points of organization, at a time when you should be blocking out the overall structure.

—Anonymous

EXERCISE 2   WRITTEN

We know one woman who can take almost any subject and break it into three logical parts. How did she pick up this skill? Well, she's the daughter of a Southern Baptist preacher whose sermons were always divided, quite logically, into three parts. As a child our friend was forced to sit through her father's sermons twice every Sunday, so she learned how to organize almost without effort.

You too can increase your organizing skills by paying attention to the structures of sermons, classroom lectures, television documentaries, and sometimes even politicians' speeches. Sometime this week while you are listening to a sermon or a classroom lecture or a chalk-talk at the office, jot down notes that outline the structure of what you have heard.

EXERCISE 3   WRITTEN

Read the following student papers from part 7, then reproduce on scratch paper the jottings each writer might have used to organize his or her paper:

Irish vs. American Education (#1)

Better to Die at Home (#18)

Borrowings from Black Culture (#7)

Who Goes to the Races? (#16)

EXERCISE 4   FOR CLASS DISCUSSION

Analyze the skeletons of the student papers in exercise 3.

> The paragraph [is] a mini-essay; it is also a maxi-sentence.
> —Donald Hall

CHAPTER 9
BUILDING PARAGRAPHS

If paragraphing hadn't been invented, just how easily could we do without it? What would it be like, for example, to read a 300-page book that was not divided up into paragraphs? Probably you wouldn't even try to read such a book; but if you did, you'd find yourself reading at a slow pace, with less comprehension than usual.

Paragraphs help readers in several ways. First of all, they ease the reader's eye by breaking up black print with restful touches of white. They assure the reader that there will be stopping points along the way. We like what the writer Donald Hall has to say about this: "Paragraphs rest the eye as well as the brain. . . . Those little indentations are hand- and footholds in the cliff face of the essay." Paragraphs help readers in another important way. They help readers visualize the shape of what they are reading. Just by looking at the way the paragraphs are blocked out, readers begin to understand how the whole has been divided into parts, and how the parts add up to the whole. Finally, paragraphs show readers how sentences are related to each other. Readers immediately understand, just by seeing a group of sentences clustered together in a paragraph, that they belong together in some way. The topic sentence of the paragraph tells them just how the sentences belong together, how they all add up.

When we talk about paragraphs in this chapter, we will limit ourselves to "body paragraphs," those used to develop the main idea of a paper. We will not, then, be considering paragraphs with special functions: introductory, concluding, and transitional paragraphs. These special-function paragraphs are discussed in other chapters.

Body paragraphs are the blocks of thought that add up to prove the main point of the paper. It helps to think of each of these body paragraphs as a mini-paper. Like a whole paper, each body paragraph needs focus, adequate development, and shape.

FOCUSING WITH A TOPIC SENTENCE

The topic sentence of a paragraph is a mini–thesis statement. It announces the main point of the paragraph, preparing readers for the sentences to come. Notice, for example, how well this student writer has focused our attention with a topic sentence:

> *The teacher had complete control over the class.* When she was in
> the room, everyone was quiet and worked in an orderly manner. When
> she left the room, noise would naturally pick up, but as soon as she reap-
> peared, order resumed. If you had a question or knew an answer, you
> raised your hand. You were not allowed to speak unless you were ac-
> knowledged. When your class left the room, you walked in an orderly
> line with your group, and talking was not permitted when passing other
> rooms.

This student's topic sentence has all of the characteristics of a good thesis statement: it is a generalization that needs to be supported by more detailed information; it is limited (not too broad); and it is precisely focused (not too vague).

Here is another well-focused topic sentence, as it appeared in a paragraph taken from a paper describing the adoption of a Vietnamese orphan by the writer's parents:

> *Because Tiet was an orphan in a country at war, my parents spent a*
> *lot of time cutting red tape and bargaining in the customary Vietnamese*
> *fashion—with monetary bribes.* The nuns of the orphanage, in a subtle
> way of course, let my parents know that if money wasn't sent for a new
> well and milking machine then the Lord never meant for Tiet to be
> adopted. Money had to be sent to village heads and Saigon officials as
> a gesture of respect. Even the President of Vietnam, who must sign all
> citations of adoption, was sent a token of esteem—namely, one thousand
> dollars.

Notice how clearly the topic sentence prepared you for the examples that followed.

Like the student writers we've quoted, generally you should put your topic sentence at the beginning of a paragraph, rather than in the middle or at the end. The topic sentence is designed to focus the reader's attention on the main point of the paragraph and to direct his or her attention to the supporting material that follows; the topic sentence should therefore come first. It makes no sense to prepare readers for a paragraph they've just finished. Another reason for putting your topic sentence first is that readers tend to look for it at the beginning of a paragraph. So when you put your topic sentence first, you are fulfilling your readers' expectations, going along with their natural reading habits.

Occasionally you will have a good reason for violating your readers' expectations. You may decide, for example, to delay your topic sentence until the end of the paragraph because you want to surprise your readers, or even sneak up on them. We recall one student paragraph that ended with a topic sentence calling for increased taxes. The student felt, quite rightly, that if he'd hit his readers right off with the main point, they'd be reluctant to read on. So the student gave his arguments first, because he thought he could get readers to go along with them, and saved his unpopular topic sentence for the end.

The writer of the following paragraph also had a good reason for delaying her topic sentence. Recognizing that her examples were more vivid than her topic sentence, she decided to dazzle her readers first, with a vivid opener, then let them know the point later, at the end of the paragraph. She judged that her readers would know, from the context, what the examples were supposed to illustrate, so by putting the topic sentence last she didn't risk confusing readers:

> Our impressionable tykes read about homicidal old ladies offering poisoned apples long before they discover SWAT. They cope with Alice's encounter with madness and Red Riding Hood's mugging without tension or discomfort. No red-blooded American child would wince during Peter Pan's battle with the pirates or Dorothy's gruesome attack by winged monkeys. *These worldly little people are not likely to faint because of television crimes: more likely they will be disappointed by the quality of the violence.*

Rarely will you have a good reason for putting your topic sentence in the middle of a paragraph, but often you'll have reason to delay it a bit. Sometimes, as you move from one paragraph to another in your paper, you'll find that you need a transitional or "bridge" sentence before your topic sentence. The purpose of a transitional sentence is to show readers the connection between what went before and what is about to come. Here is an example of a student paragraph which opens with a transitional sentence followed by the topic sentence:

> Aside from sexual incompatibility, there was another problem. *Although David was a good and decent man, he lacked initiative.* All decision-making, regardless of importance, was relegated to me. "You decide" was his answer. Home and car repairs went untended until I either insisted he make repairs or saw to them myself. If the roof leaked, it continued leaking until I had it mended. If the furnace went out, I negotiated for repair or arranged for purchase of a new one. All of our financial affairs were left for me to handle.

As a general rule, then, put your topic sentence at the opening of the paragraph unless you have a good reason for putting it elsewhere.

Sometimes you may even want to echo your topic sentence at the end of a paragraph in a "clincher" sentence. The topic sentence orients, prepares, and points ahead; the clincher sentence concludes, emphasizes, and points back. Clincher sentences work well for stressing a point, as the following student paragraph demonstrates:

> *Avoid the high class, plush, Japanese style bars filled with enchanting hostesses.* Most of them, especially those in the Ginza area, are notorious clip joints which pad their customers' bills. Often you will have to pay for untouched and unordered tidbits pushed in front of you. If you want one of the hostesses to be your companion you must pay for her as well as for her high-priced "colored drinks." Many of the waitresses and bar hostesses insist on a tip in addition to the service and hostess charges you must pay. *So unless you enjoy tourist traps, steer clear of these high class, Japanese style bars.*

FILLING OUT PARAGRAPHS

Paragraphs, like whole papers, need to be developed fully enough to satisfy a reader. Therefore, once you've focused on a topic sentence, you should ask yourself how much evidence, and what kind of evidence, your readers need to hear in support of that topic sentence. For the student who wrote the paragraph showing that her parents had to pay bribes in order to adopt the Vietnamese orphan, the decision about evidence was easy enough. To illustrate her topic sentence to readers, she simply detailed the bribes her parents had had to pay—to the nuns, the village head, Saigon officials, and even to the President of Vietnam.

Another student writer decided that a few well-chosen examples would be enough to illustrate her main point:

> *Strangely enough, instead of being academically inferior to my American high school, the Irish convent was superior.* In my class at home *Love Story* was considered pretty heavy reading, so imagine my surprise at finding Irish students who could recite passages from *War and Peace.* In high school we complained about having to study "Romeo and Juliet" in one semester, whereas in Ireland we simultaneously studied "Macbeth" and Dickens' *Hard Times,* in addition to writing a composition a day in English class. In high school I didn't even begin algebra until the ninth grade, while at the convent seventh graders (or their Irish equivalent) were doing calculus and trigonometry.

These contrasting examples—*Love Story* vs. *War and Peace,* and so on— are quite enough to convince readers that the topic sentence is true.

Sometimes a writer can get by with a less fully developed paragraph, especially if he or she selects just the right details to illustrate the topic sentence. For example, with just two additional sentences this student writer suggests the truth of his topic sentence:

> *The atmosphere of the Berwyn Cafe was easygoing, unhurried.* Some of the customers who had finished their meals were washing their own dishes, talking and sharing vegetarian recipes with the cooks. As they left, people paid for their meals by dropping their money into a large wooden bowl, retrieving the change themselves.

So sometimes, depending on your purposes, you can get by with slim paragraphs. But if your topic sentence is a major point in your whole paper, you will want to develop it with considerable detail. If the paragraph starts to look too long, you can break it at some convenient point without writing a topic sentence for the new paragraph. The writer of the following paragraphs states her main point in the opening two sentences (which work together as her "topic sentence"), then develops that main point with several examples, using two paragraphs to do so:

> *Even more offensive than the overstatements and clichés are the maudlin personal stories that sportscasters force upon us. When they deplete their supply of handy statistics, they turn to pathos.* The viewer is informed that a certain hulking linebacker was a sissy in second grade. Another bought "dear old mom" her dream house with his first playoff bonus. We hear vivid descriptions of previous injuries, and suffer through some poor guy's "excruciatingly painful" experience with a pulled groin muscle.
>
> Billy Kilmer, who was not expected to walk after his car accident, has a daughter with cerebral palsy for whom he "plays his heart out" weekly. O. J. Simpson is enduring a period of great stress. He wants to be near his family in California, but is forced by his contract to earn millions in Buffalo.

As you can see from the examples we've given you, there is a logical relation between the topic sentence of a paragraph and the rest of the sentences in the paragraph. The relation is a supporting one. So the questions to ask yourself are these: What kind of support does this topic sentence call for? And just how much supporting evidence will my readers need?

One of the most common flaws in student paragraphs is underdevelopment. Often students write the topic sentence, then have trouble filling out the rest of the paragraph with supporting examples or details. If this happens to you, maybe you are writing on a subject you know too little about; in that case you should either abandon the paragraph or figure out some way to get the material you need. But if you are writing

on a topic that you do know something about, you can fatten a too
slimly developed paragraph by simply brainstorming details on a piece
of scratch paper. Often it's a good idea to do this anyway, before you
write the paragraph. When you work from jotted-down notes, you don't
have to interrupt your flow by stopping to think up additional details or
examples.

SHAPING PARAGRAPHS

The basic overall shape of a paragraph is quite simple: topic sentence
plus supporting sentences. The most simply structured paragraphs are
those in which every sentence directly supports the topic sentence. In
the following paragraph, for example, the supporting sentences all have
exactly the same direct relation to the topic sentence:

> *Throughout history, women have resorted to many extremes in order
> to attain the standard of beauty popular at the time.* In China women's
> feet were bound, to keep them small, because men admired tiny feet. A
> tribe in Africa measured the affluence of the husband by the wife's weight,
> so women put on so much weight they could not move. In our own coun-
> try we don't have to look too far back to a time when women were prone
> to fainting spells because they had cinched their twenty-five-inch waists
> down to a fashionable eighteen.

All three supporting sentences in this paragraph directly illustrate the
writer's topic sentence.

But paragraphs are not always so simply shaped. Sometimes a writer
will want to develop some of the supporting sentences in a paragraph, as
if they were mini–topic sentences. In such a paragraph, some sentences
will support the topic sentence directly, and others will support it only
indirectly.

Let's call a sentence which directly supports the topic sentence a
"major support" sentence. Any sentences which in turn develop a major
support we'll call "minor support" sentences. The student writer of the
following paragraph has arranged her ideas into such a paragraph. As you
read, see if you can pick out the major supports, which act as mini–topic
sentences to prepare you for the minor supports:

> Hospitals are concerned with keeping the heart beating, not with the
> dignity of life. The 83-year-old father of a friend of mine, who had a
> slow-growing cancer of the prostate and whose veins were collapsing due
> to old age, was treated by the hospital staff as a collection of symptoms,
> not as a person. The nurses insisted on checking his blood pressure often,
> even though he found this very painful. In addition, they took blood
> tests every day, in spite of the fact that they had difficulty finding his

veins. Before he died, he also had to endure the torture of being X-rayed to check the progress of the cancer. Mercifully, he died after being in the hospital only a few weeks. Unfortunately, an 89-year-old aunt of mine suffered for seven months in the hospital before she died. She went in and out of comas, had pneumonia a couple of times and was pulled back to life to suffer more. She was a shrunken senile old lady begging for death when she died.

We hope you identified two sentences as "major supports"—the ones beginning "The 83-year-old father of a friend of mine" and "Unfortunately, an 89-year-old aunt of mine." Both of these sentences directly support the topic sentence of the paragraph; the rest of the sentences in the paragraph are minor supports that develop one of these two major supports.

Here is another paragraph containing both major and minor supports. The first sentence is the topic sentence. The second sentence and all of the other italicized sentences are the major supports. The rest of the sentences are minor supports:

A number of toys on the market provide safe and effective outlets for your child's aggressive feelings. *For example, you can buy a small punching bag for a small bully. In the case of fighting brothers and sisters, soccer boppers are quite effective.* Soccer boppers are a primitive form of boxing gloves that protect the children from actually hurting each other, but allow them to keep on fighting until they feel better. *When you have a child who likes to throw things, the "Nerf" airplanes and animals are your answer.* With these toys not too much can get broken, because they are made of foam rubber. *In the case of the child who enjoys biting, a rubber hand might be appropriate.* You can always find these around Halloween. With a rubber hand children can satisfy their biting impulses without hurting anyone. *When you have a child with an uncontrollable amount of aggression, one solution is a padded room.* However, these are not yet on the market for home use.

As you can see, some of the major supports required more development than others, so the number of minor supporting sentences following each major support varies. The first major support required no development, so no minor supports follow it.

In this chapter we have given you only two model shapes for a typical body paragraph: one simple and one more complex. When you are writing to prove a point, you'll be surprised how often you can pour your paragraphs into one of these two molds.

But don't expect every body paragraph you write to fit one of these models exactly. In reality there are hundreds of possible paragraph shapes. The ones that will work for you in a particular writing situation will be those which arrange your material clearly; which illustrate your point logically; and which accomplish your purpose of communicating with readers.

Much of what we have said in the chapter on shaping a whole paper applies to paragraphs as well—except that, luckily, it's easier to shape paragraphs, because they're shorter. Often you can block out the shape of a paragraph in your head, before you write it. But if you get stuck you can always scribble on scratch paper awhile until you hit on a plan that might work. Or you can just plunge in, hoping to discover a shape as you write.

If your rough draft paragraph turns out poorly shaped, what can you do? If it's hopelessly disorganized, you can always throw it out and start over. But if it's not in total chaos, a cut-and-tape revision may pull it into shape. In short, you shape a paragraph the same way you organize a whole paper. You sketch a plan in your head or on scratch paper; you write; then, if you need to, you rewrite, perhaps with the help of scissors and tape.

HOW LONG SHOULD A PARAGRAPH BE?

How long should your paragraphs be? Our general advice is that you'll have to be flexible, because there's no one consideration that outweighs all others. Using a few rules of thumb, you'll need to make decisions for yourself. All we can do is give you those rules of thumb.

Often you can tell whether a paragraph is too long or too short just by noticing how it looks on the page. Remember that one major function of a paragraph is to rest the reader's eye, so if you have a 500-word paragraph (two pages typed, double-spaced), you can be pretty sure your reader will get tired. You'll need to break up the 500 words into two or three, maybe even four paragraphs for your reader. By the same token, if you have broken 500 words up into ten paragraphs, you can be fairly certain that your readers will get too much "rest." It's like taking them on a ten-mile hike and insisting that they rest every mile; you break their momentum and wear them out from too much starting and stopping.

So you need to notice how long your paragraphs look on the page. And that, of course, depends on what kind of page we're talking about. As you write papers in college, your paragraph length will be determined to some extent by your decision to type or to write longhand. Typed paragraphs, generally, can be a bit longer than handwritten ones.

Earlier in this chapter we made the point that paragraphs help readers understand the shape of what they are reading. This is a very important consideration in determining the lengths of your paragraphs. If at all possible, let your paragraphs reflect the shape of your ideas. If, for example, you are writing a 500-word paper in which you give the reader three examples to illustrate your main point, you'll probably decide on five paragraphs: a paragraph of introduction, three body paragraphs (one for each example), and a short concluding paragraph. If one of your examples is much longer than the other two, so long that it will tire your reader's eye, you'll probably want to split it at some convenient point. The more closely your paragraphs reflect the shape of your ideas, the clearer your paper is likely to be.

One final word about paragraph length. How consistent should you be in the lengths of your paragraphs? Should you try to make them all about the same length, or should you vary your paragraphs, playing off long ones against short ones? These questions are hard to answer. Paragraph lengths, like sentence lengths, give a paper a kind of rhythm that readers can feel but that is hard to talk about. A very short paragraph can be just the right kind of short pause following a long and complex paragraph. Or a series of paragraphs of about the same length can give the reader a very satisfying feeling of balance and proportion. But let us say no more about this; you'll have to follow your own ear.

EXERCISE 1 FOR CLASS DISCUSSION

Identify the topic sentence of each of the following student paragraphs. If the writer chose not to place the topic sentence at the very beinning of the paragraph, do you see a good reason for its being elsewhere? If the paragraph lacks a topic sentence, is its main point clear to readers?

1. Now for those prepared mixes. I know that the Duncan Hines Cake mix looks very tempting, but have you ever considered what you actually get for your seventy-nine cents? Let's take a look. For seventy-nine cents you get items that are usually already in your kitchen cabinets—flour, sugar, shortening and leavening. In addition, you get certain undesirable preservatives. After getting the mix home, you find that you must add your own eggs and in some cases butter for a better tasting cake. Since the ingredients for a cake are usually in your cabinets, why not make your own mix and save your seventy-nine cents?

2. Soap opera characters are far from being realistic. They are all upper class people, living in the finest of homes and wearing the latest fashions. You never see any poor people on these shows or anyone who has an ordinary job. No, these characters are all doctors or lawyers. The cities in which these soap operas take place must have to ship people in to do the less prestigious work.

3. Another example of research aimed at preventing sexual child abuse is underway at California State Hospital. Operating under the theory that most child molesters have led highly inadequate social and sexual lives, psychologists teach offenders how to talk to and relate to adults. The California State Hospital program is so sophisticated that it even

has volunteer counselors from local gay organizations coming in to teach homosexual offenders how to pick up adult partners.

4. Today the two oldest are out of college with good paying jobs. The oldest one went into dentistry and then into the Navy. He is stationed in South Carolina, and has his own office to work in. The second child passed through college with high honors and now is a Certified Public Accountant, working for the second largest firm in the United States, making $18,000 yearly, and awaiting a $5,000-dollar raise. The youngest is still in college, planning to go into business.

5. The automobile has played a powerful role in shaping the way Americans live, and most people have always thought highly of the automobile. However, the public has recently come to realize that the automobile is actually a menace to society. It creates most of the air pollution in the United States as well as contributing to noise pollution. If citizens must drive, they should only drive cars with air pollution control devices. However, in order to really combat pollution, all commuters should use public transportation.

6. Mike was a small, frail five-and-a-half-year-old, with beautiful brown hair, brown eyes, and a laugh that was unforgettable. Mike had several handicaps. He could not walk, talk, sit up, support his head, or feed himself. He had been born severely spastic and blind.

7. As a Prepared Childbirth teachers' assistant, I've met over 60 young, first-time parents in a classroom situation. I've seen the positive effects prepared childbirth, immediate contact with the baby, and breast-feeding have on the parent-child relationship. I believe these positive experiences help prevent child abuse. The classes provide prospective parents with knowledge of what is ahead for them so they can prepare for the arrival of a third individual within their own relationship.

8. Not that the Irish were completely superior in educational standards. Many of the students at the convent had never even heard of chemistry, much less sex education. They knew by heart the exploits of Cuchulain (a legendary Irish warrior), but knew nothing of Freud or Marx or of any religion but their own. The average Irish student seemed to have a firm knowledge of the classics but was out of touch with the world of today.

9. Sake, Japanese rice wine, is as Japanese as apple pie is American. It is served at informal as well as formal dinners. Etiquette dictates that a guest should never fill his own glass, though it is proper and desirable that he should fill others' glasses. Another drink the Japanese take pride in is ochai, green tea. Japanese green tea is an indispensable accompaniment to an informal meal. It is served from a kettle which is kept on the table and frequently refilled. The Japanese do drink imported "western style" or "black" tea with lemon or milk, and the name of Lipton is famous throughout the land, but green tea is more popular. It is similar to Chinese tea and is drunk plain, without cream, sugar, or lemon.

EXERCISE 2   FOR CLASS DISCUSSION

How adequately developed is each of the following student paragraphs? If the paragraph seems too skimpy to satisfy readers (or to support the topic sentence), where might the writer find more material to fill out the paragraph?

1. The Irish convent had almost none of the educational facilities or equipment believed necessary in America. There was no cafeteria or food service. There were no science labs (although my biology teacher *did* bring a dead frog once and dissect it for us). The home economics department consisted of one stove and seven sinks. There was no library, really, just a box of paperback books that the English teacher let us borrow from. There was one record player for the entire school and a tape recorder that dated from World War II.

2. People who want to improve the environment should start in their own homes. They should change their life styles so that they consume less. Lights and televisions should not be kept on in unoccupied rooms. It only wastes energy. Junk mail should be sent back because it is only a waste of paper. These examples are only a few things that can be done in the home.

3. For a major in physical education, you need to take many science courses. It is important to know all the bones of the body. If you're a teacher and one of your students gets hurt, you have to know how to treat the injury. There is so much science required that with a few more credits you could be a pre-med major.

4. Things were just as bad for me in the outfield as they were in the infield. I always got stuck in left field, way out past any of these kids' batting range. It was so boring out there—I never did anything! Occasionally, maybe once or twice in a game, a ball would roll out my way. I would never be ready for it, though, because by that time I had lost interest in the game and was busy watching some squirrel in the bushes. So the ball would always roll on by me before I'd realized what happened. Any "fly balls" I would drop as soon as they hit my glove— assuming I was able to get them to hit my glove.

5. The main problem with this self-paced course is that I'm not pacing myself. Being a procrastinator is something I've always put off facing, but now it's beginning to catch up with me.

6. At Forestville a weekly report is sent home every Friday to inform the parents of their child's behavior and study habits during that period. If there's something that needs attention, the teacher will write comments along the bottom of the form. For instance, my daughter's teacher wrote me a note stating that Nicole's math was poor. After two weeks passed and Nicole's math hadn't improved, I suggested a meeting. When I met with the teacher she directed me to the Child Guidance Room. The storage cabinet in the room was filled with math games, word games, and science games that parents could check out to help their child. I checked out some math games, but after another two weeks Nicole's progress was still limited. Nicole's teacher then sent me a notice saying that she was receiving individualized instruction along with two or three other students who were having problems. Soon after, Nicole was consistently bringing home stars and happy faces.

7. If it's containers you're worrying about, don't! Almost anything goes. Any container that will hold water can be used as a plant container. Try painting empty coffee cans or hollowing out old pieces of wood. Just use your imagination.

EXERCISE 3 WRITTEN

Assume that the writers of the paragraphs in the last exercise worked from jotted-down lists of ideas. Reproduce, on scratch paper, the lists the students probably worked from. If a paragraph seems too skimpy, try expanding the list with jotted-down details of your own.

EXERCISE 4 WRITTEN

Browse through the topics in part 7 in search of a subject that would work for a paragraph of 150 to 250 words. (Feel free to narrow any of the topics radically.) Jot down a list of ideas which you'd use *if* you were going to write the paragraph, but don't actually write it.

EXERCISE 5 WRITTEN

Select a topic from part 7 that could be developed in a paragraph of 150 to 250 words. Before you write the paragraph, jot down a list of ideas on scratch paper. If your list shows little promise, throw it out and start another one, maybe on another topic. Once you have a workable list on scratch paper, write the paragraph. (Don't worry if the paragraph doesn't exactly fit the list—the list is there to give you control, not to straitjacket you.) Hand in your paragraph and your scratch paper list.

A reader should be able to move through a piece of writing without even being aware of the movement.

—Betty Renshaw

CHAPTER 10

HOLDING IT ALL TOGETHER

We come now to what may at first strike you as a minor detail: the coherence of your writing or how it all hangs together. Although coherence is one of the finer points of writing, it is nonetheless a very important one. If your paper does not flow along so that readers can easily follow it, they will feel confused, even lost. Readers have a right to expect your writing to flow, to move so naturally that they are not even aware of the movement. You will need to make it easy for your reader to stay with you, both within paragraphs and while moving between paragraphs.

We might define the verb *to cohere,* from which *coherence* comes, in three ways: (1) to be connected logically; (2) to be consistent; and (3) to stick together. Let's talk first about attending to the logical connections within a piece of writing.

LOGICAL CONNECTIONS

One way to achieve coherence is to establish logical connections by careful organization. How to do this is explained in our earlier chapters on focusing and on shaping. As we showed there, a piece of writing needs, first, a clear focus in its introductory paragraph. Then, once the introduction has established the promise of a paper, the shape of the rest of the paper should echo that promise, traceable through the topic sentences of the remaining paragraphs. A paper that begins with a sharp focus and follows a pattern that maintains that focus will move naturally and logically, taking the reader right along with it.

CONSISTENCY: POINT OF VIEW

Another source of coherence which can affect your paper throughout is
consistency in point of view. A paper's point of view is the perspective
from which it is written. Keeping your entire paper in the same perspective is one way to fasten it all together and to keep your reader with you.
To demonstrate why maintaining the same point of view throughout a
paper matters so much—and how jumbled writing can become when the
point of view gets off—here is a student paper, with instructor comments:

A few summers ago I had the opportunity
to jump from an airplane. And I can tell
you that sky-diving is easy to learn on the
ground--but sometimes scary to do in the air.

The equipment needed for jumping was
the first thing my instructor went over.
Most important, of course, are the parachute
and the reserve chute, then heavy ankle
boots and a crash helmet. A jumpsuit is a
good item for <u>you</u> to have, but is optional.
In going over the equipment, the instructor
also talked about ways in which it could
malfunction.

awkward
pronoun
shift:
keep paper
in first
person "I."

The next step was to learn how to get
back on the ground in one piece, following
a jump. Let me tell you about one of my
first jumps.

Once in the air, I climb out of the
plane (a Cessna 185) very carefully and
place my feet on a platform located above
the right wheel. When my feet are firmly
located on the platform, I move to get a
grip on the wing stability bar. Now I am
ready to jump at the jumpmaster's signal of
"Go!" Waiting for the signal, I wonder what
the hell I am doing 3,000 feet above the
ground with an 80-mph wind trying furiously

to break my grip from the plane. "Go!"
rings the jumpmaster's voice. Instantly my
grip is released. "Arch thousand, two
thousand, three thousand, pull thousand"--
these words driven into my head push their   *underlined*
way out of my mouth. Before I <u>could</u> collect   *verbs need*
my thoughts it <u>felt</u> like some force <u>had</u>   *to be in*
grabbed me right out of my fall and slowly   *present tense,*
but firmly brought me to a halt. To my   *as is rest*
astonishment, it <u>was</u> only the parachute   *of paragraph*
opening, otherwise known as "opening shock."   *so far.*
As I look at the ground I realize I haven't   *Do you really*
really come to a halt. During instruction,   *want to*
I was told exactly what to do after the   *suddenly take*
parachute opened in order to check for   *your reader out*
malfunctioning. I quickly check out my   *of midair -- an*
parachute for malfunctions. Thank God, I   *exciting place*
have none! As soon as I know that everything   *to be by now --*
has gone the way it was supposed to, I   *and back on to*
decide to enjoy the rest of the descent to   *the ground for*
the ground.   *instructions?*
                                                      Delete this sentence?

        The third thing I had learned about
during jump instruction was PLF (Parachute
Landing Fall). The PLF instruction didn't
help me one bit as I landed. I knew I was
supposed to sort of roll with the fall but
I didn't quite make it--I landed on my butt.
Even though that should have hurt, it didn't.
I just stood up, wrapped the parachute, and
walked back to the hangar, wondering if I
would ever jump again.

    This paper illustrates three common kinds of shifts in point of view:
pronoun shifts, verb tense shifts, and shifts in the location of what's
going on in a paper. When readers have to stop and try to puzzle out
such shifts, it is often difficult for them to get back into a paper again.
    Clear organization and a consistent point of view, then, serve to keep
an entire paper connected naturally, so that it flows. In addition, there
are some specific devices you can use to help your writing to cohere, or
to "stick together," as our third definition puts it.

THE ECHO EFFECT: REPETITION AND PARALLELISM

One device to help your writing stick together is the repetition of key words or phrases or ideas, which produces a sort of echo effect in your writing. Such repetition keeps reminding readers of the main point within a paragraph and focuses their attention on major ideas throughout a paper. In the paper you just read, for example, you kept hearing the key word *jump* echoed in various forms. In the paper printed below, the writer echoes whole sentences. "The husbands comfort their wives" is echoed at the beginning of paragraph 2 and at the end of paragraph 3. In addition, the question "Who is to comfort the husbands?" creates an echo effect to open paragraph 4.

The first thing I saw when I opened my newspaper this morning was a photograph of two sets of parents at the graveside of their young daughters, brutally murdered recently. The caption beneath the photograph, in which the mothers were clearly grieving, ended with the sentence "The husbands comfort their wives." Those last five words leave an important question unanswered: Who is to comfort the husbands?

"The husbands comfort their wives." I believe that the women in the picture are indeed receiving comfort from their men. But I believe they are getting more comfort in the open release of their emotions. Such open release allows twofold benefits. First, the women's display of emotion elicits a sympathetic reaction from others, who rush to comfort the grieving. Second, and I believe most important, their open grieving allows for a release of tensions that would otherwise build up inside. Such public display of emotion is therapeutic, and it is acceptable behavior for women.

I look more closely at one of the husbands. He sits there with his "stiff upper lip," surrounding his wife with his comfort-giving arms. I look closely at his eyes and the circles under them. In even such a poor quality photograph I can see the grief in his eyes longing for release. But that release cannot come, not in public, for he is "strong"; he is a "man." He is expected to give comfort to the "weaker" female. And so this husband comforts his wife.

But who is to comfort the husband? He is expected to "take it like a man." And he will, he will hold his grief and allow the tensions to build, until an acceptable time and place for release. Meanwhile, he acts "like a man"—in a display that is not very healthy, but that is acceptable behavior for men.

Another way to achieve the echo effect is to use synonyms, a device which also helps to avoid the monotony of simple repetition. The following paragraph uses synonyms for the word "marijuana" in this way:

The effects of *marijuana* are hotly debated. And whether the *drug* will be decriminalized largely depends on the outcome of the controversy now underway. Whether the pleasurable results from smoking *grass* should be considered worth the possible risks of its use is a real question in a free society. What are the long-term effects of the substance affectionately known among its advocates as *Mary Jane*—and how much should its detractors be listened to? Let us try to take an objective look at *marijuana*.

You can also create an echo effect by using parallel structure, in which parallel elements of a sentence or a paragraph are handled in the same way. In the following paragraph, for example, five successive sentences begin with a verb that invites an art museum visitor to enjoy a painting in various ways:

Suddenly, in the midst of your musings, you find yourself in a room ablaze with light, color, and life. There on the wall is Renoir's "Luncheon of the Boating Party." Take a seat and treat yourself to a longer look. Settle back and feel the joy and warmth of the painting. Smell the early summer breeze off the Seine. Hear the rustle of the leaves and the hum of the conversation. Stay as long as you like, but remember, there is more.

Here are the sentences listed so that you can more readily recognize the parallel structure:

Take a seat and treat yourself to a longer look.
Settle back and feel the joy and warmth of the painting.
Smell the early summer breeze off the Seine.
Hear the rustle of the leaves and the hum of the conversation.
Stay as long as you like, but remember, there is more.

In our next example, parallel structure has been combined with repetition to produce an echo effect:

You come up on the desert of the White Sands from the cultured East or the deep South or the industrial North and suddenly you breathe. The sand beneath you is white and the sky above you is blue and there is no need even to define the colors, for the white is the whitest you have ever seen and the blue is the bluest. There is nothing else. You take off your shoes and slide your feet quietly onto the whiteness and walk. You address the blue sky and walk. You breathe.

Parallel structure can also be used to carry along an entire piece of writing. In a paper by Jo Goodwin Parker, entitled "What Is Poverty?", eight of the fifteen paragraphs begin "Poverty is . . . ." Here are the topic sentences of Parker's opening paragraph, and of several of her other paragraphs:

You ask me what is poverty?

Poverty is being tired.

Poverty is dirt.

Poverty is staying up all night on cold nights to watch the fire, knowing one spark on the newspaper covering the walls means your sleeping child dies in flames.

Poverty is looking into a black future.

Poverty is an acid that drips on pride until all pride is worn away.

TRANSITIONAL BRIDGES

The final coherence device we want to tell you about is one of the simplest, and also one of the easiest to learn how to use. It is providing bridges to carry your reader from one part of your paper to the next. You can use these bridge words or phrases, sometimes called transitions, to move your reader from sentence to sentence, or from one paragraph into the next.

Here is a chart of some bridge words and phrases you can use:

TRANSITION TO INDICATE:	BRIDGE WORDS AND PHRASES:		
1. Addition	furthermore	or	thirdly
	also	nor	next
	in addition	moreover	last
	further	again	lastly
	besides	first	finally
	and	secondly	

Example: For the fruit-testing project we tasted sour green apples; furthermore, some of us consented to try very green bananas.

2. Time	while	immediately	never
	after	later	always
	when	soon	whenever
	meanwhile	in the meantime	sometimes
	during	afterwards	now
	next	following	once
	then	at length	simultaneously

Example: For the fruit-testing project we tasted sour green apples. Soon several of us developed stomach cramps.

TRANSITION
TO INDICATE: BRIDGE WORDS AND PHRASES:

3. Place:	here	beyond	adjacent to
	there	wherever	neighboring on
	nearby	opposite to	

Example: For the fruit-testing project we tasted sour green apples; nearby another group of volunteers was trying very green bananas.

4. Exemplification or Illustration	for example	for instance
	as an illustration	to illustrate
	to demonstrate	e.g. (means
	specifically	"for example")

Example: For the fruit-testing project, volunteers were expected to taste a variety of samples; our group, for instance, tried very green bananas.

5. Comparison	in the same way	in like manner
	by the same token	likewise
	similarly	in similar fashion

Example: For the fruit-testing project we tasted sour green apples; in similar fashion, some of us tried very green bananas.

6. Contrast	on the contrary	yet
	in contrast	and yet
	nevertheless	notwithstanding
	but	otherwise
	at the same time	however
	although that may be true	after all
	nonetheless	though
	on the other hand	

Example: For the fruit-testing project we tasted sour green apples; however, most of us refused to try very green bananas.

7. Clarification	that is to say	to clarify
	in other words	to rephrase it
	to put it another way	i.e. (means
	to explain	"in other words")

Example: For the fruit-testing project we tasted sour green apples. To explain, this project was part of a study to determine if green fruit can be beneficial to the body in any way.

TRANSITION TO INDICATE:	BRIDGE WORDS AND PHRASES:		
8. Cause	on account of because	since for that reason	

Example: Since we were afraid they would make us sick, several of us re-fused to try very green bananas during the fruit-testing project.

| 9. Effect | therefore
consequently
as a result | thus
hence
accordingly | |

Example: For the fruit-testing project we ate sour green apples; conse-quently, we were all in bed the next day with stomachaches.

| 10. Purpose | in order to
for this purpose | to that end
so that | |

Example: For the fruit-testing project we tasted sour green apples. In order to earn the full pay for volunteers for the project, some of us tried very green bananas.

| 11. Qualification | almost
nearly
probably | perhaps
maybe
although | |

Example: For the fruit-testing project we ate sour green apples. Perhaps I shall never feel more uncomfortable than I felt following that experiment.

| 12. Intensification | indeed
to repeat
by all means | undoubtedly
in fact
without doubt | doubtlessly
certainly
surely
of course |

Example: For the fruit-testing project we ate sour green apples; without doubt, that was one of my most unpleasant sensory experiences.

| 13. Summary | to summarize
in sum | in short
to sum up | in brief
in summary |

Example: We ate green apples for the fruit-testing project. Then we were handed very green bananas to try. Next came pears almost as hard as rocks. In brief, we were provided a steady diet of green fruit throughout the afternoon.

TRANSITION TO INDICATE:	BRIDGE WORDS AND PHRASES:		
14. Conclusion	in conclusion	to conclude	finally

Example: To conclude my report on tasting green fruits, I would simply advise my readers to find another way to contribute to the health studies of the nation.

The student writer of the following paper has learned how to use transitional bridges. Early in the course, his papers did not hold together well at all. This paper, a later one, has a problem in transition at only one point, as marked. Note the difference in the logical flow of the paper at that point with and without the bridge word. The transitional words and phrases in the paper are italicized.

If you are looking for a place to visit in the United States completely different from any other city in our country, Anchorage, Alaska, in the winter, should please you. I base this belief on five years of living in Anchorage as a military man.

First, if you arrive by air you will not be able to see the city until you are nearly on the ground, *because* it is practically surrounded by the snow-covered Chugiak Mountains. This may frighten you at first, *since* you will appear to be landing smack on top of the mountain. You will *no doubt* be quite relieved when your plane rolls to a stop at Anchorage International Airport.

Secondly, you may be somewhat surprised to find that most of the city's residents are white and black Americans, not Eskimos. You will *also* find the city itself similar to most American cities, with houses, hotels, apartment complexes, office buildings, and shopping centers—*and* not an igloo in sight. *However*, you

will learn later that there are Eskimos and
igloos farther north in Alaska.

Next, if you have never experienced
extreme cold, deep snow, and lots of ice,
you may be thrilled--*or* chilled. Tempera-
tures during the winter months in Anchorage
range from a mild zero degree to a cold 30
degrees below zero. Snow normally lies one *trans. of contrast--needed?*
to three feet deep. (The weather seems not *However!*
to be an obstacle in getting around the city.

Finally, if you like night life, you
will have plenty of time to enjoy yourself.
During the months of October, November,
December and January the nights are quite
long. *For instance*, in December the sun
rises between 10:00 and 11:00 a.m. and
usually sets between 2:30 and 3:00 p.m. It
is completely dark before 3:30 p.m.

But I must not forget to tell you that
the cost of living in Anchorage is quite
high. *In fact*, according to recent
statistics, Anchorage is one of the most
expensive places to live in our entire
country. For a holiday, *though*, I would
certainly recommend Anchorage, Alaska, to
you.

You can train yourself in how to use the transitional bridges listed in
our chart by asking yourself certain questions as you write: Does the
next thing I am going to say simply make an *addition* to something I've
just said? Or does the content of my next sentence set up a *comparison*
or a *contrast* with what's in my last sentence? Am I involved in a *cause-
and-effect* discussion? Am I about to illustrate my point by an *example*?
And so on. You can ask yourself the same questions as you begin a new
paragraph, of course.

Transitional bridges are not always merely single words or phrases.
Sometimes whole sentences or even paragraphs work as bridges to
smooth the way for your reader. You have seen an example of this kind
of transition in the student paper on jumping. The third paragraph of

that paper is a two-sentence transitional paragraph, carrying the reader between the on-ground instructions about equipment and malfunctioning and the actual jump from the plane in flight:

> The next step was to learn how to get back on the ground in one piece, following a jump. Let me tell you about one of my first jumps.

Here is another student paper that uses a transitional paragraph:

> This paper is a salute to black women all over our nation who have suffered almost unendurable hardships trying to keep their families together in the face of relentless day-to-day oppression. American history and American literature are slowly beginning to show us some of these strong black women, their struggles, their heartaches—and, always, their pride.
>
> I can think of no better example of these proud, tenacious women than Phoenix, in Eudora Welty's short story "The Worn Path."
>
> Old Phoenix was a product of the cruel institution of slavery. She had been freed by the Emancipation Proclamation, and had had no formal education. However, she was able to survive in a country hostile to freed slaves. . . .

The second paragraph, one sentence long, is a transitional paragraph. Transitional paragraphs can be composed of one or two, perhaps even three sentences, but they are unlikely to be very long.

TYING IT ALL TOGETHER: CONCLUSIONS

The conclusion of your paper, in a sense, serves to tie it all together by rounding it off. Through a summary statement, the conclusion lets your reader know that you have finished saying what you had to say. Just as your introduction introduced your main point, your conclusion drives it home. As we pointed out in an earlier chapter, your introductory paragraph should either begin or end with your thesis statement. The same is true for your concluding paragraph. Either begin or end it with a sentence that echoes your thesis.

If you decide to echo your thesis in the first sentence of your conclusion, use the remaining sentences of the paragraph to drive the point home. That's what this student has done, for example, to end a paper arguing for the rights of nonsmokers:

> Though I recognize the right of others to smoke privately, public smoking infringes on the rights of nonsmokers. It is more plausible for the smoker to curtail smoking than for the nonsmoker to curtail breathing.

The first sentence echoes the main point of the paper, that public smoking infringes on the rights of nonsmokers. The final sentence drives home that point with a witty remark: "It is more plausible for the smoker to curtail smoking than for the nonsmoker to curtail breathing."

Another student, whose paper showed how much the lifestyle of some homosexuals has changed over the past fifteen years, ended her paper like this:

> As you can see, the lifestyle of some homosexuals has changed tremendously in the past fifteen years. Homosexuals have had a long, hard struggle, but the end result has been worth it. As my friend Rhoda put it, "We feel like birds just released from our cage. We're just beginning to spread our wings and prove that we can fly."

Like the first student, this writer uses the first sentence of her conclusion to echo her main point. The other sentences, especially the quotation at the very end, drive home that point by showing what it means to one human being.

Here's one more example of a concluding paragraph that echoes the main point in the first sentence. This one concludes a paper showing readers that the Phillips Art Gallery is worth a visit:

> In any event, go to see the Phillips Collection. If you are an art lover, you can't miss at the Phillips. If you are not an art lover, you just might become one.

With her main point restated in her first sentence, our writer then uses a pair of pleasingly balanced parallel sentences in one last effort to entice readers to the gallery.

Sometimes you may decide to end, instead of beginning, your concluding paragraph with an echo of your thesis. In that case, the earlier sentences of the paragraph will build toward the restatement of your main point. Here, for example, is how one student writer built toward a final statement of her main point:

> The mother-at-home situation may produce secure, well-adjusted children. But not necessarily. It may result in a happy home. But not necessarily. The question of whether mothers of small children should work has no single answer. Since family situations are different, the answer to the question must be tailored to meet the needs of every family member —wife, husband, and children.

Another concluding paragraph, which builds toward the echoed thesis, is taken from a paper on the advantages of having twins:

> There have been many times when I've asked myself, "Why me?" But, when I stop to think that I have not one, but two beautiful, healthy six-year-old daughters, I know I'm a lucky person.

One last example. This paragraph concludes a paper on the difficulties involved in becoming a pro golfer:

Some have become millionaires playing golf. Others have made millions through advertising, writing, and investing. But when you think of the obstacles that must be overcome to make it big in the world of golf, you begin to realize that there are easier ways to make a living.

Whether you choose to echo your main point at the beginning or at the end of your final paragraph, remember that this is your last chance to drive home that main point. So don't settle for a dull restatement of your thesis. Try to put some life into your concluding words, so readers will leave your paper with a strong final impression.

This is not always easy to do, as you probably know. Strong conclusions sometimes seem to be a matter of instinct. Occasionally, as you near the end of a rough draft, just the right finish will come to you in a flash of inspiration. More often, though, you'll probably find yourself dully restating your thesis, instead of forcefully driving it home. If that happens, try to get away from your paper awhile, even for a few minutes. Then reread the paper, getting into its spirit, and try again. Hemingway claims that he rewrote one ending thirty-nine times before he was satisfied. When an interviewer asked him what the problem was, Hemingway paused for a moment, then gave this answer: "Getting the words right." You too may have to try more than once before getting those final words right.

EXERCISE 1   FOR CLASS DISCUSSION

Turn to these two student papers printed in part 8: "Time Out" (#19) and "It Was Halloween Night" (#2). The writers of both papers have skillfully used the techniques this chapter suggests for achieving coherence. Read each paper aloud, so you can hear its smooth flow. Then discuss the techniques each writer used to make her writing flow.

EXERCISE 2   WRITTEN

Read the following paragraph out loud to hear how it jolts along. Then revise it so that it hangs together better. Does your revision sound smoother when you read it aloud?

My graduation present, from my father and mother, was a new car. They said I could pick the car, as long as it was in a certain price range. I picked the Mercury Marauder X-100. My new car has a black vinyl top and is lime green in color. The Marauder X-100 has a tunnel fastback design, dual upper body paint strips, and hidden lights which open up at night. The sports car has wide oval tires with styled aluminum wheels. The car has a light brown interior with bucket seats. The following features are on my Marauder X-100: 429 4UV-8 engine, Select-Shift automatic transmission, air-conditioning, stereo-tape AM radio, power brakes and power steering.

EXERCISE 3   CLASSROOM ACTIVITY

Bring your latest rough draft to class with you. Working in pairs, check your writing for coherence, by having your partner read your paper out loud to you. Listen for rough, bumpy-sounding spots in your writing. Then, with your partner's help, try to discover the source of each problem. Is there a failure in logical connections, a lack of consistency in point of view, an absence of transitional bridges, a need for the echo effect, or what? By the end of your work session, you should be ready to revise your paper for coherence.

EXERCISE 4   CLASSROOM ACTIVITY

This one's mainly for fun. Paper number 3 in part 8 was written in class in 20 minutes. The student who wrote it was writing fast and freely—for flow. Have someone in the class read the paper aloud, someone who can read with feeling and move with the sentence flow.

EXERCISE 5   FOR CLASS DISCUSSION

For each of the following papers, printed in part 8, discuss how the conclusion drives home the paper's main point:

Nightclub Circuit (#6)
So He's Driving You Crazy (#9)
A Dangerous State of Mind (#13)
"Popsicle" (#4)

A sentence should read as if its author, had he held a plough instead of a pen, could have drawn a furrow deep and straight to the end.
—Henry David Thoreau

CHAPTER 11

CONSTRUCTING SENTENCES

If you're like most writers, your success with sentences varies. Sometimes your sentences flow onto the page smoothly, with grace and clarity. Other times they sound as if they were cranked out by a rusty machine. Listen to these sentences, for example, written by a student on a bad day. Listen out loud:

> "Prostitution" for centuries has been a word that was seldom mentioned in society, and when it was mentioned, it was in a negative manner. However, now for many reasons I feel that we as citizens of the United States of America need to take another look and to re-evaluate the positives of prostitution. The legalization of prostitution would drastically cut down the number of rape cases reported each year which is one of the worst violations that could occur to a woman's body; not to mention the psychological effect. Not only are women affected by this kind of experience, but children as well.

Pretty bad, we hope you agree. But if you're tempted to dismiss this student as a poor writer, listen to some sentences she wrote the week before:

> On a day that was of no particular significance to the country or the state of North Carolina—it was not a holiday—on May 31, 1935, I was born, the fifth of seven children. I am reasonably certain that there was nothing exciting about my birth except for the fact that Mother no longer had to "look ugly with her belly sticking out." Mother often said that she never wanted more than four children. Throughout my childhood, she let me know it.

Yes, that really is the same student writer. Here she is clearly in command of her sentences. But a week later, when she wrote the paper on   117 prostitution, she seemed to have lost her touch. How is it that a writer's command over sentences can vary so dramatically?

When we talked with the writer of the above paragraphs, she told us that she had not felt at home with the topic of prostitution. When she began to write, she had only a vague sense of where the paper was headed and wasn't sure she had enough material to develop her thesis. So, as she wrote, every sentence was burdened with decisions: "What am I going to say next, how does it connect with my thesis, where are my facts going to come from," and so on. Each new sentence was a problem, a number of problems really. She had to do so much stopping and starting as she wrote, it's no wonder her sentences sound jerky.

This student's smooth sentences appeared in a paper she obviously wanted to write, one showing the effects on a child of a mother's rejection. She knew exactly what she wanted to share with readers, and she knew where her material was going to come from—her own experience—so every sentence wasn't laden with decisions. Her writing could flow.

The more comfortable you feel about your writing, the more your sentences are likely to flow. One way to make yourself comfortable is to sit, with stacks of scratch paper, close to a wastebasket. Beginning writers often forget that wastebasket, we've discovered. Apparently feeling that they have only one chance to write a sentence, they stiffen up. If they'd move closer to a wastebasket, they might relax a bit. Good sentences are more likely to flow from a relaxed writer, one who is willing to take chances, secure in the knowledge that bad sentences can always be thrown out or rewritten.

As you write a rough draft you can't afford to worry too much about sentence structure. You should of course try to write in English sentences, but don't fuss over them. You can do that later, as you revise the paper. When you read over your rough draft—especially if you read it aloud—your ear will often tell you which sentences need revising. You'll hear that you need to weave together the too-short sentences, trim down the wordy ones, and straighten out the crooked ones.

Your ear will take you far in making sentence decisions, particularly with practice. But in this chapter we'd like to supplement your good ear with an understanding of basic sentence structure. If you understand the basic architecture of sentences, you'll be able to make more intelligent choices as you revise them.

SENTENCE CORES AND MODIFIERS

Let's begin by looking at sentences in the simplest possible way. A sentence is primarily composed of a *core*, where its message is centered, and *modifiers* that give readers additional information about the core. Simplified sentence diagrams will help you visualize the relationship between the core and its modifiers. The core appears on the top line; the modifiers, which expand the core with further information, appear on the lines below. Each modifier is attached to the part of the core that it modifies. Study these simplified diagrams of two sentences to get a feel for this very basic relationship between the sentence core and its modifiers:

Uncle Will's favorite instrument was a six-string dulcimer made out of cherry.

instrument	was	dulcimer
Uncle Will's favorite		a six-string
		made out of cherry

During most of his working life, my father held two jobs, since one usually did not pay enough.

father	held	jobs
my		two
	During most of his working life	
	since one usually did not pay enough	

Modifiers add to the meaning of the sentence core. You can think of them as answering questions about it. For the first sentence diagramed, you might ask, "Which instrument?" The modifier is the answer: "Uncle Will's favorite." And you might ask, "What kind of dulcimer?" Your answer is "a six-string" one "made out of cherry." For the second diagramed sentence, the modifier *my* tells you whose father; *two* tells you how many jobs. The other modifiers answer two questions: "When did he hold two jobs?"—"During most of his working life." "Why did he hold two jobs?"—"Since one usually did not pay enough."

You probably already have a feel for this basic structure of sentences. You may not know how to label all the parts of a particular sentence, but you have a kind of radar that detects sentence cores as you read. As you are reading these words right now, your RADAR DETECTS our SENTENCE CORE, because you know that the sentence's message is carried in its core.

Skilled readers pay more attention to the cores of sentences than to modifiers. They read modifiers quickly, understanding that they contain less important information. The function of a modifier, after all, is to expand the core with further information. Modifiers are subordinate to the sentence core; they depend upon it.

You may be wondering why we are telling you all this. Well, it's not just a grammar lesson. If you can improve your sentence radar, you'll be better able to revise weak sentences. When you write a rough draft, you may not take full advantage of the strength of sentence cores. You may put important information in the modifiers and lesser details in the sentence core. When you do this, you draw your readers' attention to the wrong part of the sentence. The following sentence will help you see what we mean:

> At 10:00 on the night of December 14, a Chinese HOME on Chien Ying WAS ENTERED by eleven Japanese soldiers who raped four Chinese women.

The sentence core is HOME WAS ENTERED, so those are the words the readers' attention is drawn to. But let's hope the writer of the sentence didn't think this was the sentence's most significant content. The sentence should be revised to emphasize its most important content:

> At 10:00 on the night of December 14, eleven Japanese SOLDIERS RAPED four Chinese WOMEN after breaking into a home on Chien Ying.

This revision puts SOLDIERS RAPED WOMEN into the sentence core, so that the sentence emphasizes its most important content.

As you revise the sentences in your rough draft, watch for weak sentence cores. One student, for example, as she read over her rough draft describing a recent visit to a prison, discovered that she could strengthen a number of sentences with more forceful sentence cores. Some of her sentences carried unimportant information in the sentence core, then buried important content in modifiers. For example, at one point she wrote:

> The VISITING PERIOD WAS NEARLY OVER when the guard tapped me on the shoulder.

The sentence core tells us that the visiting period was nearly over, but this was not the information the writer wanted to draw her readers' attention to. To stress the point she wanted readers to notice, she revised the sentence like this:

> Shortly before the visiting period was over, a GUARD TAPPED ME on the shoulder.

At another point in this paper, the writer wanted to emphasize how impersonal her visit with the prisoner had been. Her first-draft sentence read like this:

> I SAT in a chair, viewing the prisoner through the glass as we talked on the visitor's telephone.

When the writer reread this sentence, she noticed that it pulled her readers' attention to the fact that she was sitting in a chair. The information about viewing the prisoner through glass and talking to him over the phone—the facts she really wanted to emphasize—were buried in modifiers. To improve the sentence, the writer revised it to:

> Sitting in a chair opposite the prisoner, I VIEWED HIM through a glass wall and SPOKE TO HIM over the prison telephone.

Here the important information appears in the sentence core, and the lesser information about sitting in the chair has been turned into a modifier.

When you check over your rough drafts, make sure your sentences are working with you, not against you. If you want to stress your close call with death, don't write "The ROTOR HIT, gouging a hole about an eighth of an inch deep in my helmet." Write "When the rotor hit, IT GOUGED a HOLE about an eighth of an inch deep in my helmet." Or, if you want to emphasize your shock upon meeting a monstrous snake at eye level, don't write "I YANKED OPEN the DOOR, whereupon I saw a 48-inch blackish-grey snake resting at eye level on the ledge of our storm door." Write instead: "When I yanked the door open, at eye level on the ledge of our storm door LAY a 48-inch blackish-grey SNAKE."

COMPOUND SENTENCES

Whether you're conscious of it or not, the structure of a sentence—content aside—sends its own messages. Take compound sentences, for example. A compound sentence is made up of two separate statements

hooked together with a connector word (such as *and, but, or*) or a
semicolon.

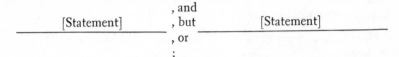

This structure sends certain messages to readers, no matter how you fill
in the blanks. First, it tells readers that they are reading about two important ideas, each one deserving its own statement. Second, it tells
readers that these two ideas are approximately equal in importance,
since they are balanced as a pair. And third, it alerts readers, depending
on the connector used, to the relationship between the two ideas. *And*
suggests that the two ideas are being added together, *but* tells us they're
being contrasted, and *or* lets us know that they're alternatives. A semicolon suggests balance between two similar or two sharply contrasting
statements.

So the structure of a compound sentence sends certain messages.
Don't let the structure of a sentence shout one message while the content shouts another. Listen to the clashing messages in this sentence, for
example:

> Once Betty was driving to our house, and her daughter accidentally
> fell out of the car window.

The compound structure of this sentence tells us that we are dealing
with two ideas of about equal importance. The content, however, suggests the opposite: the daughter's falling out of the car window is surely
more important than the fact that Betty was driving to someone's house.
Moreover, the connector *and* suggests that the relation between the two
parts of the sentence is one of addition. But is this really accurate? Isn't
the relationship more clearly expressed as follows?

> Once when Betty was driving to our house, her daughter accidentally
> fell out of the car window.

With this simple revision, we have a sentence designed to carry its message. "Once when Betty was driving to our house" is a modifier appropriate for carrying the information of lesser importance. And the time-
word *when*, placed as it is, serves much better than *and* to convey the
relation between the two ideas in the sentence.

Unfortunately it is easy to misuse, as well as overuse, compound sentences in your rough drafts. As you compose sentences for the first time,
your ideas sometimes come haltingly. To keep them going, you may
string them together with *ands*. Some of those compound sentences will

turn out to be perfectly in tune with their content, but others will need to be revised.

Here are a number of ineffective compound sentences discovered by students in their rough drafts. The student's revision, in each case, is printed following the original:

1a. I told her that this might be my last meal and I wanted to enjoy it.
1b. I told her that since this might be my last meal, I wanted to enjoy it.

2a. I entered high school, and I had a male teacher for the first time.
2b. When I entered high school, I had a male teacher for the first time.

3a. Working directly with children is an important part of my job, and that is why I enjoy it so much.
3b. I enjoy my job a great deal because it allows me to work directly with children.

4a. Nutritious foods can be easily prepared and they can give the body the basic carbohydrates, fats, minerals, and proteins.
4b. Nutritious foods, which give the body the basic carbohydrates, fats, minerals and proteins, can be easily prepared.

You'll need to revise compound sentences that are sending wrong messages to readers. But don't be too hasty about getting rid of your compound sentences. When properly used, so that the structure is working with the content, these sentences can be strong. For example:

1. Uncle Will's dulcimers disappeared as soon as he put them up for sale, but he always kept one for himself.
2. Sometimes we'd end up at a big red brick teacher's college across town, and sometimes we'd just follow the railroad tracks.
3. The children at the Goddard Day Care Center "brown bag it" for lunch, or they meet their parents in the cafeteria.
4. A man was respected for his money, power, or intelligence; a woman had to rely on her looks.

In each of these compound sentences the content fits naturally within the structure. Two important ideas, about equal in significance, are balanced together. And they are joined with a connector that reveals the relationship between them—*and, but, or,* or a semicolon.

SIMPLE SENTENCES

The structure of a simple sentence—one statement that stands alone—also sends messages to readers. It tells them that the content is fairly important, deserving a statement all to itself. The simple sentence also suggests to readers that its content does not closely depend on that of sentences close by. So a simple sentence should contain fairly important material that doesn't beg to be pulled into any neighboring sentences.

It's common to overuse simple sentences in a rough draft. Look, for example, at these sentences, taken from a student's paragraph describing the chests in a museum exhibit:

> The last chest is the most impressive. It is carved from ivory. There is a painting on the lid showing King Tut and his queen. This painting is bordered with engraved flowers and animals.

Your ear tells you that some of those simple sentences ought to be woven together. But which ones? The answer is easy. Just decide which sentences carry important ideas, and let them stand. Then find the sentences that contain less important supporting information, and hook that content into the sentences you're allowing to stand. If you followed this advice, you might pull the first two sentences together like this:

> The last chest, carved from ivory, is the most impressive.

And the next two together like this:

> On its lid, within a border of engraved flowers and animals, is a painting of King Tut and his queen.

In each of our suggested revisions we have woven supporting information into the sentence that it seemed to support naturally.

Simple sentences, like compound ones, can be effective when the content works well with the structure. Here, for example, are some strong simple sentences as they appeared in a student's paragraph. The writer uses simple sentences (those italicized) to draw the reader's attention to important content:

> *The ultimate test, in my child mind, for finding out the difference between black and white, occurred one day in a bus station in Alabama.* While waiting with my parents at the station, I studied the two water fountains against the far wall. *Side by side they stood. A big sign above one read "whites only." The sign above the other fountain read "colored only."* I decided that once and for all I would satisfy my curiosity about the water fountains which always carried the signs above them. Was the water colored in the "colored only" one, or did it taste different? Since no one was watching me, I slipped over and quickly took a sip of the water in the "colored only" fountain. When I found it was every bit the same as the water in the "whites only" fountain, I ran back to my parents and shouted, "Dad, I just drank some water from the 'colored' fountain and it tasted just the same as the other." *My father's answer was a quick, hard slap. That day I learned not to question the difference between black and white.*

Each simple sentence in this paragraph carries information important enough to deserve a whole statement all to itself. The cores of these sentences draw the reader's attention to important content, as you can hear by reading the sentences aloud:

1. The ultimate TEST, in my child mind, for finding out the difference between black and write, OCCURRED one day in a bus station in Alabama.
2. Side by side THEY STOOD.
3. A big SIGN above one READ "WHITES ONLY."
4. The SIGN above the other fountain READ "COLORED ONLY."
5. My father's ANSWER WAS a quick, hard SLAP.
6. That day I LEARNED NOT TO QUESTION the difference between black and white.

Simple sentences, especially short ones, draw attention to themselves, particularly when they follow longer, more complex sentences. Probably the most emphatic simple sentence in the paragraph we've been discussing is "My father's answer was a quick, hard slap." This relatively short sentence follows several longer sentences, so it has a blunt impact on readers. The sentence core—ANSWER WAS SLAP—overpowers everything else you've been reading.

PARALLEL STRUCTURE

When you want to stress the similarity of your content, you can put it into equal grammatical structures. Notice how similarly, for example, the first two sentences of this paragraph read:

> On March 14, 1978, Karen Riley was admitted to Suburban General Hospital with three broken ribs and a punctured lung. On July 8, 1978, Denise Porter was admitted with a broken arm and severe facial lacerations. These women were not victims of terrible automobile accidents, nor were they attacked as they walked down a dark city street. Both were products of an age-old phenomenon called wife-beating.

Here are the two sentences printed so you can see how very similarly they are structured:

On March 14, 1978,	On July 8, 1978,
Karen Riley was admitted to SGH	Denise Porter was admitted
with three broken ribs and	with a broken arm and
a punctured lung.	severe facial lacerations.

The writer of the paragraph wanted to stress the sameness of the two cases, so he structured the sentences almost identically. He deliberately used parallel sentence structure to reinforce parallel content.

Sometimes, as you are writing your rough draft, you'll think to use parallel structure to draw the reader's attention to similar content. But occasionally you may not have used parallelism to best effect in your rough draft. Then, as you revise, you can improve those sentences by presenting parallel ideas in parallel structure. For example, one of our students found this sentence in her rough draft:

> *Roots* is the story of a black boy stolen from his native land, chained and treated as though an animal, to be brought by ship here to America to be a slave.

As she read over her rough draft, the writer noticed that this sentence reports that the black boy was stolen, chained, treated like an animal, and brought to America. Since these items were similar—all brutal events that happened to the boy—she saw that she could strengthen the sentence with parallel structure, like this:

> *Roots* is the story of a black boy stolen from his native land, chained like an animal, stowed on a ship like cargo, transported to America, and enslaved.

A much stronger sentence. The parallel structure underscores the inhumanity of the treatment of the young black boy. Let's print the sentence so you can see the parallel structure more clearly. Read the sentence aloud so you can hear its strength:

> *Roots* is the story of a black boy stolen from his native land,
> > chained like an animal,
> > stowed on a ship like cargo,
> > transported to America,
> and enslaved.

Another student's rough draft read as follows:

> The Japanese barber doesn't just cut your hair. He gives you a shampoo and a shave, and he cleans your ears and cuts the hair in your nose and ears. He even places a hot towel on your face and massages your scalp and shoulders.

Using parallel structure, the student revised the sentence like this, pulling all of the details into one long sentence. The revised sentence is printed so that you can see the parallel structure:

Besides cutting your hair, the Japanese barber will
> shave your face,
> clean your ears,
> give you a shampoo,
> cut the hair in your nose and ears,
> place a hot towel on your face,
> and massage your scalp and shoulders.

Here parallel details are presented in parallel form to reinforce the sentence's point: that the Japanese barber knows no limits.

SENTENCE VARIETY

When you read through your rough draft, particularly if you read it aloud, your ear will probably pick up sentence monotony. Sentences may begin to sound monotonous if they are too nearly the same length or if they repeat the same structures over and over.

If you revise your sentences as suggested earlier in this chapter, the problem of sentence monotony may take care of itself. As you put important content in sentence cores and lesser information in modifiers, as you restructure misused compound sentences, and as you weave unnecessary simple sentences into the sentences they modify, your sentences will probably turn out varied in both length and structure.

To appreciate what sentence variety can do for your writing, read this student's imaginary letter of protest to her accounting instructor:

Dear Sir:

Do you realize that most of your students have worked an eight-hour day, rushed through dinner, and are just seconds away from collapse? If not, take a look at us.

We are the glassy-eyed night school people, whose hectic schedules would cause Olympic trainees to shudder. We rush from office to school with only seconds left to inhale a Big Mac, or worse. Our psychological state is as jumbled as our stomachs.

What we need in class is stimulation, debate, noise, excitement. You drone statistical drivel in your monotone, and we nod. You are losing us. When you darken the room to project accounting problems on the screen, the temptation to doze overwhelms us.

Tell a joke, or regale us with CPA exam anecdotes. Start an argument, or insult a student. Anything would *help*.

We balance career, family, and education in a precarious juggle of available time and energy. We have a lot on our minds, so keep us interested. We want to enjoy these hours in school, because the price we pay for them is high.

EXERCISE 1 WRITTEN

Try your hand at revising the following rough draft paragraph so that the sentences all emphasize the writer's main point, as summed up in the topic sentence. Put important ideas in sentence cores and lesser content in modifiers.

A typical hot lunch at City College has little nutritional value. For example, one day's menu might be zippy pot roast, mashed potatoes, creamy green beans, an ice cream sandwich, and milk. The zippy pot roast contains more fat than lean meat. The mashed potatoes are instant flakes mixed with water, causing them to turn out dry and thick. They contain a low amount of protein and vitamins. The creamy green beans are usually cold, watered down, and faded in color, which causes them to lose vitamins. The frozen ice cream sandwiches consist of artificial flavoring, instant milk, and nitrochloric acids. The last item on the menu is milk, which has the most nutrition. The milk is whole milk consisting of iron, certain vitamins, and calcium. So the hot lunch at City College does not provide much of nutritional value, except for milk.

EXERCISE 2 WRITTEN

Assume that the sentences below are from the rough draft of a paper describing your mandolin-playing career. As you look back over the rough draft, you notice that you have written quite a few compound sentences. Which ones do you decide to keep because their content fits well into a compound sentence? Which ones need revising? Try rewriting at least five of the compound sentences that you think were ineffective in the rough draft.

1. Owen had an antique mandolin from Italy, and it had a round back and beautiful wood inlaid on the front.
2. Owen's mandolin intrigued me, so I borrowed it in hopes of figuring out how to play it.
3. Later that weekend Owen left for England, and he took his old mandolin with him.
4. My mandolin career might have ended there, but I found a used instrument listed in the classified ads for ten dollars.
5. The mandolin had been in someone's shed for almost thirty years without a case, but the price was right.
6. The mandolin player for "The Seldom Scene" had made his own instrument, and we spent most of an afternoon in the shade of his camper pickin' bluegrass music.
7. My new mandolin was a Gibson "A" model from 1911, and it sounded, and played, like solid gold.
8. By the time I had played with "Kinfolk" for a month, I felt like a professional; after two months, I was a professional.

9. Playing at the Berwyn Coffeehouse was rewarding, and the people there loved us.

10. As my music got better my grades in school got worse, so I decided to leave my regular gig to study full time.

EXERCISE 3 WRITTEN

The following paragraphs by a student contain some ineffective compound sentences. Revise the sentences that need improvement.

I've known Sugar Ray for four years now, and he was always determined to succeed as a fighter. Each morning at about six o'clock you could find Ray jogging and training very hard. After his workout each morning he would go home, clean up and leave for school. Then, after school, each evening Ray could be found down at the community recreation center training.

Sugar Ray's training paid off, and he became one of the best young fighters in the country, and he was chosen to represent the United States in the Olympics. Ray attended the 1976 Olympics and he brought the gold medal back home with him. A few months after the Olympics were over, Ray received an offer to turn professional. Ray accepted the offer and turned pro.

EXERCISE 4 WRITTEN

Below are some passages from student papers containing too many short, choppy sentences. Rework each passage by pulling subordinate information into the sentence it seems to support naturally.

1. My father works for the Washington Trucking Company. Right now he is district manager for several different terminals. I believe he has twelve different terminals, all of which are located in the mid-eastern region of the country. Traveling is very important in his work. He travels about three times a month.

2. I had an appointment with one of my physicians. It was on a hot, humid September day. My appointment was at four o'clock in the afternoon.

3. The jewelry found in King Tut's tomb is perhaps the most exquisite of all the relics. There are gold necklaces, beaded bracelets, gold rings, and earrings. Many of the above are decorated with colored glass. This glass was usually shaped as a scarab, the symbol of the sun god. The most magnificent of all of the jewelry is the necklace that had been placed on King Tut's mummy. It is in the form of a vulture goddess with spread wings. Different shades of red and blue glass are used to decorate the necklace. This ornament was supposed to provide magical protection.

EXERCISE 5   FOR CLASS DISCUSSION

Eldridge Cleaver wrote *Soul on Ice* while serving time in California's Folsom
State Prison. In this spiritual autobiography Cleaver expresses himself pow-
erfully, often using parallel sentences. Here are four such sentences, with discussion questions for each. We have printed the sentences so that you can
see the parallel structure. As you discuss the sentences, be sure to read them
aloud:

> I'm perfectly aware
> > that I'm in prison,
> > that I'm a Negro,
> > that I've been a rapist,
> > and that I have a Higher Uneducation.

This sentence, which appears early in the book, has a powerful effect on
readers. Can you account for its power? What do you suppose Cleaver means
by "Higher Uneducation," and why does he put this item last? Why is
Cleaver putting all these facts about himself in one parallel-structured sentence?

Our next sentence from *Soul on Ice* describes the night-time longings of
a man behind bars:

> Because we were locked up in our cells before darkness fell, I used to lie
> awake at night racked by painful craving
> > to take a leisurely stroll under the stars, or
> > to go to the beach,
> > to drive a car on a freeway,
> > to grow a beard,
> or to make love to a woman.

What impact does this sentence have on you as a reader? How does the
sentence's parallel structure contribute to this impact? Why does Cleaver
order his "cravings" as he does?

The following sentence was not written by Eldridge Cleaver. Cleaver
quotes it, from Malcolm X, to explain his own one-time hostility toward
white people:

> How can I love the man who raped my mother,
> > killed my father,
> > enslaved my ancestors,
> > dropped atomic bombs on Japan,
> > killed off the Indians
> > and keeps me cooped up in the slums?

What does Malcolm X mean by "the man"? How do you interpret "raped
my mother" and "killed my father"? Why has Malcolm X included the
Japanese and the Indians as recipients of "the man's" atrocities? Why has
he ordered the atrocities in just this way, and why does he end with "keeps
me cooped up in the slums"? To which words in the sentence does the parallel structure draw your attention, and how does this contribute to the sentence's power?

For the next sentence, you need some background information. While Cleaver was in Folsom, he was impressed by the Christ-like quality of a philosophy professor who taught at the prison. Cleaver wrote this one-sentence paragraph about this man, whom he called "the Christ" as a mark of respect:

> The Christ could weep
> over a line of poetry,
> over a single image in a poem,
> over the beauty of a poem's music,
> over the fact that man can talk,
> read,
> write,
> walk,
> reproduce,
> die,
> eat,
> eliminate,—
> over the fact that a chicken can lay an egg.

This sentence should be read aloud more than once, as you discuss it; its power will grow on you. What kind of man is Cleaver describing? Why does Cleaver order the sentence as he does? Why end with "over the fact that a chicken can lay an egg"? Why begin with three lines about poetry? Why put that long list of human activities just where it is in the sentence? Why does Cleaver use "eliminate" instead of a synonym?

EXERCISE 6   FOR CLASS DISCUSSION

Read aloud the student paper printed at the end of this chapter. Listen for the effects of the varied sentences. Then discuss the writer's use of short, snappy sentences; parallel structure; and varied sentence lengths and structures.

EXERCISE 7   FOR THOUGHT

Joan Didion, in an article entitled "Why I Write," compares sentence structures with camera angles:

> To shift the structure of a sentence alters the meaning of that sentence, as definitely and inflexibly as the position of a camera alters the meaning of the object photographed. Many people know about camera angles now, but not so many know about sentences. The arrangement of the words matters, and the arrangement you want can be found in the picture in your mind. The picture dictates the arrangement. The picture dictates whether this will be a sentence with or without clauses, a sentence that ends hard or a dying-fall sentence, long or short, active or passive. The picture tells you how to arrange the words.

The difference between the right word and almost the right word is the difference between lightning and the lightning bug.

—Mark Twain

CHAPTER 12
CHOOSING WORDS

One of the secrets to building strong sentences is careful, conscious choice of words. Choosing your words carefully will make your writing clearer and more vivid.

We have placed "Choosing Words" near the end of this section of the book because we feel that writing will be easier for you if you do not worry too much about single words until late in the writing process. Stopping to think about each and every word when you first begin a paper will slow down your writing. When that happens, you risk sacrificing your flow; you may even get stuck and have a hard time getting started again. So we advise you to attend first to focusing and shaping your material into paragraphs made up of strong sentences, and only then to concentrate on your words.

DELETING EXCESS WORDS

When you are ready to think about words, we suggest that you first look for those you can delete. Deleting the excess baggage—the wordiness—from your writing is essential to building forceful sentences. Sentences full of "deadwood" drag along, blurring your meaning and boring your reader. Listen aloud to these sentences, for example:

1. The roses which grow in my largest rosebed are flame orange and pale yellow in color.

2. There were two women who ran for senator in the state of Virginia last year.

3. To our great disappointment, the circus did not get to town on time. This was because one of the elephants decided to go AWOL during the long march from the train station.
4. Judith wanted to move away from living with her parents and move to Chicago, where she wanted to go to the university and specialize in the field of law.
5. The popcorn was vacuumed up by Bruce, the chairs were stacked by Donna, and the house was aired by Lou, before the party was declared over for the night.
6. It was known for a fact by their families that John and David had left San Francisco to surf in Hawaii without enough money to live on in Hawaii.

Simply removing the deadwood from these sentences immediately livens them up. Suddenly they are clearer, easier to read:

1. The roses in my largest rosebed are flame orange and pale yellow.
2. Two women ran for senator in Virginia last year.
3. To our great disappointment, the circus did not get to town on time, because one of the elephants decided to go AWOL during the long march from the train station.
4. Judith wanted to leave her parents' home and move to Chicago to specialize in law at a university.
5. Bruce vacuumed up the popcorn, Donna stacked the chairs, and Lou aired the house, before they declared the party over.
6. Their families knew that John and David had left San Francisco to surf in Hawaii without enough money.

You will want to check all your sentences for any excess baggage they may be carrying. George Orwell, one of the most effective writers in the English language, has suggested a sort of ground rule about wordiness: "If it is possible to cut a word out, always cut it out."

Listen to the difference between the following loose, wordy student paragraph and its revision:

~~This summer~~ While I was vacationing in Switzerland, ~~the one thing that impressed me most was how kind and friendly the people were.~~ (this summer), the kindness and friendliness of the Swiss impressed me more than anything else. ~~The people who worked in~~ The hotel /~~where we stayed were extremely nice.~~ *staff*

~~They~~ went out of their way to make our stay

~~an even more enjoyable one.~~ *pleasant.* The maids and

bellboys greeted us with ʌ smile~~s~~, the women

behind the desk always asked how we were,

and ~~the people in the hotel~~ *the* restaurant

ʌ ~~always went out of their way to give~~ *personnel gave* us

excellent service. Although ~~there was~~ a

language barrier *existed,* everyone we ~~would~~ talk /to

was very patient while we tried to communi-

cate ~~and get our point across with~~ the few

~~words of~~ German and French /we knew. /*words Indeed,* The

friendly /~~people of Switzerland~~ *Swiss* added to ~~a~~ *the*

~~wonderful trip to their beautiful country.~~ *pleasure of our visit to Switzerland.*

You have probably noticed that the revisions make the paragraph considerably shorter than the original. But nothing important has been lost. When you write, don't let yourself be tempted into leaving in the deadwood just for the sake of quantity. Your rough drafts may often be too wordy, especially if you make yourself keep writing steadily to maintain your flow. Writing for flow is not a bad idea; just don't forget to trim out the deadwood when you revise.

On the other hand, we would caution you against worrying so much about wordiness that you sacrifice essential content. Leaving out needed material is not the same thing as deleting wordiness. One has to do with content—what you have to say; the other, with form—how you go about saying it.

The idea, then, is to make your writing as concise—and hence as direct and clear—as possible, while including what needs to be included. Every word you choose should be working to make your writing strong and interesting and alive. As the poet Wallace Stevens says, "Life is the elimination of what is dead."

SAYING IT SIMPLY

Writers sometimes become wordy, and their writing lifeless, because they overwrite; that is, they try to impress their potential readers with "fine writing." What usually happens instead is that these writers end up sounding pompous, and their writing stilted and artificial.

Such overdone writing has been called "doublespeak," because it generally makes so little sense by the time a reader has managed to get through it. Doublespeak is sometimes used deliberately to obscure meaning, when writers do not want to assume responsibility for their words; it often emerges from the government, the military, the educational system, and other such institutions. We bring it up here because you are so surrounded by it every day that we want to warn you against letting it influence your own writing.

For example, here is a quotation from a release by the Bureau of Land Management (BLM) of the United States Department of the Interior:

> Because the heavy mistletoe infestation in the Kringle Creek area has rendered the residual timber useless for timber production, the ultimate goal is to establish a healthy new stand of Douglas Fir.

The BLM release apparently means to say:

> Because mistletoe has taken over the timber in the Kringle Creek area, we need to plant a new stand of Douglas Fir.

When a Secretary of HEW decided in 1977 to advertise for a cook, he managed to use 402 words in the job description. OSHA (the Occupational Safety and Health Administration) wrote this 39-word definition of *exit*:

> That portion of a means of egress which is separated from all other spaces of the building or structure by construction or equipment as required in this subpart to provide a protected way of travel to the exit discharge.

President Carter, impatient with the doublespeak that creates so much paperwork in the federal government, finally sent around the following memorandum, a masterpiece of simple, direct, concise prose: "Submit the paperwork reduction recommendations on time (3/31/77)."

But government is not the only source of doublespeak. Representatives of our other institutions use it, too. The following sentence was in a letter to the editor from a doctor: "If home births are an indictment of impersonal and dehumanized health care in our hospitals' obstetrical units, then attempts should be directed toward increasing the human factor in our health-delivery systems."

Doublespeak also often plagues college textbooks. Beware of it in your books; it could creep from there into your own writing almost by osmosis. This student writer, for example, may have been unduly influenced by a textbook for a speech course:

> Effective listening requires the senses of hearing and seeing, working in harmony, to correctly interpret incoming communications. Now, more than ever before, body language—that non-verbal part of a communication—contributes significantly to the intent of a transmission and how it is received.

The student who wrote the following had spent years in the military and had gone from there into a career in business:

> As a supervisor I am charged with the responsibility of insuring maximum production through utilization of all resources, both manpower and machines. However, the increasing level of the younger employee and the state of the art in business has created a problem for supervisors in trying to find new techniques to use in motivating subordinates. This group of individuals expects rapid growth and promotion and wants to take an active role in the decision-making process.

Getting rid of doublespeak was the most difficult part of freshman composition for this writer. However, he learned to simplify his writing enough so that the above paragraph became:

> As a supervisor I am responsible for seeing that all our resources—both personnel and machines—are as productive as possible. One of my challenges is how to motivate those persons working under me. Younger employees, especially, expect to advance rapidly, and they also want to be involved in decision-making.

Doublespeak often uses euphemisms. A euphemism (pronounced: you' fuh miz em) occurs when less direct and less vivid phrasing is substituted for words that might be considered offensive. Euphemisms, then, diminish the strength and the honesty of language. Journalist Meg Greenfield refers to them as "verbal chloroform." Someone else has said that using euphemisms is like saying "That's not an elephant with a trunk under that tent; it's a mouse with a glandular abnormalization."

The doublespeak you have just been reading is full of euphemisms. Here are a few more, "translated" into "real language":

Euphemism	Real Language
selected out	fired
over-aggressive self-initiative	anger
attitude adjustment hour	cocktail hour
Society for Investigation of Human Ecology	CIA's cover organization for experiments in brainwashing and behavior control
minority-sensitive programs	reverse discrimination
therapeutic misadventure	medical malpractice
radiation enhancement weapon	Pentagon's designation for the neutron bomb, which destroys only people.

Whenever you write, you need to be constantly aware of that other human being, your reader. Doublespeak ignores the reader's need for simplicity and clarity. It sacrifices both clarity and meaning to an attempt at eloquence. We like here a piece of advice attributed to "a wise old woman": "Keep away from fancy words because you never can tell what they mean." Or, as John O'Hayre, who tried to eliminate doublespeak from the Bureau of Land Management, suggests, "To kill this big word bug, stop [writing] like a mechanical nobleman who has been stuffed to overflowing with impressive, exotic words, and start [writing] like the genuine, natural human being you are."

SAYING IT VIVIDLY

If doublespeak words are too fancy, too big and heavy, there are other words you will want to avoid because they are weak. Some of these words began their existence as slang. All of them have become "tired words"; they have been used until they are exhausted. When such words slip into our conversation, we tend not to pay much attention to them. But when someone else is reading what we have written, instead of listening to us speak, he or she can stop to question the actual content of such words. In writing, their emptiness becomes apparent; they do not say much, for the life has gone out of them.

nice	interesting	horrible	awful
pretty	big	outstanding	gorgeous
terrible	funny	wonderful	fabulous
huge	exciting	glorious	magnificent
incredible	terrific	colossal	enjoyable
fantastic	marvellous	fascinating	good
tremendous	stupendous	really	lovely
amazing	real	very	great
bad	beautiful	thing(s)	

You will probably be able to think of some more "tired words."

Using these words occasionally is of course all right; attempting to avoid completely such everyday words as these could make your writing sound awkward and unnatural. However, if you discover that your writing is dotted with weak words, you can liven it up with substitute words from a dictionary of synonyms or a college thesaurus. You will find a list of such word resource books under "Tools of the Trade" in chapter 1.

Here are two paragraphs written before the writer learned to avoid weak words and to use her book of synonyms effectively. The weak words are italicized:

> Seattle is a *beautiful* city, full of *wonderful* sights and *interesting things* to do. It is surrounded by *big* bodies of water, that the sun dances off of in *marvelous* fashion. More water greets visitors to Seattle as they discover the city's several *fabulous* fountains. Furthermore, the city has many hills, providing *really glorious* views. One of these views is of Mount Rainier, with its *gorgeous* snow-covered peaks. In addition, Seattle has some *magnificent* buildings—its public library and the IBM building, to name two. There are *interesting things* to do in Seattle, too, at its playhouse, its opera hall and its science center. And I must not forget to mention a visit to the *incredible* Space Needle, that features an *amazing* revolving restaurant at its top.
>
> The weather varies greatly in Seattle, it is true, and some people say that all those rainy days in a row must be *awful*. But, believe me, one *nice* day of *glorious* sunshine on those fountains and mountain peaks and buildings makes one forget weeks of rain. Surely, Seattle must be one of the *neatest* cities in the United States.

Although the writer of these paragraphs mentions a number of details about Seattle, the weak words she uses fail to make readers see Seattle specifically and vividly. The writer needs to put herself in the reader's place and ask herself whether the italicized words clearly and forcefully convey what it is actually like to be in Seattle. Then she needs to go to her dictionary of synonyms or her thesaurus for more precise and vivid words.

We do have some suggestions about how to use your synonyms book: Once you have located the synonym list for your weak word, be sure to read all the way through the list before choosing your substitute word; the one you most need may not be among the first two or three listed. Try, too, to find a word that will read smoothly in your sentence. If you are not sure about the exact meaning of a particular synonym, then turn to your regular dictionary and look it up, to be sure that you end up using the most appropriate word.

You will also want to be alert to clichés that may slip into your writing. A cliché (pronounced: klee shay, a term borrowed from French) is a worn-out phrase, an expression that you have heard so often that it is empty of meaning. You will probably recognize some clichés in the following paragraph:

> The mechanic rescued us, cold and miserable, from beside the road and towed our car in. He saw that we were safe and sound, and then, as the hours wore on, he looked after us above and beyond the call of duty. We found it hard to believe, in this day and age, that someone would be so kind to total strangers who had appeared in his life out of nowhere. It was indeed a moving experience.

Did you pick up the clichés? They are included in the list below:

above and beyond the call of duty	in this day and age
all walks of life	ladder of success
appeared in his life	last but not least
at this point in time	moving experience
believe it or not	on a silver platter
beyond a shadow of a doubt	out of nowhere
brought back to reality	pride and joy
cold and miserable	rude awakening
easier said than done	safe and sound
facts of life	sink or swim
first and foremost	straight and narrow
hours wore on	total stranger
	tried and true

You can add other clichés to this list—from your reading, from listening to radio and television, and from everyday conversations. Any time you hear a phrase that produces an echo in your ear, ask yourself how many times you have heard it before. Is it a cliché?

Don't let clichés weaken your own writing. Either delete such phrases entirely, or rephrase flat, cliché-ridden sentences to make them more vivid and lively.

USING JUST THE RIGHT WORD

The more you read and write, the more aware you are likely to become that words with the same *meaning* can carry widely differing *feelings*.

Words with essentially the same *denotation* can have varying *connotations*. They can be emotionally loaded, either positively or negatively. For instance, different expressions connected with growing old, though they all denote old age, carry different connotations. They affect us differently when we hear them. Consider the image and the accompanying feelings the following phrases create. To which do you react positively? To which negatively? Are any of the expressions relatively neutral?

the elderly	the aged
senior citizenship	the golden years
the declining years	old age
old man (or old woman)	old folks
growing older and wiser	older person

Here are some other sets of words with essentially the same meaning but with varying connotations. As you read a set, observe how each word affects you, what it "says" to you:

run	alternate lifestyle	determined
bolt	homosexuality	stubborn
dash	sexual deviancy	persistent
flee	sexual preference	resolute
rush	the gay life	persevering
scamper	perversion	hardheaded
dart		tenacious

Use this emotional loading of words when you write. For example, if you want your readers to visit a space museum you have just discovered, appeal to them by describing its display area as "vast" or "expansive," instead of using "cavernous," which sounds more threatening. Or if you are recommending an instructor whose only flaw is a soft voice, say that his or her delivery is "low-keyed" rather than "inaudible." On the other hand, if you are writing a letter to your local newspaper about a popular child's toy you are concerned about, referring to the toy as "hazardous" will be more effective than merely saying it is "unsafe." Use your dictionary of synonyms or your thesaurus to locate the best word for the connotation you want.

There is one more matter of word choice you will want to be sure to attend to: accuracy. The clarity of your writing depends heavily on its accuracy. If your writing is flawed by careless word choice, its entire effect may be lost, because your reader may not understand what you are talking about.

Sometimes inaccurate word choice produces hilarious sentences. We share a few such sentences with you here, just for fun:

1. A study is underfoot.
2. Bulldozers have left the earth baron.
3. We hope that all employees can remain relapsed and calm.
4. He has worked in several places. Most recently, he put in a stench at HEW.
5. The rhyme scheme makes a poem more interesting when it is re-sighted.
6. They treated him as if he had Blue Bonnet plague.
7. The Barbie and Ken dolls are so realistic that the Ken doll even has a full set of Gentiles.
8. Let's wait and see whether there is any follow-out from the incident.
9. Do you think she was speaking thumb-in-cheek?

Can you find the misused words?

No doubt you can appreciate how the misused words in the above sentences could stop a reader. And as soon as readers have to stop to puzzle out what you are talking about, they lose the continuity of your writing. Don't let that happen to your readers. If you find that you sometimes confuse words, ask a friend to read over your writing to help you find any such confusions.

FINDING MORE WORDS

We want to remind you here that increasing your supply of words, by whatever means, is absolutely basic to becoming a good writer. A writer needs to be on the lookout for new words all the time: while listening to TV or the radio, during conversation, while reading, during lectures and class discussions, even eavesdropping while traveling—wherever he or she encounters words, written or spoken. If you truly want to develop a rich vocabulary, this kind of word awareness is one of the easiest and most pleasant ways to achieve one.

You can train yourself to be aware of words in exactly the same way you train yourself to concentrate on anything else, whether it's basketball, singing, cooking, or karate. The payoff for taking the trouble to build up a rich vocabulary is that you will be a better writer—because a more precise one—for the rest of your life. It doesn't have to cost you any extra money, and you can start right away. Turn to the editorial page of your newspaper, or leaf through *Time* or *Newsweek*, to see if you can find words you don't ordinarily use. Use some of them, as you talk and as you write, as often as possible during the next two weeks. They will soon belong to you.

EXERCISE 1   WRITTEN

Remove the deadwood from the following sentences, taking care not to change the meaning of the original sentence. Bring your revised sentences to class.

1. When Carlos and I first started dating a couple of years ago, it was a bit of a problem for me to grasp his ideas and ways of thinking into my ideas and ways of thinking.
2. The important factor in the working world now is to have useful knowledge and skills that are in demand.
3. My brother is a fine Christian man and is one who is able to say the right words at the proper time.
4. He then proceeded to purchase a gas station, so he could make more money to be able to support his family and to give them what they wanted.
5. Most of the individuals who claim to have true religious faith are only afraid to go forth in life without the assurance that some external power has full control over them.
6. The food that is included in a Cuban meal is quite a bit different from that in an American dinner.
7. Making a four-string dulcimer is something that a lot of people today would not even consider doing, since no one ever got rich doing it and it's doubtful that anyone ever will.
8. With reference to the question of equal rights, I think women should have equal rights.
9. Sociologists claim that in the case of hardened criminals rehabilitation is rarely achieved.
10. The image of the American Indian through the eyes of the TV media is, to put it mildly, an insult to the American Indian.

EXERCISE 2   WRITTEN

Look over the list of weak words in this chapter and choose five that you feel you use too often. Develop a list of synonyms for each word. Write down all the synonyms you can think of on your own *before* you go to a synonyms dictionary or a thesaurus, so that you can see how many substitute words you already have. Then expand your lists by using a book of synonyms. Share your lists with the class.

EXERCISE 3   WRITTEN

Make a list of all the words you can think of that mean the same as any five of the words below. Work first without your dictionary of synonyms or thesaurus, then go to that source to complete your list.

1. advise	7. fat	13. serene
2. agree	8. fix	14. straightforward
3. ask	9. get	15. thin
4. conscious	10. inactive	16. walk
5. disagree	11. sensitive	
6. evaluate	12. sentimental	

Bring your sets of words to class for a discussion of connotation.

EXERCISE 4   WRITTEN

Connotation can be used to slant a piece of writing. Write on one of the following topics, in two ways: In one paper, attempt to prejudice your reading audience *for* the idea; in the other paper, attempt to prejudice your audience *against* the idea. Deliberately choose words with either positive or negative emotional loading to strengthen your position.

1. A mother of a 2-year-old wants to go to work. The income she would make is not required for the family to live. In one paper, support her going to work; in the other, argue against her taking a job.

2. Introductory psychology is being considered as a *required* course for all first-semester freshmen in a community college. Argue in one paper in support of the requirement; in another, attempt to defeat the requirement.

3. A university establishes a coed dormitory for unmarried couples to live together. Write papers (perhaps letters) from two sets of parents with students enrolled; one set supports the idea, the other rejects it.

4. An excellent teacher has a brief period of silent prayer every morning in her fifth-grade classroom. The Board of Education learns of this activity, and tells her to discontinue it. She threatens to resign if she cannot have the prayer time (which has been optional for her students). Write one paper to support keeping her on and allowing her to continue the prayer time. Write another paper supporting her being released from her position.

EXERCISE 5   CLASSROOM ACTIVITY

Try to translate the following euphemisms. Listen for others to bring to class to challenge your classmates. (Advertising, political statements, work memoranda, and hospital language are some likely sources.) Be ready to discuss how euphemisms can be dishonest, sometimes even immoral.

1. adult entertainment	10. for motion discomfort
2. correctional facility	11. grief therapist
3. culturally deprived child	12. inner city
4. deteriorating residential section	13. inoperative statement
5. downsized car	14. nervous wetness
6. encore telecast	15. powder room

7. Egyptological pornoglyphic   16. preowned automobile
   sacrophagi   17. protective reaction strike
8. engage the enemy on all sides   18. twilight years
9. expired, passed away, left us

Translations of the euphemisms will be found in the Appendix.

EXERCISE 6 FOR VOCABULARY BUILDING

The following paragraphs are from an editorial about Britain's celebration of the twenty-fifth anniversary of the reign of Queen Elizabeth II. We are making a guess that you will find in the paragraphs five to ten words not now in your everyday vocabulary that could become useful working words for you. Read the paragraphs to see whether there are words you want to learn. If there are, begin a word list, and try to use some of the words as you talk and write during the next two weeks.

Events in the past few years have mainly drawn attention to Britain's well-advertised troubles. There is the unending guerrilla warfare in Northern Ireland and the rise of separatism in Scotland. There is the increase of violent crime and the emergence of racial antagonism. There is the poor economic performance, the inflation, the precipitous slide of the pound. As you read about these things from a distance, it's easy to get a sense that the country is coming unraveled. But it's not. That was the message of the tremendous turnouts for the Jubilee processions in London and the spontaneous celebrations in hundreds of neighborhoods.

It's necessary not to get sentimental. The troubles are real. But there's an analogy to the recent experience of the United States, which, after a decade of bitterly divisive war, political scandal and race riots, astonished itself last year with an amiable and most enjoyable birthday party. The popularity of these civic celebrations is a corrective to the dire states of mind into which democracies sometimes talk themselves. Americans tend to judge Britain's condition by comparing it with the phenomenal prosperity of France and West Germany. But, as our London correspondent, Bernard Nossiter, has been arguing for some time, most Britons judge it in comparison with their own recollections of the 1930s and 1940s. Since then, for most of the population, everything has been constant—if slow —improvement.

—*The Washington Post*, June 14, 1977

EXERCISE 7 JUST FOR FUN

My husband had lost his temper at the church ballgame on Saturday, resulting in an embarrassing scene, so I decided to pay an impromptu visit at the pastor's house and apologize for his temper.

The pastor and I chatted momentarily; then, intending to emphasize my husband's good qualities, I blurted out, "I sure wish Allen could learn to control his temper. He is good in so many ways. He's thoughtful. Kind-hearted. Very generous. But *most* of all, he is so passionate!"

Unaware of the inevitable phone call, I returned home feeling satisfied that my mission had been accomplished. Opening the front door I called out, "Hon, I'm home."

There he stood in the kitchen with arms folded and a Cheshire grin to greet me. With a chuckle he said, "Hi, hon. By the way, the word is— *com*-passionate!"

CHECKLIST FOR WRITING TO SUPPORT A POINT

1. Have I established an unmistakable focus early in my paper?
2. Does my paper progress in the best possible sequence? Is it organized so that it is easy to follow?
3. Is there any content in my paper which does not belong there? And have I said anything more than once?
4. Is my paper developed enough that it fulfills the promise of its introduction? Have I left out anything essential?
5. Does my paper hang together well? Does it flow so smoothly that a reader could not get lost in it?
6. Does my conclusion clearly let the reader know the paper is finished?
7. Are my sentences clear? Do they say exactly what I mean for them to say?
8. Have I emphasized the major points in my sentences, and deemphasized the minor ones?
9. Do my sentences read smoothly individually and together? Are they varied enough in pattern and in length?
10. Are there any words I should delete?
11. Have I used fancy language where I should have been more direct and clear?
12. Are there any weak words or clichés I should replace?
13. Is my word choice as precise as I can make it?

PART IV

Describing, Narrating, and Informing

It is a good deal easier for most people to state an abstract idea than to describe and thus recreate some object they actually see.

—Flannery O'Connor

CHAPTER 13
DESCRIBING

Let's say your uncle gave you for graduation a thirty-day bus pass to travel around the United States, and you want to thank him by sending him your impressions of the Grand Canyon, a part of the country you know he especially likes. Or, the department for which you work will be renovated, and all employees are being asked to describe in writing their ideal new working quarters. Or, your daughter has just moved into a new home, and you want to tell her grandmother, who is not well enough to visit, all about the house.

Perhaps your history professor has assigned a project in local history, for which you are to write about some building at least 100 years old. Or, the editor of the Family Weekly section of your local newspaper has called to ask if you would like to send in a feature article about your family's recent reunion. Or your father's friend who owns an inn needs some paragraphs for an ad about his menu specialties and has offered to pay you to do the job. Or a friend, who has applied to serve on a local commission on human rights, has asked you to write a personal recommendation for her.

In each of these situations, you will be doing descriptive writing. How will you go about it?

OBSERVING AND SELECTING DETAILS

When you get ready to write a description, you need first to be sure you are familiar enough with what you are describing. You need to have *observed* carefully enough to be able to convey to someone else—your reader—an *exact* picture. You will want readers to experience what you are describing in relatively the same way you did. The writer Flannery O'Connor, in her statement at the beginning of this chapter, recognizes that this kind of "recreating" in description is not easy. But careful observation—"actual seeing," as O'Connor puts it—is the key here.

As you observe details, try to be clear about the *focused effect* you want your description to achieve. For instance, if you wanted to share with your uncle how awesome you found the Grand Canyon as a spectacle of nature, you would focus on details of size, and perhaps the overwhelming variety of texture and color the canyon presents. However, if you were most interested in emphasizing the canyon as a geological phenomenon, you would highlight details of its rock formations, the variation in color created by different minerals in the rock, and the way in which water continues to carve away the rock bed. Keeping your desired effect in mind throughout your paper will help you to keep the paper unified; it will aid you in deciding which details to delete, as well as which to include.

FRAMING YOUR DESCRIPTION

Think of your description as being inside a frame. Once you decide exactly how much you want to include in the space you are "framing" and what you want your "picture" to emphasize, you will know that anything that slips outside your frame or away from that emphasis does not belong in your description. Your frame, then, "contains" your description.

The writer of the following descriptive paragraph knew that she wanted to write about her mountain retreat. She could have included anything on her mountainside: the forest, the meadow, a stream, her cabin, hiking trails, flowers and trees, birds and animals. But our writer also knew that she wanted to highlight the serenity of her retreat. To achieve that focused effect, she decided to include in her frame only three major features of her retreat: the meadow her cabin faces (including its rocks, trees, and flowers), the cabin itself, and the mountain stream beside the cabin.

> The place where I feel most at home—and most contented—is in the
> mountains; my "heart's home" is there. I like best a spot just where the
> timberline begins, with a wide, spreading meadow in front of me and
> the forest just behind me. Meadow flowers dot the grass, and big rocks,
> for sitting and musing, jut up here and there. It is summer, and the
> flowers are mostly bright, open-faced daisies and black-eyed Susans. On
> the upper edges of the meadow are maples in full leaf and pines that sing

in the wind and drop their needles to make a forest floor behind my cabin.
My cabin is an old-fashioned log one, with a huge chimney of mountain
rock. When I sit by my fire and read at night I can hear the mountain
stream trickling over the waterworn rocks in its bed. The music lulls me
to sleep, or rather to that stage between waking and sleeping when I briefly
experience real serenity, despite the world's worries beyond my mountain.

Here is the writer's working list for her paper:

Focus: My favorite place: in the
         mountains (meadow, cabin and
         stream)--why my favorite

   (7) mountain stream, and its "song"

       mountain spring, for keeping food cold

   (3) flowers--black-eyed susans/violets/
            dandelions/daisies

   (1) exact part of mountain -
            meadow in front of cabin
            mention forest--?

       hiking

   (2) season of year-- Summer

   (4) trees--changeable ones: elm/willow/
                                maple
            evergreens: pines/cedars

   (5) housing--old-fashioned/ log cabin/
            mountain rock chimney

       access road

       rocks in meadow

   (6) fire in fireplace for reading by

   (8) effect on me of being in mountains--
            end with this

When she made up her list, this writer was not sure which season of the year she wanted to write about, so "summer" was written in later. That decided, she realized she would have to delete the spring flowers, violets and dandelions. Under "trees," she settled on mentioning only two, one deciduous and one evergreen. She eliminated three major items (mountain spring, hiking, and access road), as distracting details that could take her reader outside her intended framing of mountain meadow, cabin, and stream. Because she was building her focused effect toward the nighttime peacefulness of sitting and reading inside her mountain cabin, she did not want to bring in either the physical activity of hiking or practical items like an access road or a spring for cooling food. Once she had arranged her remaining details in sequence by numbering her list and moving "rocks" up with "meadow," our writer was ready to write her description.

FILLING IN THE FRAME

Once you have established the frame for your description and have decided on the focused effect you want it to achieve, how will you develop the details you've selected to fill in your frame? Because well-done description plays on a reader's five senses, you will want to take particular care to get as much sensory detail as possible into your descriptive writing. When readers encounter strong descriptive writing, they find themselves experiencing with the writer what is being described; they identify with the situation through sight, smell, sound, touch, taste, or some combination of these.

For example, this student writer manages to appeal to four of our five senses (all but touch):

I shall always remember those Sunday morning breakfasts I used to have as a child. At seven in the morning the smell of fresh-perked coffee would snake its way down the long hall which led to my room and fill it with an indescribable aroma, awaking me to tell me breakfast was ready and waiting. And what a breakfast it was! I first see a tall frosty glass of just-made orange juice filled with orange pulp. Steaming hot coffee is being poured into a small mug with sugar and country cream already in the bottom. Pancakes cooked to a golden brown are stacked almost a foot high, with butter oozing down the sides. Warm maple syrup covers the cakes with a soft glaze and slowly drips down to form a small pool in my plate. In a side dish are oven-baked apples sprinkled with cinnamon, nutmeg, vanilla and raisins and served hot with the cooking juices still bubbling. Thick-sliced country bacon rounds off the meal. Whose mouth would not water, just thinking about this kind of breakfast served on a cold wintry morning—an "old fashioned breakfast"?

We would guess that your mouth did indeed water when you read that paragraph, especially if you were hungry. And that is exactly what the writer intended. He wanted to involve you, to take you back with him to the Sunday morning breakfasts of his childhood.

The breakfast paragraph illustrates the heightened sense of detail that characterizes effective description. One of the ways you can involve a reader in your descriptive writing is by piling detail on detail, so that the description is packed and its effect intensified. Furthermore, each detail should be as precise and as vivid as you can make it. For example, the breakfast paragraph refers to the smell of coffee "snaking its way down the long hall," and to a "tall frosty glass" of juice and baked apples with their "cooking juices still bubbling." A useful rule of thumb to follow in descriptive writing is "Show your readers, don't just tell them." The breakfast paragraph does that, through its specific sensory details.

We do want to warn you against overdoing the pile-up of detail that we have just advised. Overdone description tends to become so lush that you risk overwhelming your reader; there is simply too much to digest. The following sentence, about the cliffs around a lake in Oregon, is an example: "The shores are lined with searing, blood-red clay cliffs that produce a staggering display of fluorescence and kaleidoscopic colors at sunset." A reader could feel overpowered by that sentence. And here is an overdone paragraph:

On a summer morning Eagle Rock Camp is the most captivating and blissful place in the world. The camp, located high in the mountains of upper New York state, is tucked away in the midst of mighty oak trees that seem to be reaching out elegantly in a creative dance movement. The exquisitely sweet summer breeze floats softly through the air, bending the slim blades of grass and kissing the golden buttercups.

However, even overdone description is better than abstract, "floating off" description that lacks concrete sensory details that a reader can identify with. You need to keep a description externalized so that your readers will stay with you. If you allow the writing to float off into a kind of abstract philosophizing inside your own head, your readers will become confused; they cannot follow you there. So keep your descriptive writing sensory by using concrete sensory details. Concrete description might be said to be grounded, so that a reader can get hold of it, while abstract description floats off into vagueness.

An example of such vague, "floating off" writing is the following paragraph by a student who started out to describe a walk on the beach:

> When I take a walk on the beach I am a king surveying his kingdom. Gulls soar ahead to herald my approach and the waves bow at my feet. The sea belongs to me as far as I can see. And yet I am lonely, as lonely as a man lost on an empty desert. The seagulls have become hawks circling above their prey. The waves are mirages that retreat as I move toward them. And the expanse of the sea merely intensifies my loneliness. I realize my intense aloneness, my place as an almost nonexistent speck in the universe. I am a king no more.

Too much of the above takes place internally, inside the writer's head; he leaves the physicalness of the beach, and with it, the kind of details a reader could identify with: the gleam of sun on water; the feel of sand and pebbles underfoot; the plaintive sound of a bell buoy.

CREATING WORD PICTURES

In descriptive writing, you can often use word pictures to good effect. Word pictures give your reader a concrete image on the page to identify with. You can use three major devices to produce word pictures: the simile, the metaphor, and personification.

A *simile* creates a word picture by comparing what is being described with something else, using "like" or "as" to express the comparison. In his novel about migrant workers, *The Plum Plum Pickers*, Raymond Barrio uses a simile to describe apricot harvesting: "The plump orange balls plopped pitter patter like heavy drops of golden rain into his swaying, sweaty canvas buckets." Annie Dillard, in *Pilgrim at Tinker Creek*, finds two similes to describe the translucent entrails of a rotifer (a water creature): "Something orange and powerful is surging up and down like a piston, and something small and round is spinning in place like a flywheel."

In a *metaphor*, the thing described becomes the object with which it is being compared. In a passage from Frank Walters's novel *The Man Who Killed the Deer*, a sacred lake becomes an eye as an American Indian describes it: "We wanted the mountains, our mother, between whose breasts lies the little blue eye of faith. The deep turquoise lake of life." In a student paragraph about Washington in midspring, a cloud formation becomes "little sheep flocks" of cloud, and the Washington Monument is "a sharp, clean sword." And one more especially effective metaphor: "A burning silver sword slit through the heavy cloud's fat stomach and it bellowed in rage . . . and then cried like a child." Do you recognize the image?

Personification makes descriptive writing more vivid by giving life to inanimate objects. Sappho, a poet of ancient Greece, makes dawn perform a human act in these lines: "Standing by my bed in gold sandals/ Dawn that very moment woke me." In a paragraph about a deserted house, a student writer personifies the lawn, weeds, and rosebushes: "The lawn waves with long grasses, and tangled weeds choke the struggling rosebushes." Another student gives life to the sun as she describes an afternoon on the beach: "The sun takes an afternoon break while the clouds bluff a storm. Now the sun returns to work, laughing at his naive victims below." Playful images, like this one, are often especially appealing to a reader.

You can increase your skill at creating word pictures if you consciously try to do so. First, you concentrate on what it is you want to describe—an object you see while driving, an aroma you pick up during a walk, the sensation you experience when sand runs through your fingers. Then you set your mind to work trying to think of different ways you could compare the object or the aroma or the sensation with something else. Your skill will increase with practice, and you will develop a store of images to draw on when you need them.

We should caution you against getting too caught up in creating a word picture. This one, for example, may be overdone: "Morning comes over the bay like a young woman gowned in palest blue chiffon trimmed with billowing white lace, as cloud puffs drift across the sky." Your reader may get lost in trying to follow your image all the way through, if you overdo it.

It is also possible to create an *absurd image*, a word picture that doesn't quite make sense. Here are some illogical, nonsensical images: "You can hear the ruffling of lifeless leaves as the trees embrace you"; "She accepted her husband's death with open arms"; "The audience was a restless sea of legs and laps." *Mixed images* don't make sense either —images like:

At this point in my life I sit in a stew that smacks of irony. (a stew cannot "smack")

The talk I had with my grandmother helped to dissolve the generation gap between us. (a gap is bridged, not "dissolved")

Gales of the late November wind glide around you. (gales would not
"glide")

Or the wrong word, or words, might find their way into your images:
"My going to school has put some fire on the skillet." "When I told
my husband I was taking this course, he told me right off the back not
to discuss anything I had learned with him." "My being away from
home and in the college library so much was one of the main flaws in
the ointment." Can you see how an image has become confused in each
of these sentences?

Finally, let us warn you to beware of tired images or clichés in your
writing. "Cliché" (klee-shay) is a word borrowed directly from French,
to mean an overused comparison or other expression that has become
trite, empty, and therefore lifeless. Here are some clichés: "white as a
sheet," "cool as a cucumber," "pretty as a picture," "hungry as a bear,"
"hot as hell," "tired as a dog," "cold as a clam." One way to test for
clichés is to consider how often you have heard or read a comparison
you are about to write.

SOME OTHER DEVICES

Word pictures are one way to involve a reader in a description. Another
useful device is to take your reader along with you inside the frame of
your description. To do so, you write the description in the present
tense, from either a first- or second-person point of view ("we" or "you").

In the following description of a summer thunderstorm, the student
writer begins to place his reader inside his frame with the second sentence:

> The summer afternoon is hot and sultry. Your clothes cling to your
> clammy skin and humidity drains your energy. You search the sky for
> signs of relief—but there is no response. Detached clouds, dense and with
> sharp outlines, invade the blue of the sky. You watch as their bulging
> upper parts become cauliflower heads—then suddenly mountains, whose
> tops flatten out like anvils. You hear the gentle wind becoming angry.
> Thunder and lightning clash as if vying for your attention. The thunder-
> storm climaxes.

By using we, the student writer of a paper about a Mardi Gras parade
includes both the reader and herself in her opening paragraph about
the crowd anticipating the parade:

The crowd waits anxiously; the parade is already an hour late. We are like sardines in cans—so close together that we can smell the alcohol on each other's breath. The crowd is waving back and forth while the people in the front row act as a flood wall trying to keep the river from spilling over.

Notice that both paragraphs are in the present tense: you are there as you read.

Another device for involving your reader in your description is to use names. If you are writing about a person or an animal—any animate being—your reader will become involved with your subject much more quickly if you name him or her. In her book *In the Shadow of Man,* anthropologist Jane van Lawick-Goodall writes about observing some chimpanzees in East Africa:

The easiest individual to recognize was old Mr. McGregor. The crown of his head, his neck, and his shoulders were almost entirely devoid of hair, but a slight frill remained around his head rather like a monk's tonsure. . . . He reminded me, for some reason, of Beatrix Potter's old gardener in *The Tale of Peter Rabbit.*

Right away, we as readers feel closer to Lawick-Goodall's chimp because she calls him by name—and so can we.

In describing a person, you of course do not have to use the person's real name if doing so makes you uncomfortable. You can change the name. Indeed, if you happen to be describing someone you think doesn't "look like" his or her name, your description might be more effective if you rename the person.

CHECKLIST FOR WRITING DESCRIPTIONS

1. Observe carefully.
2. Decide on your focused effect.
3. Frame your description.
4. Use concrete sensory details.
5. Consider using word pictures, similes, metaphors, and personification.
6. Consider using *we* or *you*, the present tense, and names.

Refer also to the checklist inside the back cover.

EXERCISE 1   FOR CLASS DISCUSSION

Below are several pieces of descriptive writing by students. Be ready to discuss in class why each is either effective or ineffective, citing specific strengths and weaknesses.

1. In the early sixties, Framingham, Massachusetts, was a small town with bicycle paths worn into the grass wherever the sidewalk didn't go. Sometimes in my dreams I ride back over those trails, feeling the bumps, the jars and the tree-roots just as they were under the wheels of my new English racer. I can even recall some of the places where if I didn't duck I'd get a mouthful of clothesline.

2. The most interesting city I know is Jacksonville, Florida. I made my first trip there when I was 14 years old. We have relatives there and went there for our summer vacation. I was amazed to see how crowded the beaches were, because I was so used to seeing Bayside's beaches. Also, in Jacksonville there is no boardwalk with all the side stores and pizza parlors. Another interesting thing is that the cars drive right up to the beach to the edge of the water, which is rather unique compared to other beach resorts. Jacksonville is really a great city full of many wonderful sights and people, and I hope to go there again in the future.

3. We're on our way down the Hudson on the Manhattan Excursion Line. When the motor revs up, the band revs up, and the excitement begins. As the boat slowly pulls away from the dock, it is already vibrating with rock music. The buildings and people behind us look smaller and smaller and soon disappear as though they were never there. Our boat rides so smoothly through the water that the city seems to be moving instead of us. The skyline is like a Rembrandt, as the setting sun casts an orange glow along the shore.

4. Watching the little sail boats on the edge of the lake, I sit in the grass and feel a cool fall breeze brush dry leaves across my back. The sun ducks behind a cotton cloud only for a moment, then its lemony rays burst out again on my head. On the opposite bank several ducks are squawking over a piece of bread two kids have thrown in the water in hopes of touching just one of their snowy backs. I spy a little robin who has just landed, hidden only slightly by a dancing branch. He hesitates and suddenly pulls up a plump worm from the muddy shore. His bright black eyes see me and he flits away.

5. The wind rushes again almost like the surf. The air feels like a rainstorm—but the sun won't let me down. I wish I were a leaf, tossing about, free and flying. Up, up, up from the ground into the blue and white sky, and then I'd float back, touching on a jeweled lake. I guess I shouldn't ask myself what it's all about so often. I feel the wind coming up stronger now. It's almost dark—I'll have to work tomorrow.

6. A stroll into the forest at sunset is almost like walking into a vast ca-
thedral. The trees, looming high above, stretch their branches to form
splendid arches. Others point skyward as if to acknowledge the presence
of God, a presence one can easily feel within the calm, stately solitude
of the woods.

It is autumn. The air is clean and crisp, with a faint hint of pine.
New fallen leaves crunch underfoot, while those still aloft explode into
bright fall colors in the last golden rays of the afternoon sun. Deep blue
twilight sky above provides a contrast of depth and majesty in space.

Everywhere there are telltale signs of a cold, hard winter ahead. The
forest dwellers, flora and fauna alike, seem to sense the impending
wrath of Nature. The squirrels are wearing thick coats of fur, and are
gathering as many hickory nuts as they can find. There is an abundance
of woolly black and auburn caterpillars, along with multitudes of shiny
ebony crickets. The dogwood seed pods are harder and thicker this year,
and the black walnuts are falling early.

As darkness descends, there is a subtle, almost undetectable, change
in the forest. While creatures of the day are quietly going to sleep,
those of the night are just emerging. A rustle in the leaves overhead, a
faint flapping of wings in the cool, dark air, betray the presence of owl
and opossum. The feeling is one of calm mixed with fear, fear of the
unknown. There is a compelling urge to return to home, safety,
warmth.

Emerging from the forest is much like entering it. Except that by
now one is inclined to acknowledge, with the trees, the presence of
God, instead of merely feeling it.

EXERCISE 2 WRITTEN

Make up word pictures for 8 to 10 of the following sensory situations, using
similes, metaphors, and personification. Observe carefully first. Be as creative
as possible; don't let yourself resort to clichés. Bring your word pictures to
class to share with your classmates.

1. chewing taffy
2. stroking a longhaired dog or cat
3. listening to *little* waves as they reach the shore
4. watching a fire burn down
5. feeling polished marble, bronze, or aluminum
6. smelling ripe peaches, watermelon, or bananas
7. feeling fine rain hit your face
8. smelling charcoaled hamburgers
9. tasting curry, spinach, bittersweet chocolate, or cinnamon
10. hearing rock music
11. seeing tulips, lilacs, or dogwood
12. walking barefoot on packed wet sand
13. walking barefoot on dry sand

14. motorcycling on a bumpy road
15. seeing an horizon of trees of five different shades of green, or seeing the same horizon in autumn

EXERCISE 3   FOR CLASS DISCUSSION

When you first begin to write descriptions, you may be tempted to overdo them, as you learn how to use sensory detail and to create word pictures. Don't be discouraged if you find that you need to restrain yourself somewhat as you write. To help you distinguish between effective and overdone description, read the following student paragraphs and be prepared to discuss their use of sensory detail and their word pictures.

1. Picture the sunrise over the bay. You are standing on the beach. Bulky waves bounce between the ancient towering rocks with a deafening crash, while the undersized ripples wash the miniature boulders of earth from beneath your feet. Suddenly, the dark, peaceful, moonlit sky is filled with a kaleidoscope of light and color. Now you can see a colossal fiery and luminous sphere rising from the hidden depths of the ocean. As you look up into the endless space, morning brings you a multitude of seagulls who seem to be gazing back down at you in the early morning light.

2. You can smell the pier before you can see it. Walking up the narrow oyster shell road bordered with high marsh grass and cattails, you pick up the odor of old wood, fish, and creosote tar. The crunch of the oyster shells underfoot gives way to a hollow sound at your first step onto the plankings which formed ragged vertical lines between the pilings. Here and there a new board of bright tan breaks the seemingly endless rows of older boards, brown and rough from years of wear. The old timber creaks and sways as the rushing tide pushes against the pilings driven deep into the bottom of the bay.

3. Small groups of people huddle under umbrellas to protect themselves from the burning sun, waiting for some sound, some movement. Then it happens. The street dancers, so beloved in Trinidad, round the corner ahead. Suddenly you feel a surge of energy, like an explosion throughout your body, as each nerve makes itself known. Everyone rises and starts to dance, throwing up their arms and shouting for the favors being tossed by the official dancers. You forget the heat and the wait as you are caught up in the excitement—and you know it is worth everything to be here.

4. Like a multicolored centipede inching its way, the jammed traffic crawls through the choked, rain-drenched streets. Furiously dancing rain ricochets off everything in sight. The dark and menacing sky, seen through blurred windshields, rests on the tops of buildings like a filthy layer of gauze. Swirling wisps of gray, shaved off the billowing clouds by the buildings' granite edges, spill over into the deep concrete canyon. In the floor of the canyon, amber taillights ignite brilliantly all along the curving spine of the centipede. A line of hazy headlights hangs in

the air like shimmering disks suspended from an invisible wire, reflected in water-spotted mirrors. Blaring horns add a shuddering wail of protest to the already clamorous language of the city. Undaunted, the wet, sluggish mechanical creature continues its methodical journey home.

EXERCISE 4 WRITTEN

Improve the following description by deleting any overdone or "floating off" portions and then applying techniques learned in this chapter. Bring your revised version to class for discussion.

I am now a confirmed mountain lover. This belief came about as a result of a weekend trip that I took to the mountains of Virginia. From one of the highest peaks of the mountain, the rainbow of colors in the valley below reminds one of a patchwork quilt. This surely must have inspired the mountain women creating their very imaginative quilts. The cows grazing peacefully in the field below blend into the background of colors quietly as if they, too, are in awe of Mother Nature's abundant generosity surrounding them. Driving slowly along the winding roads, we gaze at the lush green foliage flanking the roadbed, with intermittent flecks of sunlight breaking through the leaves overhead. Completely surrounded by woods for miles, we come to a bend, and the road narrows abruptly, bordered on both sides by a majestic ridge; it is as if the earth has been completely swallowed up. These scenes will forever be imprinted on my mind. I think I must have felt like the first settlers of our country did when they tamed the wilderness. They must have been overwhelmed with its beautiful trees and valleys as they made their first home. I hope so—because I was.

EXERCISE 5 WRITTEN

Write a descriptive paragraph on one of the following topics. Be sure to observe your material carefully before you begin to write. Use the devices you have learned about in this chapter to make your description as vivid as possible. And beware of the traps in descriptive writing you have been warned about.
  1. an unusual piece of furniture
  2. a walk down your block
  3. an animal or a bird
  4. some physical feature of your college you especially like
  5. a holiday celebration
  6. a geographical scene
  7. something you have made
  8. a garden
  9. some family treasure
  10. a striking building

EXERCISE 6 WRITTEN

Turn to the long list of topics in part 7 and select one which would require you to write a description of several paragraphs. Decide how much to include in your description by carefully "framing" it first, keeping in mind the focused effect you want the description to achieve. Use a working list to write your paper from, and hand in your list with your paper. Try to use at least some of the devices you have learned about in this chapter for writing effective description.

> I was trying to write . . . and I found the greatest difficulty . . . was to put down what really happened in action; what the actual things were which produced the emotion that you experienced.
>
> —Ernest Hemingway

CHAPTER 14
NARRATING

Your daughter is away with the Peace Corps, and you want to send her a full report of her younger brother's first high-school band parade. Or you are involved in helping to expose police corruption in your town, and you plan to relate what happened during a raid on a music store that was fronting for a drug supply source. Or you have been invited to speak to a civic group that may be interested in sponsoring a scholarship for your college, and you have decided to begin with a funny anecdote.

You are interested in becoming a sports announcer, and the local station where you are training has asked you to prepare a five-minute account of the Little League playoffs. Or you are planning to argue before your city council for a stoplight at a street corner in your neighborhood, and as part of your evidence you want to highlight a fatal accident that occurred there last month.

Each of the above situations will involve you in narrative writing. You do narrative writing whenever you tell about something that happened within a defined time span. Narrative writing, then, relates an event, usually in simple chronological order. In some instances, it might be said to tell a story.

SOME GROUND RULES

There are a few ground rules you can apply to most narrative writing: (1) Put your readers on the scene immediately and clearly, and then get on with your story. (2) As you narrate, select out details for a focused effect. (3) Keep your narrative moving. These ground rules can be diagramed like this:

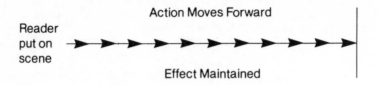

This brief narrative follows these ground rules very well:

It happened at the dinner table, at the Greenbrier Hotel, a fancy resort where I, a young bride from the country, felt even less sophisticated and more awkward than usual. My new husband and I were on our honeymoon, and the social manager of the hotel had invited us and three other honeymooning couples to a celebration dinner in the main dining-room. For my dinner I ordered Beef Burgundy with Noodles.

After a while, the very French waiter returned from the kitchen, and said to me, in rather breathless Parisian English, "The beef, it is strucken off."

"Oh," I responded, "that's okay. I'll have Ham in Pineapple Sauce, then."

"Oh, no Madame, the beef it is all right, but it is strucken off!"

"Ham is fine," I said again.

"No, no, no, Madame! Beef, beef—but is *strucken off!*"

This dialogue continued for longer than I care to remember—until finally another, more sophisticated new bride "translated" for me, in a tactfully quiet voice, "I believe he is saying the beef dish is Beef Stroganov, rather than Beef Burgundy with Noodles."

"Oh-h-h." My eyes must have been as wide open as my mouth, in my surprise.

So, I had Beef Stroganov for that celebration dinner, instead of either Beef Burgundy with Noodles *or* Ham in Pineapple Sauce, but you can be sure that I have never eaten it since without remembering with a chuckle the Greenbrier Beef Struckenoff.

Here is the working list the writer of this paper made up as she prepared to write:

```
Focused effect:  My relative lack of
                 sophistication in a setting
                 that assumed a certain
                 amount of sophistication

       where event happened ⎞
       when event happened  ⎬    background
       the circumstances/   ⎠
          situation
```

~~why we chose the Greenbrier~~
~~what I wore~~
~~describe other couples~~--no, keep focus
        on me and my funny story
what I ordered originally
~~what others ordered~~
conversation between waiter and me
        --ham as alternate dinner
~~my new husband's discomfort~~
another bride, ~~from St. Louis,~~
        "rescues" me
my reaction when I realized what was
        going on
~~how beef dish tasted~~

characterize waiter--briefly--to add
        humor

You the reader learn right away that this narrative is going to occur at the dinner table, at an exclusive hotel during the honeymoon of an unsophisticated young woman. You are on the scene immediately and ready to get on with the story. If the writer had told you why she and her husband had chosen the Greenbrier, or what she was wearing at dinner, you might have felt impatient, bogged down in needless, boring background information.

Now note what else our writer decided to delete before she began to write. For her focused effect, she wants to emphasize her relative lack of sophistication in a setting that assumed a certain amount of sophistication. So she gets rid of such details as what the others ordered, her new husband's discomfort as the situation got more and more out of hand, and where her "rescuer" was from. The focusing spotlight needs to stay on the action between herself and the waiter. Details about her dinner partners are irrelevant. They would blur her intended effect and distract you as you read.

The deletion of irrelevant details is one reason this piece of writing keeps moving. Another is the use of dialogue, a device that helps to give a reader the you-are-there effect. The paper moves rapidly enough that you want to keep on reading to see what happens next.

You will probably choose to write narratives in chronological order most of the time. But occasionally you may decide to begin in the middle or near the end, then flash back to an earlier part of your story. The student writer of the following football narrative opens his story at its climax, as an overtime field goal is being placed, at the end of a tied game. Then he pauses to take his readers back through some of the semiclimaxes of the game, to build them up to whether the field goal wins the game.

> The game is tied. The date is December 14, 1975. The place is Baltimore's Memorial Stadium. Everyone in the stands is on their feet for the overtime play. Down below, Toni Linhart, behind a wall of Colts, is set to kick the field goal.
>
> For a moment before Linhart's snap, I see the game so far in my mind's-eye. At one point, my team, the Baltimore Colts, is behind 7–0. Then, late in the fourth quarter, the Colts seem to hear the pleas of the shouting crowd and start to move. Like a machine, Bert Jones marches the Colts over a determined Miami defense. Then, from the six-yard line, Lydell Mitchell bursts into the end-zone. Touchdown! Linhart adds the extra point and the game is tied. The gun sounds, ending regulation time.
>
> In sudden-death overtime, the young Colt defense freezes Miami's offense and the Colts take over on their own four-yard line. Once again the Colts seem to grow stronger from the crowd's screams. Jones throws to Chester, then to Mitchell, and completes a third pass to Carr. As the Colts get nearer to the goal line, the noise becomes almost deafening.
>
> And now a strange silence falls over the stadium. I realize that Linhart is ready to try to win the game. The ball is snapped and an unbelievable roar pours out of the crowd. The stadium seems to rock and then explodes with screams of joy and excitement. The referee's raised hands only confirm what 60,000 frenzied fans already know. The field goal is good. The Colts have won.

FINDING A LIVELY OPENER

It's a good idea to involve your reader in your narrative right away, with a lively opener. In her narrative about the honeymoon incident, our writer catches readers at once with her opening words: "It happened at the dinner table. . . ." To what does "It" refer? she wants readers to ask. A student writer about to narrate his wife's delivery of their first child began with this dramatic opener: "I was awakened suddenly one morning at four A.M. by my wife."

Generally, it is wise to avoid beginning a narrative with something like "I am going to tell you a story about . . ."—unless what follows "about" is so intriguing that a reader could hardly resist it. The original opening sentence of the honeymoon dinner narrative read: "One of my favorite funny stories on myself has to do with my lack of sophistication in a very sophisticated setting." Pretty flat, isn't it?

Here are some more lively openers taken from student narratives:

While I was running an EEG (electroencephalogram) one day, the pens started clacking and throwing ink around the room.

It was a warm day of about 80 degrees as we sped along into some part of the Pacific unknown to me.

Damn, I wish Bill hadn't gone and done that, gotten his head blown off like that.

Standing in the early morning light of October in Ohiopyle National Park, I studied the swollen river below me. The water level was higher than usual, from heavy rainfall. And this was to be the day of my first white water rapids trip.

We would guess that you would want to hear each of these narratives once you had read their opening sentences.

BUILDING SUSPENSE

Once you have caught your reader's attention with a lively opener, you want to hold it throughout your narrative. You achieve that by building suspense. Think for a moment about a recent TV segment that totally involved you. Suspense no doubt helped to keep you in front of that TV screen.

In building suspense, you involve readers through their emotions. As Ernest Hemingway suggests in the quotation that opens this chapter, you want your readers to share the emotions *you* experienced while your narrative was actually happening. Recall again that TV segment that totally involved you. It doubtlessly featured a great deal of action—but action that *mattered* to you, for one reason or another. You were there, your emotions were involved, you were identifying with the characters participating in the action because you were *feeling* with them. As a writer of narrative, try to get this high sense of drama into your writing. Involve your readers' emotions by building suspense.

One way to tell whether your narrative is dramatic enough, suspenseful enough, is to test it out on a listener before you write it down. As you tell it, you can also check for how well you have observed the ground rules we discuss earlier in this chapter. Watch your listener's face as you speak. Does he or she seem puzzled as you begin to get into your story? Do you hold his or her close attention throughout? Do you see any evidence of your listener's "wandering off" at any point? The answers to these questions should tell you whether you located your listener clearly enough as you began, whether you included anything in your narrative that would be better left out, and whether you built in enough suspense.

After telling your narrative, don't forget to tighten up your expression when you begin to write. Conversational storytelling does not equal narrative writing.

We think you will agree that the student who wrote the following narrative about a barracuda chase builds suspense skillfully. You might like to know, though, that the first version of her paper had much more background information on learning how to scuba dive. Also, at the end of paragraph 3 she had included several anatomical details about barracuda, which were distracting. With the deletion of these two chunks of material, her narrative moves much more dramatically.

After completing all the difficult tests involved in learning to scuba dive, my father and I thought we were ready for almost anything. Little did we know what an adventure we were headed for.

For three days we had been taking trips into the sea to gaze at the beautiful sights the ocean holds. Swimming with a school of fish and squeezing through jagged-edged caves of pink and purple coral had provided considerable excitement. We decided we were ready to sign up for the barracuda chase.

On the day of the chase we left shore just as the sun was coming up, our equipment and weapons having been double-checked for air leaks, pressure, and maneuverability. Five miles away from the Florida coast we plunged into the choppy water. Sticking together, we quietly cruised the ocean bottom searching for our target. My father motioned toward a huge field of ocean grass. A large barracuda was lurking in the waving strands of seaweed. He must have seen us first, since he was already glaring at us.

As we slowly approached, the narrow body darted from the weeds into open space. Instinctively I felt the intense danger. Since I had no weapons I immediately slinked to a coral enclosure and watched my father join the group in surrounding the huge fish. I was terrified as they closed in for the catch, since all I could see were air bubbles from the divers' air tanks.

Suddenly it was over. The barracuda was trapped in the iron cage brought along for his capture. A surge of joy rushed through me as I helped escort the awesome fish to our boat.

Now when I go to Key Largo Aquarium House I can visit Spike—the barracuda I—or rather my father—helped to chase and capture.

MAKING IT HAPPEN NOW

As you think about ways to involve your readers in your narrative, you might decide to cast it in the present or to use dialogue, or both. If your narrative is written in the present tense, your readers will feel as if it is happening while they are reading, so it will be easier for them to identify with what is going on. You can also make readers feel as if your narrative is happening in the here and now by using dialogue. If you do decide to use dialogue, you will want to be sure it rings true; otherwise it may distract readers instead of further involving them. Skillfully done dialogue often makes a narrative seem more real; it will surely liven one up.

The student writer of the following narrative both casts it in the present and lets us hear his characters conversing so that we feel a part of the action:

"Breaker one nine . . . breaker one nine!" It's two o'clock in the morning on Route 50 and I am heading toward the beach.

"Go, breaker one nine," comes the welcome response, a female voice that is crisp and clear.

"You got the Wild Turkey here," I offer. "What's your 20?"

"Hey, Wild Turkey, I'm eastbound on 50 just past the bridge, come back!" she replies.

"You must be on my back bumper. What are you driving?"

"I'm in a Ford van . . . blue and yellow. Is that you in the bronze Dodge just ahead?"

"That's me," I answer, "in the number two lane. What's your handle there?"

"You got the Eight Ball here. Where are you heading?"

"Ocean City, by the sea. And I got a problem. My speedometer isn't working and I'm worried about the smokies, come back."

"You say your speedometer went bad?" Eight Ball comes back. "Well, let me cruise past you and you can hitchhike on me all the way."

"That's a big 10-4," I reply as I sign off.

The handsome Ford van roars by me in a blink and I barely make out a quick wave from the woman behind the wheel. The next thing I know, I am staring at her rear bumper and the fatigue I was starting to feel is gone. In the next twenty miles we change lanes three times to chatter about a variety of subjects. All I have to do is steer and throttle and talk. What I forget to do is think. When the flashing lights go on behind me, I suddenly realize that Eight Ball and I have forgotten about the "double nickels" speed limit.

"Hey, Eight Ball, there's a smoky on my butt," I let her know. "How fast were we going?"

"Sorry about that, Wild Turkey, for sure. Catch you on the flip-flop."

I pull the Dodge van over on the shoulder and play that old familiar scene again. I fumble for my license and registration. I smile weakly. My mind races for all the right things to say.

"What's the trouble, officer?"

"I just clocked you at 68," replies the Maryland State Patrolman, pleasantly but firmly.

While he writes my ticket, I decide to save the story about the broken speedometer and the woman in the Ford van I was trailing. It wouldn't matter anyway, I'm sure, I tell myself.

As I sign the ticket, I can't resist the pun. "I guess this is what it means to be behind the eight ball," I say, smiling.

"I guess," he answers. "Take it easy now."

I start my engine, turn off my CB, and head off—slowly—toward my destination once more.

PACING YOUR NARRATIVE: SENTENCE CHOICES

Your narrative writing will be more dramatic if the form in which you write it reflects the content that you are writing about. You can achieve this happy combination by being aware of the pace of different kinds of phrasing.

For example, note how this student's choice of expression reinforces the event she is narrating—the escape of a horse from her uncle's corral:

> The horse races away in exultation. He runs as if the world is his, his head trying to touch the sky, his body strong with spirit and muscles, his mane and tail flying as if to tell the wind which way to go. His skin glistens in the sun, his feet hit the ground in perfect rhythm, never missing a beat, never slowing down, but going faster and faster until the forest stops him.

The following sentence, with which Edgar Allan Poe opens his short story "The Fall of the House of Usher," demonstrates the pacing effect you can achieve with a long sentence piling detail on detail:

> During the whole of a dull, dark, and soundless day in the autumn of the year, when the clouds hung oppressively low in the heavens, I had been passing alone, on horseback, through a singularly dreary tract of country; and at length found myself, as the shades of the evening drew on, within view of that melancholy house.

This long, heavy, slow-moving sentence is exactly right to establish the despairing mood into which Poe wants to plunge his readers.

This paragraph, on the other hand, immediately establishes for the reader the detached attitude of the central character who will narrate Albert Camus' novel *The Stranger*:

> Mother died today, or maybe, yesterday; I can't be sure. The telegram from the Home says: YOUR MOTHER PASSED AWAY. FUNERAL TOMORROW. DEEP SYMPATHY.

We are not surprised, as we read on, by the uninvolved quality of a hero who begins his story with such short, stark sentences.

One of our student writers uses short sentences in another way to pace a narrative. Here is her account of the final inning of a softball game for which she was catcher:

> Here comes the first pitch. It's outside. Ball one. The ball goes back to the pitcher. I return to my position behind the plate. My mind is racing. Relax. Keep your glove out there. Don't take your eyes off the ball. Here's the second pitch. It looks good. It's coming right over the plate. Smack! She hit it. I can't see it. I'm up off my knees in a split second. My glove is open. It seems like an eternity and then suddenly it's all over. The ball falls right on target into my glove. The game has ended and we have won.

The student writer of the following paragraph invites readers to ride with him in a fantasy about the Grand Prix. He maintains the movement of that heady race through the steady, almost rhythmical pace of parallel structure, as he begins three successive sentences: "To feel . . ."; "To go flat out . . ."; "To know . . ."

> To feel the wind in your face and hear the tires scream as you slide through the S-curves at Monza. To go flat out through the streets of Monaco, hearing the roar of that mighty engine and accelerating till you think you are going to be pushed through the seat. To know you are one of only twenty-four men in all the world who drive the giant V-12 Formula-1 cars in the Grand Prix International Circuit.

Sentences of different kinds and different lengths can be used to vary the pace of a narrative, reflecting what is happening at a particular moment. The following paragraphs from a student narrative about a cross-country marathon use pacing in this way. Listen to how the sound of the writing echoes exactly what is happening as the race progresses:

> The runners are already at the line-up, pawing the ground like horses at a derby. The starter readies his pistol. He fires. Adrenalin surges through the runner's body, exciting every muscle into spontaneous movement. Dirt and gravel fly in faces as the human steeds head toward home.
> The first mile removes some of the competitive element of the race, as some runners overheat and retire to barking coaches and sympathetic parents. Others fall victim to injury and lack of stamina. But some persevere. They run. Run like they have never run before.
> The next turn marks halfway. The runners quicken their pace as the thundering hooves round the bend. The mind recognizes the hill ahead and instinctively shifts to a traction mode. Arms pump and spikes dig in while the words "work that hill" echo through the mind.

We want to conclude this chapter with the following well-done narrative by a student who works as a plainclothes police officer:

> One busy Friday evening the police department had me assigned to the Bureau of Patrol at Woodland Grove. There weren't even enough seats to go around for all the prisoners. I was working the desk, and another shoplifter had just come in. With a recent directive requiring him to be handcuffed and with no space left on the bench, I was at a real loss. So I went into a nearby office and came out with a chair. Setting the chair next to the coatrack, I handcuffed the shoplifter to the rack until I could get to him. After all, I thought, he's only a shoplifter and the rack stands nearly six feet high. Where's he going to go?
>
> It hadn't been ten minutes until someone went to get his coat. All the coats and jackets were on the floor and both rack and man were gone. The ultimate embarrassment had befallen me—an escaped prisoner. We searched the neighborhood for the rack-laden shoplifter, and after an hour I would have settled for almost anyone who happened to be handcuffed to any six-foot coatrack. Then the call came. A lady near Central Avenue had seen a man climbing backyard fences carrying what looked like a coatrack. A quick run to her house—but the man and the rack were gone. How could anyone move so fast with such a cross?
>
> I rode around for about another hour or so and then pulled into an empty lot to sit a while. I looked down Central Avenue and suddenly there he was. Coatrack and all. The tired shoplifter was cautiously making his way up the street. I was in a dark spot so I decided to sit it out and watch him for a few minutes. I couldn't believe it. He stopped at the Metro bus stop, and with his own jacket covering the handcuffs, pretended to be leaning against the coatrack waiting for the bus.
>
> Almost immediately a bus showed up, and there he was—a 160-pound, five-foot-four man trying to maneuver a six-foot coatrack onto the bus and trying to be cool about the whole thing. After he had made several unsuccessful attempts at boarding, one of which knocked the driver's hat off, I pulled up next to the bus. The exhausted shoplifter was almost relieved to see me. His burden had been too much, even for the search for freedom.
>
> Once back at the station, the shoplifter found himself facing charges of escape, but even that didn't keep him from rolling with laughter as he recounted his trials at crossing all those backyard fences with his special companion. With my own embarrassment gone, I could laugh too.

CHECKLIST FOR WRITING NARRATIVES

1. Put your reader on the scene at once.
2. Select details for a focused effect.
3. Keep your narrative moving.

4. Look for a lively opener.
5. Build suspense.
6. Consider using the present tense and dialogue.
7. Pace your narrative with varied sentences.

Refer also to the checklist inside the back cover.

EXERCISE 1 CLASSROOM ACTIVITY

Jot down some notes for a narrative you would be interested in writing, and use them to tell your narrative to a classmate, to test it out. Watch to see if your narrative holds your listener's attention throughout. If it does not, talk with your partner about how you can improve the narrative.

EXERCISE 2 WRITTEN

Below are several possible topics for narratives. Write lively, dramatic openers for at least three.
  1. Christmas Day in a big house where seven cousins between two and twelve years of age, along with their parents, are spending the holiday with their grandparents.
  2. The morning before the final swim meet, scheduled for noon, at a camp for young teens.
  3. A human rights rally being cosponsored by American Indians, gay rights activists, Chicanos, union organizers, and exprisoners.
  4. A dog show about to begin in a fine rain.
  5. A noisy party, the fifth in a month, that is disturbing your quiet neighborhood.
  6. The opening of a county fair, complete with agricultural exhibits, livestock competitions, sideshows with hawkers, daring rides, and the like.
  7. A sailboat race about to get underway in unpredictable winds.
  8. The day before your best friend is to go into the hospital for open heart surgery.

EXERCISE 3 FOR CLASS DISCUSSION

Read the following student paper, then go back and analyze how its writer builds suspense.

My five children, ranging in age from two to ten, and I were vacationing on Brigantine, a rather secluded little island off New Jersey. We had all walked to the end of the island looking for shells, and had strolled leisurely back to our spot on the beach. I bent down to straighten our

blanket and then counted noses—1, 2, 3, 5, no #4. My four-year-old,
Danny, wasn't with us, although I knew he had returned from our walk.
We searched the sand dunes, and looked in the water. No Danny. About
five minutes had passed when I approached the lifeguard stand, trying to
appear calm. The lifeguard was talking to three young women. After
several attempts, I finally got his attention.

"My four-year-old son is lost—he's gone."

Reluctantly he looked toward me. "He's probably around here somewhere; maybe he's playing in the dunes," he said, and immediately re-
sumed his conversation with the young women.

"No, he's not around here," I insisted. "He may have gone into the
water."

"Oh, no, we watch the little ones closely."

I could see who he watched closely. I realized that I was no competition for his attention. I was trying not to become hysterical when I saw
a beach patrolman in his jeep. I flagged him down and explained. He
radioed all the beach stations. A little boy had been found 30 blocks
farther down the beach and was waiting at one of the stations. Is it
Danny? raced through my mind.

I told the other four kids to sit on the blanket without moving, and
added the threat "The next one that get's lost, is staying lost!" Then, the
beach patrolman and I took off down the beach, dodging sunbathers as
we went. The question echoed and re-echoed through my head during
the interminable wild ride.

When we were within ten feet of the station, I saw a very short lifeguard wearing a long droopy sweatshirt and a long droopy face, sitting
high up on the lifeguard stand and eating a hotdog. Was it—yes, it was
—Danny.

EXERCISE 4   WRITTEN

Write a narrative about one of the following. Pace your narrative by deliberately constructing various kinds of sentences to reflect what is happening
from moment to moment.

1. A motorcycle race over a bumpy course which includes several
   obstacles
2. A five- or ten-minute segment of a three-ring circus
3. The final minutes of a Little League softball game, with a top
   pitcher on the mound and a star batter at homeplate; the score is
   nearly tied
4. Some frightening encounter you have had—with an animal, an authority figure, a machine, or the like
5. A trip in a canoe or a rowboat down a river with changing currents
   and small rapids
6. Giving birth (if you are female)
7. Being with someone else who was giving birth
8. Skiing down a challenging slope
9. A hurricane or other natural disaster you have lived through
10. Some exciting moments in an adult sports event you attended
11. The death of someone who died gracefully

EXERCISE 5 WRITTEN

Turn to the long list of writing topics in part 7, and find a topic that you can develop by including a true-to-life narrative. Write the paper, using what you have learned in this chapter about narrative writing.

EXERCISE 6 SMALL-GROUP ACTIVITY

Read the following student papers in part 8 outside of class. Come to class prepared to discuss, in small groups of three or four, how well these papers succeed as narrative writing:

Charlie's Carry-Out (# 5)

A Warning (#11)

The Youghiogheny River and Me (#14)

An EEG Emergency (#15)

Light Action Today in South Viet Nam (#17)

Never underestimate your readers' intelligence or overestimate their information.

—an old newspaper saying

CHAPTER 15
INFORMING

A friend of yours wants directions for making wreaths of nuts, cones, and other natural materials, to sell at a Christmas bazaar. Or, you need to write to your insurance company to claim compensation for several expensive items missing from your car. Or you have just discovered a new bluegrass singer, and you want to tell your friend on a submarine—a bluegrass fan—about the unique banjo-picking style of your find.

Your art history instructor believes in comprehensive exam questions; you expect one something like this on your final: Tell me everything you know about Chagall—or Rembrandt—or Georgia O'Keeffe. Or the owner of the summer camp where you serve as a counselor has asked for a report on all the special activities you designed for your campers this summer, to help her determine who to hire next year. Or your sister, who has a partially deaf 10-year-old, knows that a family on your block also has a youngster with hearing problems, and she has written to ask you about a hearing device that child wears.

To meet the needs of these situations, you will write to inform. That is, you will be passing on information to someone else. Informative writing explains, and often it instructs. It is intended to be useful and practical. And you, the writer, may know a great deal more about your subject than your readers do. That's why you're writing in the first place: to send information from someone who does know to those who don't know. So when you write an informative paper, keep in mind this old newspaper saying: "Never underestimate your readers' intelligence or overestimate their information."

COMPLETE, ACCURATE, AND CLEAR

Because your readers do not already know the information you are
176   sending them, you'll need to take special care to be complete, accurate,

and clear. To help you understand the importance of being complete, accurate, and clear, we'd like to show you a sample informative paper on a subject you probably know very little about. Notice that the writer has kept in mind the old newspaper saying—she doesn't assume her readers are unintelligent, but she does assume they lack information.

Our writer's purpose in this paper is to inform readers about hypoglycemia, a rather common metabolic condition that can radically affect the everyday lives of its unsuspecting victims. She wants to explain what hypoglycemia is, what symptoms might indicate it, why diagnosis is important, how to find out whether one has it, and what diet to follow if the tests are positive. The paper's focus is determined for her by what she wants to explain and how much information she chooses to convey.

> Facing the fact that you have hypoglycemia is somewhat like an alcoholic's facing the fact that he or she is an alcoholic. From that day forward, if you want to feel good and to function well, you know that you must generally avoid sugary foods—just as the alcoholic must avoid alcohol. And just as with alcoholism, hypoglycemia is much more prevalent than many people realize.
>
> "Hypoglycemia" (high po gly seé mee uh) means, to put it simply, that you suffer from low blood sugar. What actually happens is that pure sugar in your blood stream makes your pancreas overproduce insulin, which in turn burns sugar very rapidly. This explains why the "pick-up" candy bar so popular with the unaware lethargic-feeling hypoglycemic provides the desired sudden spurt of energy—but at the price of a new low as soon as insulin gets to the sugar in the candy bar.
>
> The hypoglycemic person—depending on the rate at which he or she burns sugar—may have functioned fairly well for years prior to suspecting hypoglycemia. But even with a reasonable level of functioning, having yourself tested if you have certain symptoms—irritability, depression, fatigue, lassitude, blurring of vision, difficulty in concentrating—is very important. For hypoglycemia sometimes precedes diabetes, a much more serious condition.
>
> It may not be easy to talk your doctor into the blood sugar test used to discover hypoglycemia; for some reason, many doctors refuse to acknowledge hypoglycemia. If your regular doctor won't cooperate with you, go to another physician, probably an internist. If your sugar test does indicate hypoglycemia, then you will need to attend carefully to what you put into your body—if you want to be a healthy hypoglycemic.

The paper continues with a discussion of foods and beverages the hypoglycemic should include in his or her diet and those to be avoided. These are listed, under appropriate headings:

Include: *Avoid:*   *May be used sometimes:*

The effect of both alcoholic beverages and drugs is mentioned. Finally, the writer explains that the hypoglycemic will probably need to eat more frequently and in smaller portions than formerly, to slow down the insulin overreaction.

Let's look at the above paper in terms of our three standards for informative writing: completeness, accuracy, and clarity.

The paper seems complete enough. It defines hypoglycemia, mentions some of the common symptoms, points out its relation to the more serious diabetes, talks about the sugar test used for diagnosis and tells how to get one, and details both an approved food and beverage diet and recommended eating habits for the hypoglycemic. It even notes that hypoglycemics are likely to be more susceptible to drugs than are other people.

How accurate is this writer's information? We, her readers, are not really in a position to know. The writer certainly sounds as if she knows what she's talking about. Though she doesn't overwhelm us with medical terminology, she does give us enough technical information about blood sugar, insulin, and pancreas, and so on, to inspire our confidence in her discussion of hypoglycemia.

The paper is clear enough so that most readers could follow it and use the information if they needed to. Several specific factors contribute to its clarity. First, the writer has used everyday language, rather than a lot of technical words that many readers might not understand. Second, she has been careful to define "hypoglycemia" early in the paper. She does not assume that her readers are familiar with the word. She has even taken the trouble to show the reader how to pronounce this big, rather strange-looking word—a minor tactic that can be more important than you might think. Letting readers in on how to say possibly intimidating words can make them feel more in command of what they are reading.

By referring to the "pick-up" candy bar so popular with hypoglycemics, our writer gives her readers a common hypoglycemic situation that they can identify with. This real-life situation helps to clarify, early in the paper, how hypoglycemia affects human metabolism. Finally, the information about what a person with hypoglycemia should and should not eat and drink is presented in list form, for easy readability and quick reference.

You might want to try out your informative writing on a test reader before you write your final draft. In fact, you might want to use *two* test readers—one to check your rough draft for accuracy, another to test it for completeness and clarity. Choose an expert on your subject to test read for accuracy. The writer of our sample paper might have asked a doctor or a medical student to check her rough draft for accuracy. But to check for completeness and clarity, she would need to ask an average, uninformed reader to help her out. Only an uninformed reader—her real audience, remember—could help her see where to fill in the information gaps and where to clarify. It is probably more important to test your paper on an uninformed reader than on an expert. Why? Because it is too easy to assume that your readers know more than they do.

OPENING DEVICES: ANALOGIES AND RHETORICAL QUESTIONS

The writer of our sample informative paper opens the paper with a device that often works well in informative writing: an analogy. In an analogy, an unfamiliar subject (in this case, hypoglycemia) is made clearer by comparing it with a more familiar one (here, alcoholism). In addition to clarifying unfamiliar content, an analogy helps to make readers feel at home with new material. Many readers of this paper may never have heard of hypoglycemia before; however, the chances are good that they know at least something about alcoholism.

Using analogies can be tricky, though, especially if you try to push an analogy too far. Notice how our writer qualifies her comparison of hypoglycemia and alcoholism:

> Facing the fact that you have hypoglycemia is somewhat like an alcoholic's facing the fact that he or she is an alcoholic. From that day forward, if you want to feel good and to function well, you know that you must generally avoid sugary foods—just as the alcoholic must avoid alcohol.

She says that facing hypoglycemia is *somewhat* like facing alcoholism, and that hypoglycemics must *generally* avoid sugary foods in the same way that alcoholics must avoid alcohol. Both *somewhat* and *generally* are qualifying words; that is, they keep the sentences they appear in honest.

Nor does our writer try to extend her analogy too far, another trap one can fall into when using analogies. No analogy will be valid for comparing every point about an unfamiliar subject with a familiar one. For that to be true, the two things would have to be identical. Actually, this particular analogy could be applied at certain other points in this paper. However, it has served its purpose once it has made the reader feel at home with the unfamiliar subject it has been used to introduce. If you try to extend an analogy too far, it can "take over" your material, so that you risk losing the focus on your main points as you—and in turn your reader—get caught up in the fascination of the analogy.

Analogies are fun to experiment with. Try one out the next time you need to explain unfamiliar material to someone. But don't push your analogy so far that it either becomes dishonest or overwhelms what you wanted to explain in the first place.

There is another opening device you can use in informative writing to whet the curiosity of your readers and make them want to read on: the rhetorical question. This device poses a question that will be answered by what follows. A reader begins to wonder about the answer as soon as the question is asked—and right away you have an involved reader, one who is in the right frame of mind to absorb your information.

The student writer of an informative paper about some problems in owning an aquarium of live-bearing fish began her paper with two rhetorical questions:

> You wish to start an aquarium of live-bearing fish? Are you aware of how prolific certain live-bearing fish can be?

Here are some other rhetorical questions calculated to engage readers:

1. Does extraterrestrial life exist?
2. Looking for a movie that will keep you laughing all the way home?
3. How can you locate a doctor who believes in "treating the whole person"?
4. How—if at all—should pornography be controlled?
5. What is cloning, and how near is science to being able to clone humans?

Before we leave our discussion of general informative writing, we want to share with you a student's informative paper intended to help a Western host or hostess give a Japanese dinner party:

> Traditional Japanese architecture and furnishings are so different from those of the West that it is virtually impossible to reproduce the style of a formal Japanese dinner party outside Japan. Nevertheless, I would like to venture a simple account of certain essentials, which a Western hostess can adapt.
>
> In a traditional Japanese room there are no chairs and the guests kneel —or, in the case of men, sit cross-legged—on zabuton (large flat cushions). The zabuton are placed directly on the tatami mats which form the floor. The Japanese table is about the height of a coffee table but has a larger top. This table is usually used for dinner, but for very formal occasions each guest will have his or her own small laquered table. The place of honor in a Japanese room is in front of the tokonoma, or alcove, which usually has a hanging scroll or a flower arrangement placed in it. The hostess usually occupies the place in front of the door or the one on

the opposite side of the table. With the exception of a large wooden paddle used for serving rice, chopsticks are the only utensils in sight.

Prior to the meal each guest is presented with a tightly rolled hand
towel which has been dampened with very hot, sometimes scented,
water. It is not improper to bury one's face in the oshibori—as this towel
is called—for a few seconds, in addition to using it to wipe one's hands.

The food at a Japanese dinner party is always served in individual
lacquered or china bowls carefully chosen for shape and color to comple-
ment the food that goes in them. Bowls are lifted in the hand for eating
from them. Since there are no spoons, soup is drunk from the bowl, and
chopsticks are used to eat the fish or vegetables often found in the soup.

The basic Japanese dinner consists of clear soup with a few pieces of
meat or vegetables floating in it or a thick soup containing miso (bean
paste). The soup is followed by a main course, which ends with plain
boiled rice and pickles. Sake, Japanese rice wine, or ochai (green tea) is
the beverage. It is rare to have dessert. If dessert is served it is usually
fresh fruit in season—or out of season if the hostess is trying to impress
some of her guests.

EXPLAINING A PROCESS

When you tell someone in writing how to do something—how to repair
a guitar, execute the backstroke, groom a dog, carve a totem pole—you
are doing a special kind of informative writing known as process writing.
For process writing we would add three more standards to our original
three of completeness, accuracy, and clarity: Be direct, concise and
orderly. By "direct," we mean strictly straightforward and to the point;
by "concise," don't waste words; and by "orderly," put the steps of the
process in proper sequence. After all, we usually explain a process so
that someone else can do exactly the same thing in exactly the same
way.

In the following paper, a student gives directions for constructing a
piñata:

> To set the theme for a "south of the border" fiesta, you might make a
> colorful piñata, a figure filled with edibles and/or party favors, borrowed
> from Mexico. You will need to start your piñata several days ahead of
> time, since it contains paste that must dry.
>
> To make a piñata, you will need:
>
> a large balloon (any shape you want)
> paste (regular household starch will do)
> strips of newspaper
> paint (any kind that will stick to newspaper)
> decorative materials, such as crepe paper, ribbons, sequins (optional)
> assorted treats: candy, nuts, miniature party favors, etc.

a small amount of colored paper, to match paint
transparent tape

Inflate the balloon. Then dip the newspaper strips in the paste and apply them one at a time to the balloon, leaving a small space clear to put in the party treats later. Continue this procedure until you have four or five layers of newspaper strips on the balloon. Set the balloon aside to dry for a day or two.

When the paste has dried completely, paint your creation any color you want. If you like, you can add such materials as crepe paper, ribbons, sequins, and so on, to make the balloon resemble some figure—perhaps a donkey, or a drum, or a football. To finish off the piñata, fill it with assorted treats and patch up the hole with colored paper and tape. Your piñata is now ready to be hung from the ceiling for your fiesta—and to be smashed to bits for all the goodies to fall out, as the high point of your party.

Illustrations of various kinds—diagrams, charts, graphs, and the like —can often help to clarify process writing. We encourage using this kind of visual reinforcement. However, don't assume that your illustration will explain itself. It won't, for a reader unfamiliar with your subject matter.

INFORMING WITH HUMOR

Sometimes students complain—and with reason—that informative writing is boring to do. And sometimes instructors grow weary of reading relatively dull, flat informative papers. The student paper that follows will prove to you that informative papers can be cleverly written—and pleasant to read—and still achieve their purpose of conveying information.

Here is the paper on live-bearing fish whose two opening sentences you read earlier in the chapter:

You wish to start an aquarium of live-bearing fish? Are you aware of how prolific certain live-bearing fish can be? Black mollies, guppies, sunsets, and swordtails, for example. You may return from the pet shop with a pair of these fish only to wake up the next morning and find thirty new arrivals squirming through the filter's air bubbles—as happened to me. Soon these newcomers grow and contribute to the mass production of live-bearing fish that knows no forty-hour work week. They will fill your bathtub and your kitchen sink; and the sewers of this country must know plenty of their cousins.

You may answer with, "I'll just buy one, or all the same sex." That logical solution is struck down when your single, but once impregnated, female mollie has three broods of fifty fish each without a father in sight;

she left him back at the pet shop. Once a live-bearer is pregnant, she may seem to be so continuously. If you do find a group of non-pregnant females, don't be surprised if, within a week, a few have changed their sex. This common little trick is accomplished only by the females. The fact that males never achieve this feat poses the question, why not have all male fish? Because they will chase each other in dizzying circles, getting so confused that they will eventually commit the ultimate in aquatic suicide—and jump out of the tank!

But don't despair, red velvet swordtail fans, because I have found the solution to the underwater population explosion. Supply your tank with two or three large angel fish, who will delight in a feast of newborn delicacies of swordtails. If you do decide to raise some live-bearing offspring in this same tank, plop a few plants on the surface for their protection from the angel fish. Or, if you become a really serious breeder, set up separate maternity tanks for the expectant mothers. There will be plenty of future occupants waiting in line. Plenty!

CHECKLIST FOR INFORMATIVE WRITING

1. Decide on exactly how much information to convey.
2. Be complete: don't leave out anything essential.
3. Be accurate: make sure your facts are correct.
4. Be clear.
5. Consider opening with an analogy or a rhetorical question.
6. In process writing, be direct, concise, and orderly.
7. Consider using some humor.

Refer also to the checklist inside the back cover.

EXERCISE 1 FOR CLASS DISCUSSION

Below are two informative papers on the same subject. Compare them according to the standards for informative writing discussed in this chapter.

Anyone can learn to play pinball. All you need is a good eye, a controlled arm, perseverance in practicing, a pocketful of loose change—and a lot of luck.

You should approach the magic machine with respect; after all, it does contain all the answers to the riddles posed by its buttons, bumpers, and bells. After you have bowed before it with proper courtesy, pull back the arm—and say a prayer for luck. If you're lucky, your ball will stay in play and away from the flippers for a long time.

You are bound to score points when you play pinball. But to be really good at it, you will have to "pop" the machine. To learn how to "pop," stand and watch what several experienced players do in order to increase their scores; it never hurts to learn from the competition! If you pop regularly enough, you will soon feel that the money you have fed into the maw of this mechanical monster was well spent.

Although it looks rather easy, playing pinball well is an art few can master. Not many players can be termed "Pinball Wizards"*—although many lay claim to the title. On the way to becoming a wizard, first you need to understand how to play the game.

After placing your quarter in the machine, gently pull back on the spring-loaded knob which sends the little steel ball into the playing area. The object is simple enough: to keep the ball in the playing area while scoring as many points as you can by hitting buttons, bumpers, bells, even moving targets. To help keep the ball in play, there are two button-controlled flippers, which flip the ball back into the playing area if it should near one of three or four exit holes. You do not want to let the ball get past a flipper and out of play.

Scoring points in pinball isn't hard. You will always score at least 1,000 points per ball played, and there are five balls to a game. But, to become a great player, a master, you will have to consistently "pop" the pinball machine. Popping the machine means scoring beyond the point total needed to get a free game. This range is usually between 64,000 and 151,000 total points, depending on the machine. While even a good player may score 12,000 to 15,000 points per ball, to pop the more popular machines, you would need at least 20,000 to 25,000 points per ball. Only one player out of 1,000 can accomplish this with regularity. And only that one can proclaim himself or herself a Pinball Wizard.

EXERCISE 2 WRITTEN

Here are ten possible topics for informative papers. Write out an analogy or a rhetorical question that you could use to begin a paper on at least three of these topics.

1. Keeping a guinea pig or a hamster or some other small animal as a pet in a two- or three-room apartment
2. What to do if you are the first person to arrive at the scene of an automobile accident in which three persons have been injured
3. A job you have held or now hold
4. A new musical group you have heard recently and like
5. A hobby you pursue in which you would like to interest others
6. How to conduct a study of your family's history from colonial times forward
7. Tennis as a mental game as well as a physical one
8. Directions for making something unusual

---

* Pinball Wizard: the greatest player of all; the movie "Tommy" was about him.

9. Ways a person could discover the most appropriate occupation for himself or herself

10. Seals as playful creatures, or big cats as restless ones, or pandas as shy ones, or some other such topic—if you can get to a zoo to gather your information

EXERCISE 3 CLASSROOM ACTIVITY

Write an informative paper (not one explaining a process) about something that probably at least one person in your class does not know about. Bring your rough draft in for uninformed persons to read. Is the rough draft complete and clear enough to satisfy your test readers? Is it accurate enough to satisfy you? If the answer to either of these questions is "no," do whatever additional background work you need to before writing the final version of your paper.

EXERCISE 4 WRITTEN

Write a process paper on one of the following topics. Assume that someone will use your directions to do whatever activity you write about.

1. training an animal
2. decorating a cake for a special occasion
3. building a piece of furniture
4. repairing a fence—or a lamp—or a bicycle
5. learning to play a simple musical instrument
6. creating decoupage
7. building a fire indoors
8. building a fire outdoors
9. making a clay or ceramic pot
10. creating a flower arrangement
11. carving or sculpting some object
12. explaining how to use a small electronic device
13. teaching a youngster to swim
14. planting a vegetable garden
15. making a quilt
16. creating a needlework design
17. teaching a friend to sail

EXERCISE 5 CLASSROOM ACTIVITY

Read the following student papers in part 8, outside of class. Come to class prepared to talk about the papers as informative writing, based on what you have learned from this chapter.

"Popsicle" (#4)

Nightclub Circuit (#6)

Water-skiing to Signals (#10)

PART V
Research Writing

What is research but a blind date with knowledge?
—Anonymous

Much of the writing you will do in college and in your career will require or be improved by the use of information from sources. This use
may be very extensive, as when you cite a number of magazine and
newspaper articles to argue that there are several alternatives to power-
ing automobiles with gasoline. Or this use may be very limited, as when
you quote one line from a Bob Dylan song to illustrate a statement you
are making about the need for students at your college to evaluate their
professors.

In either case, certain rules for using and identifying your sources
have evolved—rules designed to assure accuracy, gain your reader's confidence, and give proper credit to a source. If a number of sources are
used and the identification methods are the formal ones stressed in this
chapter, the paper is usually called a "research paper"; but what is "research" and what is not is more a matter of degree than a clear-cut distinction between types of writing. If, while writing an essay about an
injury that you sustained playing football on artificial turf, you cite one
statistic about the frequency of certain types of injuries on artificial
turf, you are in a way doing research, and you must in some way,
whether formally or not, identify the source of the statistic.

Almost all freshman composition courses devote a section to research
writing, a section designed to teach you both how to find information
and how to identify the sources of the information. For most students,
at first, finding such information and documenting it correctly seems
an awkward and bewildering process. But a sincere attempt at the paper
your instructor assigns should begin to convince you that information
on almost any subject is readily available; library systems are designed
not to confuse, but to lead you quickly to answers. The attempt should

also teach you that incorporating information from sources in a paper need not be much more difficult than repeating in a paper a story your grandfather once told you. Basically the statement, "When I was ten my grandfather told me . . ." is replaced by "According to the *Statistical Abstract of the United States* . . . ." If the paper is a formal research paper, a footnote is added to indicate exactly where in that volume the information was found.

Although students tend to exaggerate the difficulties in writing research papers, some of the protests instructors hear are understandable. It does take time to write a research paper, and almost everyone has at some time cursed the awkwardness of taking notes from that necessary modern monster, the microfilm machine.

One protest, however, is less and less valid: the protest that "I will not have to do research in my job." It may have been true in the past that work involving formal research techniques was not demanded of most people, even college-educated people; but that day, for better or worse, has passed. Because society is so complex today, because new information is accumulated so fast, and because the firms or government agencies for which we work are so large, the more casual approach of the past is less and less possible. Nurses may have to participate in studies that compare their pay scales to the pay scales of nurses in other area hospitals. Police may be called upon to evaluate the accuracy of various kinds of lie detector machines. Even so seemingly simple a decision as the brand of electric typewriter a firm should buy may today involve the expenditure of thousands and thousands of dollars; and the budget-minded executive may well demand a thorough study of the long-term costs of upkeep and of ribbons for a particular brand.

Even if you are never asked in your job to submit a report on the safety of recreational equipment or on advances in computer technology, learning your way around a library will give you a sense of confidence, an assurance that you will know how to find information when you need it. And, unlike writing the report on typewriter brands, writing the college research paper can be enjoyable, if you choose your subject carefully, for it gives you an ego-boosting sense of expertise on a particular subject.

THE RESEARCH PAPER THESIS

Although papers using sources look different because of all their paraphernalia (footnote numbers and references to sources), such papers do exactly what is done in many shorter papers; they back up a thesis that appears early in the paper, a thesis that is a limited, precise generalization. The research paper thesis may, however, differ from the theses you have been writing in three ways: (1) Because the subject may be more complex, the thesis may be several sentences long; (2) Because the paper may be longer than papers you have been writing, the research paper thesis is more likely to set up the major divisions of the paper, as an aid to both you and the reader; (3) Because a research paper is usually based on objective information, the thesis will be derived from and supported by information from sources other than your opinions or personal experience, although both opinions and personal experience may be used if relevant.

Even though the research paper thesis is not usually developed until you have read a number of sources, it is important that you look on the thesis as your own, not just as a repetition of something someone else has said. Don't make the mistake of accepting the first written opinion you find and trying to write a paper to back up that one writer's opinion: other writers may think differently; you may change your mind; and accepting the first opinion you read violates a basic principle of research, that you choose from and use a number of sources.

For instance, following are three possible but different thesis statements for a paper on Laetrile, a controversial cancer drug that is legal in Mexico but illegal in the United States as of 1977. All three students may conceivably have read the same articles, but have come to somewhat different conclusions:

Although individual cancer patients claim to have been helped by Laetrile, scientific study after scientific study has found no evidence that its use stops or slows down the spread of cancer.

No scientific evidence exists that Laetrile retards the growth of cancer, and, therefore, the United States government should continue to ban its use. Its legalization would only encourage people with cancer to avoid legitimate treatment and to put money into the hands of unethical physicians.

Although no scientific evidence exists that Laetrile stops or slows down the spread of cancer, neither does sure scientific evidence exist that its use is harmful. Until evidence that it is harmful does exist, the government should allow its use, for Laetrile at least provides victims of cancer a hope, a hope that could give them strength.

All three students seem to agree that there is no scientific evidence—at least in 1977—that Laetrile is effective in fighting cancer, and each will establish that through references to books and articles. The second student, however, has decided also to argue that the ban on its use in the United States should continue, a position that he or she will probably bolster with the arguments of government officials, physicians, and the student's own observations about human nature. The third student seems to agree with the other two about the scientific evidence, but has decided that legalizing the drug will do no harm and might even help patients psychologically. If this student can find arguments to support that position, he or she would use them; if not, the student should not be afraid to go ahead and argue on his or her own for the position.

All three of these theses are legitimate. The important point is that each student decided *after* reading a *number* of sources what he or she wanted to say and organized the thesis and paper accordingly.

MAKING THE THESIS YOUR OWN

Students who otherwise write clearly often seem to lose their voices and their control in a research paper. They then turn in papers that resemble patchwork quilts or scrapbooks more than essays to which the student contributes.

That contribution may seem small and may consist primarily of a thesis statement and topic sentences (as it might, for instance, in a straightforward account of whether there is scientific evidence for the effectiveness of Laetrile), but the thesis statement and the topic sentences are *your* conclusions, even if all your supporting evidence comes from sources. For instance, it is you who must decide how seriously to take personal testimonials on the effectiveness of Laetrile; it is you who must decide how conclusive scientific research has been; it is you who must group the opinions you find into types. And, in most research papers you write, your opinion will play a much larger role than in a straightforward account of Laetrile research.

Admittedly opinion plays a smaller role in research papers than in some other kinds of writing, and, admittedly, you will want to avoid subjects so subjective that little but opinion is possible (like "What Was the Greatest Rock Band of the 1960s?"); but if your paper is to be more than a simple report, opinion may become very important in producing a good paper.

For instance, let's say that you have chosen to write your research paper on the controversy over grizzly bears in the national parks. You will find as you read that attacks on people by grizzly bears have increased dramatically in Yellowstone and Glacier National Parks in recent years, mostly because more people are in the parks and the bears are becoming aware that food may be found where humans camp. Some individuals have even advocated removing the bears from areas where they might come in contact with tourists or campers. Others argue that if the national parks are to preserve what is left of wild America, visitors to the parks must accept the possibility of danger—that to remove all dangers would turn Yellowstone and Glacier into Disneylands.

Unless you have encountered a grizzly bear yourself, you will probably take all your information on attacks from sources. You will read different opinions on what should be done. But in the end it is you who must formulate the thesis, a thesis that will depend on how you personally feel about dangerous wildlife and their importance, and on what you feel the function of a national park should be.

Even in a paper on Laetrile, which seems to leave less room for personal contribution than others, your opinion and experience could become important, depending on your thesis. For instance, you may have decided to write on Laetrile because an uncle who had cancer went to Mexico in the last year of his life for treatment. What you know about your uncle's treatment and death may add little to the scientific knowledge about Laetrile, but it might be very relevant to your deciding whether you want to argue that Laetrile should be banned or not.

FINDING SOURCES AND LIMITING YOUR SUBJECT

An instructor will usually assign a general subject for the research paper or suggest specific subjects of current interest. Your first task, therefore, is to trek to the college library and begin making a list of sources. This list is called a preliminary *bibliography*.

As you locate a source, write down all the necessary information for finding the source and for footnoting later. For books you will need: (1) the author or editor; (2) the title of the book; (3) the place of publication; (4) the publisher; (5) the date of publication; and (6) the call number. For magazine articles you will need: (1) the author; (2) the title of the article; (3) the name of the magazine or newspaper; (4) the volume number; (5) the date of the issue; and (6) the page numbers.

Most writers find it handy to keep the information for each source on a file card like the sample on the following page.

QL
696
S8
M23
1966A

Faith McNulty
The Whooping Crane
New York
E. P. Dutton & Co.
1966

What sort of material you are going to locate and read will depend on the subject you have chosen or been assigned and how much you already know about the subject.

You may at times feel like the foreign student in a physical education class who is assigned a paper on American football: he not only does not know the rules but has seen no football game other than the tag game running continually outside his dormitory window. If he cannot persuade his instructor to allow him to write on soccer, this student is obviously going to have to begin with general reading about football, which many American students would find unnecessary.

Don't despair if you find yourself in a similar situation. The sample research paper that follows this chapter is from a class in which students were asked to investigate the status of an endangered species. Many knew nothing about the species they chose before writing the paper, but still produced good research papers.

Step One General Reading
If you know very little about a subject or need to brush up on what you once knew, go first to an encyclopedia or other general reference work. These, which cannot be checked out, are usually kept in a separate section of the library.

The encyclopedia most widely used by college students is the *Encyclopaedia Britannica*, which is now divided into a ten-volume micropedia (with brief articles on tens of thousands of subjects) and a twenty-volume macropedia (with longer, more detailed articles on thousands of subjects). The micropedia will indicate where in the macropedia you will find more detailed discussions of your subject. Probably handier but briefer will be the articles in the one-volume *Columbia Encyclopedia*. If you are someone who responds more readily to illustrated articles, you may want to try *The Random House Encyclopedia*.

Almost all areas of study have encyclopedias and reference works that go into more detail than even such a large reference work as the *Encyclopaedia Britannica* can. There are hundreds of these, and there is no reason for you to learn the names of all of them, but you might want to know the names of some of those in your major. For instance, if you are a biology major it might be handy later to know of the *Encyclopedia of the Biological Sciences*; or, if an engineering major, *The McGraw-Hill Encyclopedia of Science and Technology*; or, if you are in any technical field and like lots of illustrations, *The Way Things Work: An Illustrated Encyclopedia of Technology*.

Following this chapter is a sample research paper on the whooping crane, a bird the student first read about in two reference works on endangered species, *Wildlife in Danger* and *Extinct and Vanishing Birds of the World*. Such reference works can be located in one of four ways: (1) consulting the card catalog; (2) going to the reference shelves directly (reference works are generally arranged by subject); (3) consulting a reference work on reference works (there actually are such books); or (4) consulting the reference librarian, whose job is to help you find source material.

Step Two Locating Magazine Articles

Instructors often like to assign subjects of current controversy, and current controversy is most readily found in magazine articles. The place to look is the indispensable *Reader's Guide to Periodical Literature*, an annual compilation by author and subject of articles in about 160 periodicals of general interest in all subject areas. (Articles published in the current year may be found in paperback indexes, which come out every two weeks.) Don't give up if you don't find what you are looking for under the first heading you try; whooping cranes, for instance, are listed under CRANES, as in this entry from the 1974 edition:

CRANES (birds)
Captive breeding: boon or boondoggle; the endangered whooping crane. D. Zimmerman. il Natur Hist 83:6-8+ D '74
Day of the crane; sandhill cranes; with photographs. J. Madson. Audubon 76:46-63 Mr '74
Programmed extinction of the sandhill crane. R. S. Miller. il Natur Hist 83:62-9, bibl (p90) F '74
Rare and endangered species in the lake states: Hiawatha's goony chicken; sandhill cranes. W. E. Taylor. il por Am For 80:42-4 S '74

The shorthand technique of the *Reader's Guide* may appear puzzling at first, but it is easy to read once you get the hang of it. The first entry under CRANES above, for instance, is the title of the article, "Captive Breeding: Boon or Boondoggle?" Next is the author's initial and last name, D. Zimmerman. The *il* indicates that the article is illustrated. Next comes the name of the magazine, *Natural History*. (If you can't figure out the abbreviation for the magazine, turn to the list of abbreviations at the front of each *Reader's Guide*.) "83:6–8+" indicates that the article is in volume 83, begins on page six, runs to page eight, and is continued on later pages. "D '74" gives the date, December 1974. Except for the *il*, you should write down all this information.

The student who wrote on the whooping crane went to the *Reader's Guide* after he had read two articles in reference works. He looked at the *Reader's Guide* for the last six years and discovered, as you probably will, that there were more articles listed than he needed, and so tried to eliminate those that did not seem very pertinent or that were repetitious of other articles.

For most undergraduate papers the *Reader's Guide* will provide you with sufficient material, but there are periodical indexes in specific fields, indexes that cover the many scholarly and technical publications that the *Reader's Guide* does not. A nursing student might want to know of the *Cumulative Index to Nursing Literature*; a sociology student, of *Sociological Abstracts*. These specialized indexes should be on the shelves near the *Reader's Guide*.

Indexing today is marvelously efficient, but there is still no easy way to find articles on an event that took place within the last month. In that case go to the magazine section of the library and start thumbing; *Time* and *Newsweek* at least will have articles on any very recent event of importance.

Step Three **Locating Books**
With almost any subject, you will want to check the card catalog for the library's book holdings. The student writing on the whooping crane found in the card catalog under the subject heading *Whooping Crane* one book entirely on the crane, one partly on it. If your subject is Thomas Jefferson, abortion, or Stoicism, you will find a great many more books than you would on the whooping crane and will be forced to select carefully those you are going to note. (Later in this chapter we will discuss a process you might follow if you must work primarily from books and there are a great many books on your subject.)

On the next page is a sample of a card catalog entry under the subject *Whooping Crane*:

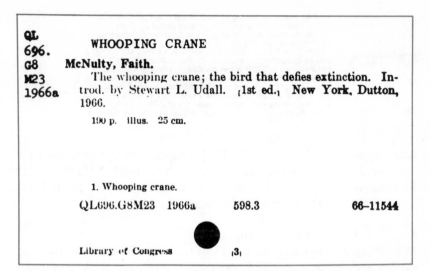

QL.
696.
G8   McNulty, Faith.
M23   The whooping crane; the bird that defies extinction. In-
1966a   trod. by Stewart L. Udall. ₁1st ed.₁ New York, Dutton,
          1966.

          190 p. Illus. 25 cm.

          1. Whooping crane.
          QL696.G8M23   1966a   598.3   66-11544

          Library of Congress   ₍3₎

WHOOPING CRANE

The catalog card gives a great deal of information, including the size of
the book and its total number of pages, but you will need to copy down
only the author's name, the title, the place of publication, the publisher, the date of publication, and the call number, which appears in
the upper left corner.

Step Four **Locating News Stories**
If you need for your paper up-to-date information or an account of a
recent event of importance, the newspaper is probably your best bet, as
it was for the student writing on the whooping crane. Although several
American newspapers—the *Washington Post,* for example—are now
publishing indexes, the *New York Times Index* is the oldest (going back
to 1851) and is still the most thorough. Like the *Reader's Guide,* the
New York Times Index is an annual compilation with biweekly compila-
tions for the current year. As can be seen in the sample below, the index
also includes a handy one- or two-sentence summary of the story's content. Don't despair if there is nothing under the first subject heading
you try; whooping cranes, for instance, are listed here under BIRDS
and the subheading *Cranes:*

> **Coots. See also** Hunting, F 24
> **Cranes**
> Wildlife biologists reptdly are hopeful that 4 young
> whooping cranes that were born in Idaho during summer of
> '75 and recently migrated into wildlife refuge near Monte
> Vista (Colo), will form nucleus of new flock of endangered
> species (S), Mr 6,50:2; birdwatcher John Savage describes

visit to Bosque del Apache Natl Wildlife Refuge (Sorocco,
NM); notes 2 young whooping cranes raised by 'foster
parent' sandhill cranes during '75 in Canada are wintering
in area; says they are 1st whoopers to visit NM since
1850s; Tom Smylie notes there are only 48 wild whooping
cranes in existence, excluding '75 hatch; illus (L), Mr 7,X,
p9; Patuxent Wildlife Research Center head Dr Cameron
Kepler says whooping crane chick was hatched May 5;
birth expands whoopers' world population to 85; if chick
survives, it will be 1st whooper successfully hatched and
grown from parents raised in captivity (S), My 6,23:1
Fed Appeals Ct, New Orleans, refuses to consider decision

A shorthand entry like "Mr 6,50:2" above gives first the date, then the
page number, then the column, and would be translated March 6, page
50, column 2. Note that titles and authors are not usually given; those
you will have to take down when you read the story.

Step Five Finding Other Information

Most if not all the source material you need may be found in the card
catalog and in newspaper and periodical indexes, but if at some point
you need further information it almost certainly can be found in the
library. There are, for instance, a number of sources for statistics. The
United States Bureau of the Census each year publishes the *Statistical
Abstract of the United States,* a compilation of the principal statistical
information produced by the federal government. Statistics for the past
may be found in *Historical Statistics of the United States, Colonial
Times to 1957. Statistics Sources* will show you where to find data on
industrial and business matters.

Just ask the librarian!

A REVIEW OF THE PROCESS

Let's move through the above process with a student who has not been
assigned a specific topic like "The Status of an Endangered Species"
and who has a subject that requires using more books than would the
whooping crane paper.

Let's say that you are assigned a paper on some aspect of American
history from 1776 to 1865. The professor obviously does not want a
summary of George Washington's life or the sequence of events at Bull
Run, but rather a paper that develops a fairly precise thesis. You obviously do not want a subject like "The Causes of the Civil War," which
would involve vast amounts of reading and to which you could contribute few comments of your own.

What you should do is find a subject which has caught your interest
—for instance, Thomas Jefferson—and then find a topic about Jefferson

limited enough (his interest in music, his theories of architecture, his relationship with Lafayette) for you to emerge from the paper with a reasonable expertise. You are best off if you also find a topic about which you can make some observations of your own—such as comparing Jefferson's views on States' Rights to those prevalent today.

If you are interested in Jefferson but know little about him, you might first go to an article on him in either the *Encyclopaedia Britannica* or the *Dictionary of American Biography*, a standard reference work with articles on most notable Americans of the past. While reading one of these reference works, you might become interested in the fact that Jefferson frequently condemned slavery and yet owned slaves until the end of his life. (In all probability, he even had several children by one slave, Sally Hemmings.) You decide at this point that your specific subject will be "Thomas Jefferson and Slavery."

The best approach now is probably to go to the card catalog or to the shelves where the books on Jefferson are kept. You will certainly not have time to read many of these books, but by using their indexes you may be able to read parts of what a number of authors say about Jefferson and slavery. These books will probably also lead you to those places in Jefferson's writing where he commented on slavery. This is not the most thorough approach, of course, but you as an undergraduate work under great time limitations and your instructor knows that.

With a subject like Jefferson and slavery, most of the material will be in books, but you will also want to consult the *Reader's Guide* for recent years to see if writers are still commenting on the paradoxes of Jefferson's attitudes toward slavery.

TAKING NOTES

You will not be far into your reading before your thesis will begin to take shape, however much it may later have to be modified. At this point you should begin taking notes. The best method of taking notes is to put each quotation, piece of information, or observation of your own on an individual note card, giving that card a label that will correspond to one of the sections of the paper.

The student writing on the whooping crane realized early in his reading that his thesis would be a generally optimistic statement about the hopes for the crane's survival. He did not change that thesis, but at one point in the reading he did become more pessimistic than he had been initially. As it turned out, the successful 1977 breeding season, which the student read about last in the *New York Times*, returned him to something of his initial optimism.

The student writing on the whooping crane also realized early what the major sections of his paper would probably be and labeled his cards accordingly. He soon could even see subheadings developing—for instance, "Tex-Can Flock—Danger from Hunting."

The most important thing to remember in taking notes is to be accurate. Be sure your summaries reflect what the text actually says; be sure when you quote that you quote *exactly*; be sure that you will be able to tell later what is *directly* quoted and what is not; be sure you note the *exact* page or pages on which the information appears. Such care will help avoid later trips to the library for checking—and burns from your instructor's red pen.

There are three general ways of noting a passage. The first is to summarize part of the article, as on the following card:

> Texas - Canada flock — Hunting Dangers
> Pressure to open up more access to
> swan and sandhill crane hunting
> could endanger whooper because of
> its similarity to these birds.
>   Author thinks, however, that
> fear of public wrath if a
> whooper shot will prevent this.
> North Dakota, e. g., will not allow
> sandhill crane hunting until
> certain all whoopers gone for year.
>   — Sherwood, 84

Be certain when you summarize that you do not "half-copy," that is, rely too much on the wording of the text. Obviously you will be repeating in your summary some of the words in the text, but normally when a series of words on your note card follows exactly a series of words in the text, these should be put in quotation marks. To prevent half-copying, it may be best to summarize without looking at the article and *then* check for accuracy.

The second method of noting is to quote directly. This method is most frequently used with statements of opinion, for it is very important that someone's opinion not be distorted by your rewording. The following directly quoted passage could have been summarized, for it is not opinion but observation, but the student was impressed by the quality of the author's description:

Life-Cycle — Aransas

"It appears that the presence of the youngster stimulates a quicker temper and a fiercer attachment to home. Thus parents will defend their territory with greater determination than a childless couple, and usually triumph in dispute. A mated pair, though childless, in turn makes stronger territorial claims than do either the lonely "singles"--who may be widowed or adolescent birds--or "companions," birds whose relationship is purely platonic. Singles or companions surrender their territory to the first challenger. They then wander, living hand to mouth as it were, chivied by the lords of whatever territories they chance to invade.'[19]"

McNulty, pp. 69-70

The third method, probably the most useful, is to summarize, but to quote in that summary key words and phrases, especially words or phrases skillfully used:

Life-Cycle — Mating Dances

Mating dances begin in late December — but only become intense 2-3 months later. In dances birds leap, bow, posture. Because of crane's "immense size," this is "one of the great dances of the bird world." By March dances are "an almost daily occurrence."

Allen, pp. 68-70

With the development of duplicating machines, other methods of note-taking are being used more and more. Particularly if you are working from magazine or newspaper articles, some or all of these articles may be duplicated inexpensively, allowing you to work from them at home rather than taking notes in the library. One Soviet researcher now living in the United States calls our duplicating machines "the best thing about working in the United States." In the Soviet Union, he says, "I spend 50 per cent of my time sitting in the library copying notes out of books."

Duplication, however, does not make the traditional methods of taking notes completely obsolete. With a large number of duplicated pages, you will still need to locate specific information in articles quickly. In recent years, some students have developed ingenious methods of avoiding the laborious task of note taking. One student, writing on Stanley Kubrick's film *2001: A Space Odyssey*, decided what the divisions of her paper would be and bought eight different-colored pencils with which she marked the duplicated articles as she read.

Most likely, however, even if you are going to duplicate articles, you are best off sticking to some variation of the traditional method of note-taking, as the student writing on the whooping crane has done in the following note. He has described part of an article briefly and has indicated, exactly to the column, where the discussion may be found.

Life - Cycle — Summer
    Describes in detail nesting,
hatching, rearing process.

                                    —Guthery, p. 19,
                                            col. 2

If your articles are long, you may even want to note the paragraph in which the information appears (for instance, "Green, p. 67, col. 1, para. 3").

Although duplication may enhance accuracy because you can check the sources quickly, it may encourage the rushed student to rely too heavily on the wording of the source, sometimes unintentionally. *Don't* —both because this is plagiarism (copying someone else's work without giving proper credit to the source) and because such heavy reliance on someone else's wording will interrupt the smooth flow of your own style through the paper.

As you approach your final thesis, the tendency is to note only those opinions or that information that will support it. But remember also to note information and opinions that may weaken or oppose your position, both out of fairness and because arguments are most impressive when they face up to the strength of their opposition.

WRITING THE PAPER

After you have finished taking notes and have some rough idea of your thesis, you will want to polish the thesis and sketch an outline before beginning your rough draft. By this time you will know a great deal about your subject, probably more than you realize. It is therefore best to set aside your notes and work on your thesis and rough outline without them. With so many facts, figures, and opinions in front of you, it is sometimes difficult to see the forest for the trees. A good way to start— and to prove to yourself how much you know—might be to take a friend aside and tell him or her what you plan to say about your subject in the paper. If you feel you have presented a reasonably well-organized oral argument, that presentation probably can become the basis for the first draft of your outline.

Once you have polished the outline, after again referring to your notes, you should be ready to begin writing. As you write you will for the most part simply back up the statements in your outline with your own observations and material from your notes.

WHAT TO FOOTNOTE

Except for common factual knowledge (of which there is a great deal), all information taken from a source, whether it is quoted directly or put in your own words, must be followed by a footnote—all quotations, all ideas and opinions, all precise factual information such as statistics. (In some cases you yourself may know statistical information, but in such a case you are usually best off checking on your own memory by finding a source for the information.)

Much that you have read, however, is common knowledge and need not be footnoted, whether you knew the information prior to your reading or not. No absolute distinction exists between what is common knowledge and what is not (if you aren't sure, footnote), but information can usually be called common knowledge if it passes two tests: (1) if such information (that whooping cranes mate for life, that William Faulkner won the Nobel Prize for Literature) appears in general reference works and is mentioned without footnotes in more than one article you have read; (2) if you can honestly say, "I know this." Thus, what you tell your friends in the cafeteria about a subject (for instance, the grizzly bear) is in all likelihood common knowledge.

At times, however, you may wish to footnote even common knowledge. For instance, it is common knowledge that there is no verifiable evidence of a wild wolf ever attacking a human on the North American continent, but there are so many myths to the contrary that writers may wish to protect themselves by citing a source. Remember, however, that even if something is common knowledge, you *must* footnote if you are using someone else's actual wording of this information.

INCORPORATING SOURCE MATERIAL
INTO YOUR PAPER

When incorporating source material into a paper, be sure that you make clear to the reader what is from a source and what is not. As a general rule, quotations, opinions, and ideas that appear in your paper are preceded by a signal phrase such as "According to Carl Jung" or "As Mario Pei has observed"; the quotation, opinion, or idea is then followed by a footnote number, indicating to the reader that everything between the signal and the footnote number is from the source, whether directly quoted or put in your own words.

Here are two examples of the proper form for introducing direct quotations:

In June of 1977, Keith M. Schreiner, associate director of the Fish and Wildlife Service, said of the whooping crane's future, "The outlook has never been brighter."[1]

> So successful have hunting regulations and educational campaigns been that *Wildlife in Danger* could say in 1969 that "the losses on migration by uncontrolled and ignorant shooting have certainly become small."[13]

Notice that the writer of these sentences was careful to let his readers know in the text itself the source of the quoted material. The reader understands immediately that the first quotation is from Schreiner and the second from *Wildlife in Danger*. In addition, the reader learns who Schreiner is. (If referred to later, Schreiner's position need not again be mentioned, just as it was not necessary to identify *Wildlife in Danger* as an important reference work, for this had been done earlier in the paper.)

Factual material is also usually preceded by a signal phrase and followed by a footnote number, but it is often put in one's own words, as in the following examples.

> According to Faith McNulty, by 1938 there was only one migratory flock of 22 birds left.[6]

> Although some chicks will not survive, at one point in the spring of 1977, according to the *Washington Post*, the total in the wild and in captivity numbered 126.[8]

Except for numbers, the writer is not borrowing wording from his sources and doesn't need to use quotation marks. The footnote exists to let the reader know just where the writer obtained his information.

On occasion, the signal phrase may be omitted, and factual information included in the text followed only by a footnote number. This may be done especially if you have a cluster of brief bits of information from different sources (population figures, for instance); *but*, if you omit the signal phrase, make certain that the context makes clear what is from a source and what is not. If this is your first research paper, you are probably best off never omitting the signal phrase.

To keep from sounding like a stuck record repeating over and over, "Faith McNulty says," you will want to have at hand a variety of signal phrases and learn to place them at various points in the sentence. In the following sentence, for instance, the student has cited the author in the middle of the quotation: "If chimpanzees have consciousness, if they are capable of abstractions," Carl Sagan asks, "do they not have what until now has been described as 'human rights'?"

Incorporating the wording of others into your own writing may be a bit awkward at first, but you will quickly learn how to work such material into the texture of your paper. Following is a quotation about human hatred of wolves and three examples of ways the quotation could be used in a paper:

Wolf Hatred

"How can one hate the wolf and love the dog as
his best friend at the same time? Without the
wolf on the evolutionary ladder, there would be
no dog. Yet there are people in Minnesota and
Alaska who would lay down their lives for their
huskies and German shepherds and forgetting the
origin of things, go gladly into the great void
still ungrateful to the wolf."

                                                 Mitchell, 20

1. Many people feel very differently about the wolf and its descendant
   the dog. John Mitchell points out that "there are people in Minnesota
   and Alaska who would lay down their lives for their huskies and German shepherds," yet die "still ungrateful to the wolf."[3]
2. A puzzled John Mitchell asks, "How can one hate the wolf and love
   the dog as his best friend at the same time?" As he observes, the dogs
   for which humans even risk their lives are descended from wolves.[2]
3. Since dogs are descended from wolves, this human hatred of wolves
   seems inconsistent and irrational. John Mitchell points out that the
   same Minnesoteans and Alaskans who hate wolves would risk death
   for their huskies and German shepherds.[1]

Once you have learned how to use signal phrases, you will find it fairly
simple to incorporate material from several sources into one paragraph
and yet always make clear to the reader which information is from what
source, as in the following passage from the sample research paper on
the whooping crane. Any material between the signal phrase and the
footnote number, whether quoted directly or put in the student's own
words, is from the specific source indicated:

   This bird [the whooping crane] of which so few remain has a long
   history. *Wildlife in Danger* describes it as a "Pleistocene relict": bones
   found in Idaho are 3,500,000 years old by potassium-argon dating and
   "are not distinguishable from modern bones of the species."[3] According
   to Fred Guthery, when glacial ice was receding from North America
   10,000 years ago, whooping crane numbers were high, "perhaps at their

strongest point in history," and the bird was distributed over all of North America except eastern Canada and New England. The receding ice, however, meant the replacement of marshes by forest and grasslands, so that the whooping crane population had greatly declined even before humans began to further diminish its numbers.[4] As early as 1860–1870, before there was "significant human interference," the late Robert Porter Allen, this century's leading authority on the whooping crane, estimated that there were only 1300–1400 individuals.[5]

FOOTNOTE FORM

The nearest thing to a standard guide to footnote form for students is the MLA *Handbook for Writers of Research Papers, Theses, and Dissertations*, which is probably on sale at your college bookstore.* This guide or any of the others on the market will tackle such tough problems as how to footnote unpublished letters, radio and television programs, and telephone interviews. Most of your footnotes, however, will follow the basic format for a book, a magazine article, and a newspaper article given below. Learn these and worry about the other forms only as you need them:

1. A book:

    [8] Lillian Feder, *Ancient Myth in Modern Poetry* (Princeton: Princeton University Press, 1971), p. 51.

2. A magazine article:

    [9] Edward Abbey, "The Crooked Wood," *Audubon*, Nov. 1975, p. 26.

Note that the title of the magazine article is put in quotes and that the name of the magazine is italicized (or underlined). A newspaper article is footnoted in exactly the same way as a magazine article, except that you put the section number between the date and the page number.

Following are examples of some less frequently used footnote forms:

3. A book by more than one author:

    [10] Daniel Berrigan and Lee Lockwood, *Absurd Convictions, Modest Hopes* (New York: Random House, 1973), p. 18.

4. An edition other than the first:

    [11] John Hope Franklin, *From Slavery to Freedom*, 3rd ed. (New York: Alfred A. Knopf, 1967), p. 348.

---

* Certain disciplines, for instance, anthropology, have developed different documentation techniques.

5. A book with more than one volume:

    [12] Robert Graves, *The Greek Myths* (New York: George Braziller, 1967), II, 69.

6. A book with an editor:

    [13] *The Letters of Virginia Woolf*, ed. Nigel Nicholson and Joanne Trautmann (New York: Harcourt Brace Jovanovich, 1975), I, 413.

7. A work in a collection of pieces by different authors:

    [14] Richard Wright, "Bright and Morning Star," in *Short Stories: A Critical Anthology*, ed. Ensaf Thune and Ruth Prigozy (New York: Macmillan, 1973), pp. 387–88.

8. Articles in reference works:

    [15] "Minerva," *The Oxford Classical Dictionary*, 1970 ed.

    Rules for citing reference works vary greatly. For well-known alphabetized entries (like "Minerva" above), no other information is necessary, but in other instances you may wish to give further information.

9. Personal and telephone interviews:

    [16] Personal interview with O. J. Simpson, 18 April 1979.

Once you have given the complete information about a source, that information need never be given again. However, you will more than likely be citing a source several times, and in that case, your later footnotes need consist only of the author's last name and the page numbers (for instance, McNulty, p. 88). If there is no author, you repeat the name of the article to identify the source.

In the past a good many Latin terms were used in footnotes, but today most of those have been dropped. Some writers still prefer to use the term *ibid.*, followed by the page number, when there are successive footnotes from the same source, but we suggest always using the author's last name, however delightful *ibid.* may sound to you.

BIBLIOGRAPHY FORM

In addition to footnotes, you may be asked to submit a bibliography (an alphabetized list of your sources placed at the end of your paper). Bibliographical form is slightly different from footnote form. If you are required to submit a bibliography, be sure to check the commentary on the page facing the bibliography for the sample research paper.

SOME ENDANGERED SPECIES TOPICS

If you would like to investigate the status of an endangered species, the following are good subjects for research papers:

1. Bowhead Whale
2. Kirtland's Warbler
3. California Condor
4. Grizzly Bear
5. Bald Eagle
6. Peregrine Falcon
7. Timber Wolf
8. Red Wolf
9. Alligator
10. Porpoise
11. Mountain Lion

SAMPLE RESEARCH PAPER

On the following pages is a sample research paper, written for a class in which the students were asked to investigate the current status of an endangered North American animal species. This paper is approximately 3000 words in length, not an unusual length for an undergraduate research paper, though good papers can be written with far fewer words. If you feel your paper is going to require more pages than you want to write, it is usually possible to narrow the topic further. This student, for instance, could have written his entire paper on the controversy over the captive breeding of whooping cranes.

Unless your instructor specifies otherwise, the following is submitted with the research paper:

1. A *title page*. The title page should include the title of the paper, your name, the name of the course and the instructor, the name of the college, and the date of submission.

2. An *outline*. The outline is discussed on the page facing the sample paper's outline.

3. *The text of the paper*. Most instructors require that the research paper be typed. It should be typed with fairly large margins left on all sides of the paper. The footnotes usually appear at the bottom of the page, although some instructors will allow you to type the footnotes on separate pages at the end of the text. The text itself is double-spaced; footnotes are single-spaced.

4. A *bibliography*. The paper will be followed by an alphabetized list of your sources, the form of which is discussed on the page opposite the sample paper's bibliography.

A Miracle Almost Achieved:
The Status of the Whooping Crane in 1977

by

Nick Culver

English 101, Mr. Dudley
Prince George's Community College
October, 1977

In an outline, the thesis appears first, although it may be preceded by introductory material in the paper itself. The major headings of the outline are logical divisions supporting that thesis. Therefore, in this outline, the four divisions are the four major reasons for the new optimism about the whooping crane's survival. It could be argued that the fourth overlaps the other three, but the student decided that the success of 1977 was significant enough to deserve a section to itself.

Introductions and conclusions are best set aside from the numbering system of the outline, as they are here, for neither is a clear division of the thesis. This student preferred simply to state what he was going to say in the introduction and in the conclusion. If your introduction or conclusion is more complex, you may want to number its sections 1, 2, 3, etc.

The logical division system of this paper is an ideal, but, frankly, not all subjects can be divided so neatly, at least not without a great deal of manipulation of words. There is a danger that the student, in trying to satisfy the instructor's demands for a logically divided outline, will oversimplify or distort the truth about his or her subject. If you are having difficulty in developing a logically divided outline, you may want to ask for suggestions from your instructor.

Outlines may be done in either sentence form, as this one is, or in topic form, which does not use complete sentences. If a paper is expressing opinions or drawing conclusions from material, a sentence outline is best; it forces you to decide exactly what you are going to say before writing the paper. If a paper is primarily a report on clearly factual material, a topic outline may be adequate.

A Miracle Almost Achieved:
The Status of the Whooping Crane in 1977

Thesis: Although the whooping crane's survival in the wild is far from
           absolutely assured, no one any longer sees extinction as
           inevitable and many are optimistic about the crane's future.
           Developments in three locations and the success of the 1977
           nesting season are the reasons for this optimism.

Background: The background material briefly describes the whooping crane's
             life cycle and briefly summarizes its history until its numerical
             low point in 1938.

I.   The Texas-Canada flock has grown, and its protection is assured.

        A. The flock has steadily increased in number, especially in
            the last decade.

        B. The protection of the flock is assured.

            1. The nesting and wintering territories are now on
                government-protected land.

            2. Public protests would greet any threat to the whooping
                crane.

            3. Hunting losses have become very small.

II.   Despite controversy, problems, and failure to meet proposed
        goals, the captive breeding program at Patuxent, Maryland, now
        appears to be a success.

        A. In 1977, after long years of partial failure, the captive
            whooping cranes are now producing eggs.

        B. Some of the fears about the captive breeding program have
            been allayed.

        C. The successes in 1977 indicate that the Patuxent program
            may be able with adequate funding and more knowledge to
            overcome some of the problems that have beset the program
            in the past.

        D. Goals set in the past now seem feasible within a decade.

III.   Although it is too soon to know if the birds will successfully
        breed, there have been initial successes in establishing a second
        migratory flock in Idaho and New Mexico.

IV.   The number of eggs hatched in 1977 at Wood Buffalo, Canada; at
        Patuxent; and at Grays Lake, Idaho, has been called by officials
        "spectacular."

Conclusion: The conclusion briefly argues that humans should continue to
             protect the whooping crane.

The thesis of the paper usually appears in the first paragraph, though it sometimes is preceded by an interest-catching introductory paragraph. The wording of the thesis in the text of the paper need not exactly parallel the wording in the outline, though it should closely parallel that wording. In this paper the student has expanded the two-sentence statement in the outline to two paragraphs, the second of which sets up the major divisions of his paper. The longer your paper, the more important it is that you announce to the reader what the divisions of the paper will be.

Be sure to word your thesis carefully, and don't hesitate to change the thesis if while writing the paper you decide that it is not quite what you want to say. In the process of his research, this student twice reworded his thesis. He reworded it first when he became more pessimistic about the whooping crane's survival than he had been after initial reading. Later he returned to something of his original optimism when he read the most recent news reports on the successes of the 1977 breeding season.

In writing this paper, the student read one entire book on the whooping crane and sections of another book on endangered bird species; two fairly short articles in reference works; five short news articles; and five magazine articles. This is not an unreasonable amount of reading for a research paper: your topic may demand more reading or less.

The footnote numerals are Arabic numerals, numbered consecutively through the paper. The number is typed slightly above the line and always appears at the *end* of a citation. The footnote number corresponds to the same number at the bottom of the page where all the necessary information about the source is given.

Because this is a fairly long paper, the student has decided to help the reader follow his organization by inserting a subtitle before each of the paper's main sections, as he has done here with the background section. The background section describes the whooping crane's life cycle and history. Not all of it is directly related to the paper's thesis, but the student has decided that it is needed, both to attain the reader's interest and because the reader may not be familiar with the whooping crane. How much material is needed in a paper depends on your subject and your audience. In a research paper on changes in the rules of football, for instance, it would normally not be necessary to explain in great detail the history of football. However, if one were writing on American converts to Eastern religions in the 1970s, it might be necessary to give some background on these religions.

A Miracle Almost Achieved:
The Status of the Whooping Crane in 1977

In the 1930s the whooping crane seemed almost certainly doomed to
extinction. But today, though the bird's survival in the wild is far
from absolutely assured, no one sees extinction as inevitable and many
are optimistic. In June of 1977, Keith M. Schreiner, associate director
of the Fish and Wildlife Service, said of the whooping crane's future,
"The outlook has never been brighter."[1]

Three developments (all of which seemed to reach their high point
in 1977) have led to this new optimism: (1) the assured protection and
numerical increase of the wild whooping crane flock which nests in
Canada and winters in Texas; (2) the successes of the captive breeding
program at Patuxent Wildlife Research Center in Maryland; and (3) the
initial successes in establishing a second migratory flock in Idaho and
New Mexico.

Background

On the Texas gulf coast in mid-March, 1977, I boarded a converted
deep-sea fishing boat with two or three hundred other tourists, most of
them carrying binoculars and cameras. Our objective was to sight whooping
cranes from the last remaining wild flock, a flock the people on the boat
far outnumbered. On that day we saw 25 of the 69 whooping cranes which
were wintering at the Aransas National Wildlife Refuge.

---

[1]"A Spectacular Year For Whooping Crane," New York Times, June 23,
1977, p. 14.

Although personal experience and the *I* appear less frequently in papers making use of sources than in more subjective writing, there is no reason why they should not be used if relevant. Indeed, you will probably enjoy writing a paper more if you can make personal comments on the subject.

The information on the whooping crane in these paragraphs is "common knowledge" and thus does not have to be footnoted. The student has seen the information repeatedly during his reading and can honestly say that he "knows" this information. If the student had presented a more detailed description of the incubation process, it might have become necessary to footnote.

Footnote number 2 is an information footnote rather than a source footnote. The student has placed in the footnote further information about the whooping crane. He thought this information was interesting, but felt it might clutter the text of the paper itself. This sort of footnote is frequently used when the writer feels that a term or an allusion will not be understood by all readers and needs explanation.

If your instructor allows you to type the footnotes on separate pages at the end of the paper, you should still type an information footnote on the page itself. In this case the footnote is indicated by an asterisk (*) rather than a number. If there is more than one information footnote on a page, indicate the second with a double asterisk.

-2-

We did not hear the distinctive call audible for miles that gave
the bird its name (it was once called "Bugle Crane"), nor see the elaborate
courtship dances that occur a month or two earlier, but we did see the
majesty of this tallest American bird as it stood in hunting stance. We
did see the magnificence of the whooping crane in flight, the size of its
black-tipped snow-white wings. We did see its serene glide, long neck
and legs fully extended, over the Texas salt flats.

The whooping cranes arrive in Texas in late October, some singly,
others in pairs, and others--the most eagerly anticipated--in pairs with
a youngster. Each pair or group establishes a territory of around 400
acres, which it will defend against intruders and rarely leave.[2]

In April the whooping cranes migrate over 2000 miles to Wood Buffalo
Park in northern Canada. There the pairs, which mate for life, establish
a nesting territory, usually the same one year after year. Two eggs are
usually laid, and the parents alternate in incubating.

This bird of which so few remain has a long history. Wildlife
in Danger describes it as a "Pleistocene relict": bones found in Idaho
are 3,500,000 years old by potassium-argon dating and "are not distinguishable from modern bones of the species."[3] According to Fred Guthery,
when glacial ice was receding from North America 10,000 years ago,

---

[2]According to Faith McNulty, whooping cranes are among the few
birds in which the family does not fully break up at the end of the
breeding season. If a pair returns to Aransas with a youngster, they will
"defend their territory with greater determination than a childless·
couple." A mated pair, though childless, will in turn defend their
territory more fiercely than single birds. Faith McNulty, The Whooping
Crane: The Bird That Defies Extinction (New York: E. P. Dutton & Co.,
1966), pp. 69-70.

[3]James Fisher, Noel Simon, and Jack Vincent, Wildlife in Danger
(New York: The Viking Press, 1969), p. 223.

Notice how the writer tells the reader through the use of signal phrases and footnote numbers where the use of material from a particular source begins and ends. The general rule is that all the information between the signal phrase and the footnote number is from the source indicated in the footnote. Therefore the reader can assume that all information from the signal phrase "According to Fred Guthery" to footnote number 4 is from Guthery, page 18.

Notice what the writer has decided to quote directly and what he has decided to put into his own words. In general he has used direct quotations when opinion is involved or when the precise word used in the source is significant. He thus quotes Guthery's opinion that 10,000 years ago whooping crane numbers were "perhaps at their strongest point in history" and Greenway's judgment that "the survival of the species would be a miracle."

The chapter on research writing warns you that you should be careful of accepting opinions as facts, even when they are found in standard reference works. The Greenway quotation can be used to illustrate the reason for this warning. If the student is correct in his thesis, Greenway was obviously overly pessimistic in his prediction about the whooping crane's future.

-3-

whooping crane numbers were high, "perhaps at their strongest point in history," and the bird was distributed over all of North America except eastern Canada and New England. The receding ice, however, meant the replacement of marshes by forest and grasslands, so that the whooping crane population had greatly declined even before humans began to further diminish its numbers.[4] As early as 1860-1870, before there was "significant human interference," the late Robert Porter Allen, this century's leading authority on the whooping crane, estimated there were only 1300-1400 individuals.[5]

In the nineteenth and twentieth centuries, destruction of habitat and hunting radically sped up the decline. According to Faith McNulty, by 1938 there was only one migrating flock of 22 birds left.[6] The only other flock, a nonmigratory group in Louisiana, had even fewer birds and would be almost entirely destroyed by a storm in 1940, never to recover. As late as 1967, James C. Greenway, Jr., in Extinct and Vanishing Birds of the World, said that even with protection "the survival of the species would be a miracle."[7]

Today that miracle may have been achieved. Although some chicks will not survive, at one point in the spring of 1977, according to the Washington Post, the total in the wild and in captivity numbered 126.[8]

---

[4] Fred S. Guthery, "Whoopers in Idaho," National Parks and Conservation Magazine, Oct., 1976, p. 18.

[5] Robert Porter Allen, On the Trail of Vanishing Birds (New York: McGraw-Hill, 1957), pp. 33-34.

[6] McNulty, p. 15.

[7] James C. Greenway, Jr., Extinct and Vanishing Birds of the World, 2nd ed. (New York: Dover Publications, 1967), p. 208.

[8] "The Whoopers Flap Back," Washington Post, Oct. 18, 1977, p. A-18.

At the conclusion of the background section, the student repeats his thesis in a modified form as a transition to the main sections of his paper.

-4-

Despite the persisting threats of oil spills, hurricanes, disease, and
even the potential mistakes of well-intentioned biologists trying to
replenish the whooping crane stock, the whooping crane is surviving.

The Texas-Canada Flock

The first reason for the new optimism about the whooping crane is
that the Texas-Canada flock has grown and its protection now seems assured.
A growth from 22 cranes in 1938 to 80 in the summer of 1977 may seem small,
but it is greater than was anticipated even ten years ago.

Despite small declines in individual years, the Texas-Canada flock
has steadily increased in number, especially in the last decade. Not only
has the overall number increased, but the 69 birds at Aransas in the
winter of 1976-77 included more first-year young brought back from the
nesting grounds in Canada than in any year since accurate records have
been kept. Audubon magazine reports that in the summer of 1977 the flock
in Canada produced at least 11 chicks.[9] Thus, with the continued good luck
of the last few years, 80 or more whooping cranes could winter at Aransas
in the winter of 1977-78.

For three reasons, this increasingly large flock will be much safer
than were its ancestors in the 1930s. First, although much of the bird's
former habitat can of course never be recovered, the preservation of its
wintering and nesting territories now seems "reasonably well assured," to
use the words of Wildlife in Danger, an internationally sponsored survey
of the world's endangered species.[10] In 1937 the United States government
purchased the approximately 50,000 acres on the Blackjack Peninsula near
Corpus Christi, Texas, where the bird wintered. (Much of the land was being

---

[9]"Whooping Cranes," Audubon, Sept., 1977, p. 155.

[10]Fisher, Simon, and Vincent, p. 244.

If a quotation is a complete sentence, as with the Allen quotation that concludes this paragraph, it is preceded either by a comma (Allen pointed out, "The welfare. . . .") or by *that* (Allen pointed out that "The welfare. . . ."). The period at the end of the sentence goes inside the quotation marks, and the footnote number outside.

It may be helpful to remember that the period and the comma *always* occur inside the quotation marks. Some other marks of punctuation may occur either inside or outside the quotation marks (see the "Punctuation" section of the handbook).

If the quotation is more than one sentence in length, as with the Allen quotation on hunting in this paragraph, it is usually introduced by a colon rather than a comma.

If phrases are being quoted, no punctuation mark precedes the quotation marks unless that mark would occur there in a sentence without quotation marks.

-5-

used for cattle-grazing and hunting.) When the nesting grounds of the
whooping crane were finally found in 1954, they were in an already
established Canadian national park, Wood Buffalo, on the Alberta-Mackenzie
border. So swampy and isolated is the area that danger from human interference is minimal.

Not only are these areas government-protected land, but today a
public outcry would greet any threat to the crane's territory in either
Canada or the United States, as there was, for instance, when United
States Air Force bombing ranges were activated near Aransas. As Robert
Porter Allen pointed out, "The welfare of the whooping crane has become
front-page news."[11]

Conservation groups, however, must continue to push for legislation
protecting the Aransas refuge from oil spills. They must continue to
alert the public to the danger to the whooping cranes from industrial
waste and nearby irrigation canal projects.

Hunting, particularly during migration, was also a major cause of
the whooping crane's decline in the last century. Allen says: "They
were shot on the breeding grounds as they sat on their eggs, and they
were shot on migration as they came to earth to feed and rest. On the
wintering grounds they were shot when they raided sweet-potato fields in
Louisiana, and for sport along the Texas coast."[12]

Severe penalties now exist for shooting whooping cranes, and public
and private groups conduct intensive campaigns to educate hunters along
the migration route in bird identification. One National Audubon Society

[11]Allen, p. 30.

[12]Allen, p. 38.

The student remembers the phrase "any large white bird" from an illustration in one of the articles he read. There is no need to footnote this particular kind of quotation.

When you use quotations of three or more sentences in length, they are usually set apart from the text of the paper, as this one is. Introduce the quotation with a colon, then double-space, then indent three spaces from the left-hand margin and single-space the quotation.

It is generally not good practice to include in your paper a large number of extended quotations such as this one. The student decided to do so in this case because he wished to stress in some way that all people are not as concerned about the whooping crane as he is.

Frequently you will want to omit something that appears in the middle of a quotation you are using. If the omission is a group of words, it is marked by an ellipsis [. . .]. If the omission occurs at the end of a sentence or consists of an entire sentence, an extra dot for the period is added. In the long quotation from Allen, the student omitted an entire sentence.

Frequently in quoting, you will need to explain or identify a word or reference for the reader. So as not to confuse the reader as to who is saying what, your insertion in the middle of someone else's quotation is enclosed with brackets, as "the wrooping crane" is here. If your typewriter has no brackets on its keyboard, put them in with ink.

When you are quoting material that was quoted in another source, this is indicated by using first quotation marks, then an apostrophe. Note in footnote 15 that the source is preceded by the phrase "quoted in."

When the source material is taken from more than one page, the abbreviation *pp.* (for "pages") replaces the abbreviation *p.*

-6-

poster exhorts hunters not to shoot "any large white bird." So successful

have the hunting regulations and educational campaigns been that <u>Wildlife</u>

<u>in Danger</u> could say in 1969 that "the losses on migration by uncontrolled

and ignorant shooting have certainly become small."[13]

Strange as it may seem in the conservation-conscious 1970s, the

attempts to bring about this protection did not always go unopposed.

Robert Porter Allen describes a time of despair in 1949:

> It seems unbelievable, but in spite of the great amount of
> public good will that had been generated during the first years
> of our campaign, there were still many people who took an
> entirely different view. It is not often that we see or hear
> an outright expression of this other attitude, but several
> incredible samples have been sent to me. One was a letter from
> a distraught farmer in Saskatchewan. He told of certain of his
> neighbors who were outspoken in their opinion that all this
> fuss about the whooping crane was a lot of nonsense. They
> proposed that the best way to put a stop to it would be to kill
> the few birds that remain and then forget the whole thing, thus
> saving the taxpayers a lot of money. . . . They likewise
> announced their intention of using their guns at every opportunity
> to promote such results.[14]

One writer to a "leading newspaper" said, "'From what I have observed and

heard he [the whooping crane] is a dim-witted gawk of a bird whose pate

has become more less addled in the course of time until now he is not

quite sharp enough mentally to be up to the fundamentals of procreation.'"[15]

I hope to give my children a view of an even stronger flock than my

parents showed me, and therefore, do not begrudge the relatively small

amount of tax money spent on protecting the Texas-Canada flock.

---

[13]Fisher, Simon, and Vincent, p. 225.

[14]Allen, pp. 74-75.

[15]Quoted in Allen, p. 75.

The three paragraphs following the introductory paragraph of section II consist of explanatory material that the student feels he must present before developing his first subheading.

This paragraph may be used as another illustration of what is "common knowledge" and what is not. The information in this paragraph is not, for two reasons, and is thus footnoted. First, unlike the fact that the whooping cranes migrate over 2000 miles, the figures here are very specific ("15,000 of the 140,000 waterfowl"). Second, although the student now knows about this near-disaster, he read about the incident only in the article in *Science News*.

Because the material in this paragraph is factual, the student decided to introduce the source material with nothing other than the phrase "for example." Some instructors may prefer, however, that a signal phrase, such as "According to *Science News*," also precede the source information.

-7-

Captive Breeding at Patuxent

Despite controversy, problems, and failures to meet proposed goals, the second reason for the growing optimism about the whooping crane has been the captive breeding program at Patuxent Wildlife Research Center in Maryland. After years of its not living up to expectations, 1977 has been a bountiful year for the center, though many questions about captive breeding remain.

The captive flock was established because biologists and conservationists were aware of the Texas-Canada flock's fragility even with maximum government protection. For example, in the spring of 1975, just before the whooping cranes flew north from Aransas, a severe epidemic of avian cholera broke out among waterfowl at Nebraska wildlife refuges where the whoopers customarily stop to feed and rest. The disease had already killed 15,000 of the 140,000 waterfowl at Sacramento Game Refuge. Only by scaring the whooping cranes away with airplanes was contact with the contaminated birds in Nebraska avoided.[16]

Because of such threats of disaster, proposals were made to maintain a reserve flock in captivity, a flock whose young or eggs might replenish the wild stock. These proposals were supported by research which seemed to show that if the eggs of captive birds were removed soon after they were laid, birds could be stimulated to produce more eggs.

The plan was to retrieve one of the two eggs usually laid by whooping cranes at Wood Buffalo, and to transport the eggs with great care to Patuxent for hatching. In 1966 that egg-taking began.

---

[16]"Whooping Cranes Survive Disease Threat," Science News, April 26, 1975, p. 27.

-8-

  After ten years of egg-taking the Patuxent flock now numbers around

twenty birds. From January through May of 1977, that flock produced 21

eggs, more than the wild flock of 69. Four pairs of whoopers are producing

eggs, and up to three more pairs are expected to produce eggs next year.

In addition, Patuxent is aiding in replenishing the wild stock. Fourteen

of this year's eggs have been shipped to Grays Lake National Wildlife

Refuge in Idaho to be hatched by sandhill cranes as part of a project to

establish a second migratory flock.[17]

  If this paper were being written as little as two years ago, the

Patuxent program could not have offered so much assurance. Although

whoopers were being successfully hatched from eggs flown from Wood Buffalo,

none of the captives were breeding, and the only chick born of an artificially

inseminated Patuxent female had died a few days after birth.

  The successes at Patuxent in 1977 have allayed some, though not all,

of the fears about captive breeding, a very controversial subject.

  In a 1974 Natural History article, D. R. Zimmerman (a writer who has

misgivings about captive breeding) describes the bitter debate that ensued

when the Patuxent program was proposed, a debate between the "protectionists"

and the "propagationists." "Protectionists," according to Zimmerman, felt

there was too little proof of success in captive breeding to warrant

removing eggs from the wild. They saw risks in releasing captive-bred

birds or their eggs into wild flocks, for these birds might be unable to

adjust to the wild and might carry disease. "Propagationsits," on the

other hand, argued that the cranes were "too close to extinction not to

---

  [17]"Maryland Wildlife Center Reports Whooping Crane Egg Bonanza of
21," New York Times, May 31, 1977, p. 32.

-9-

try captive breeding to increase their numbers, particularly as a hedge
against a natural or manmade disaster that could kill many or all of the
wild population in a single blow."[18]

All of the questions raised have certainly not yet been answered,
but at least it can be said that the taking of eggs did not diminish the
number of wild birds, as Dr. Ray Erickson, who heads the Patuxent program,
had anticipated. Erickson maintained that only one chick usually survives
anyway because "newborn whooping cranes are so hostile and aggressive toward
each other that when there are two, one often kills the other."[19]   (Further
answers to the questions raised by the Patuxent controversy may be found
at Grays Lake, to be discussed later in this paper.)

The successes in 1977 indicate that the Patuxent program may be
able, with adequate funds and more knowledge, to overcome some of the
problems that have beset the program in the past.

For instance, the death rate for birds at Patuxent has been considered
high by such critics as D. R. Zimmerman (who, incidentally, seems to me
a constructive critic rather than a debunker). Some of these deaths
clearly could have been prevented by the more adequate facilities Patuxent
now has. As late as 1973 none of the Patuxent buildings had air conditioning.
Erickson attributed the death of three of the ten whoopers hatched in 1968
to their "being out in the hot Maryland sun at six weeks of age--when
they were too young to stand the heat."[20]

---

[18]D. R. Zimmerman, "Captive Breeding: Boon or Boondoggle," _Natural
History_, Dec. 1974, pp. 7-8.

[19]Zimmerman, p. 8.

[20]Zimmerman, p. 10.

-10-

One other problem may serve to illustrate both what Patuxent seems
to be overcoming and the difficulties of captive breeding. A number of
the Patuxent whooping cranes have died of bacterial infections contracted
from other birds. The obvious solution might seem to be to segregate the
birds from both fellow whoopers and their sandhill crane foster parents.
However, the aim of Patuxent is to get the birds to breed, and Erickson,
according to Zimmerman, feels young birds fare better with parents and
that "firm pair bonds and successful matings are more likely if the birds
can pick their own mates from a flock, rather than have a mate imposed by
their keepers."[21]

Although Patuxent has not met the production goals anticipated ten
years ago, this year's successes make that goal seem possible within
another decade. Faith McNulty, writing in 1966, said that the program
anticipated having by 1977 "at least ten breeding pairs of birds, as
little inbred as possible, who should be able to produce fifty or more
young birds in a season."[22] Too much may have been anticipated too soon.

Initial Successes in Idaho and New Mexico

The third reason for the new optimism about the whooping cranes is
the initial success of biologists in establishing a second migratory flock.
Although this experiment has not been without disappointment, each of three
summers (1975, 1976, 1977) has seen new birds join in migration and some
of the first and second year birds come nearer to breeding age.

In 1974 Canada and the United States approved what has been called
"the biggest gamble ever in the . . . 40-year effort to save the whooping

---

[21]Zimmerman, p. 12.

[22]McNulty, p. 181.

-11-

crane from extinction."[23]   The plan was to move eggs from Wood Buffalo and
Patuxent to Grays Lake Wildlife Refuge in Idaho, where the eggs would be
hatched by sandhill cranes acting as foster parents, and hopefully the flock
would follow the sandhill crane to wintering grounds in New Mexico.

In a 1977 Natural History article, Rodney Barker cites four major
reasons for the gamble. First, in 1974 Patuxent did not seem to be meeting
its goals. Second, many subadult whoopers were disappearing in the
Canadian wilderness for unexplained reasons. Third, cranes summering in
Idaho and surrounding areas would have a much shorter--and thus less
dangerous--migration route to wintering grounds. Fourth, and perhaps most
important, new developments in biology suggested that such a plan might
succeed. After a long study of sandhill cranes, the nearest American
relative of the whooping crane, biologists Rod Drewien and Elwood Bizeau
had come to the conclusion that crane behavior was primarily learned
through early experience rather than being innate; and that, therefore,
young whooping cranes could learn to survive and to migrate from sandhill
crane foster parents.[24]

Thus, in May of 1975, at just about the same time the first baby
whooping crane was being born to the captive flock in Maryland, fourteen
eggs were taken from Canadian nests and flown to Idaho--flown with many
questions. Would the whooping cranes, if they hatched, survive in a
new environment? Would the chicks be rejected by their foster parents?
Would the whooping cranes take on the traits of sandhill cranes to such a
degree that they might even interbreed, producing sterile hybrids?

---

[23]Linda Scarbrough, "The Ugly Duckling Updated," New York Times
Magazine, Nov. 30, 1975, p. 88.

[24]Rodney Barker, "A Whooper Rally," Natural History, March 1977,
pp. 24, 26.

-12-

Some chicks did survive, and they were not rejected by their foster parents, but the last question will remain unanswered for several years, until the whooping cranes reach breeding age. However, in 1976, the second year of the project, refuge manager Pete Bryant observed that "the whooping cranes appeared to be dominant in the juvenile groups," suggesting to him "that a pattern of segregation was already developing that would eventually lead to natural separation when the birds reached sexual maturity and selected mates."[25]

As can be seen from the following figures, Grays Lake has not been without disappointment, but the flock has increased in size with each summer.

In 1975, according to Barker, of the fourteen eggs placed under carefully selected sandhill crane pairs, nine hatched (three eggs were infertile, two were eaten by coyotes); six reached flight stage; four of these would successfully migrate south and return northward in 1976, one other bird having been reported but not sighted by wildlife officials.[26]

In 1976, sixteen eggs were brought from Canada to Grays Lake, and two eggs produced in captivity were brought from Patuxent. Because of drought, it was, as Rodney Barker says, a "poor year" for all cranes at Grays Lake. However, three of the 1976 crop lasted the summer and reached the wintering grounds at Bosque del Apache in'New Mexico, where they were joined by four of the 1975 crop, with one of the 1975 birds reported elsewhere. (Both of the Patuxent eggs were thought to be infertile, but no one can be sure, for both were eaten by ravens before hatching.)[27]

---

[25] Barker, p. 26.

[26] Barker, p. 26.

[27] Barker, pp. 28-29.

-13-

In the summer of 1977, according to the September 1977 <u>Audubon</u>,
nine chicks were hatched at Grays Lake from eggs placed under sandhill
cranes, these eggs coming from both Patuxent and Wood Buffalo. These
chicks joined five yearling birds which had returned to Grays Lake for the
summer.[28] A few others may have been summering elsewhere, but one, according
to the <u>New York Times</u>, was found dead in Wyoming of an injury "commonly
caused by barbed-wire fences."[29]

Enthusiasm Over 1977

In the summer of 1977, at least eleven chicks were hatched at Wood
Buffalo; between January and May of 1977, twenty-one eggs, many of which
would go to Grays Lake, had been produced at Patuxent; in the summer of
1977, nine chicks were hatched at Grays Lake. These figures have caused
such enthusiasm that in June of 1977 the United States Fish and Wildlife
Service was reported as announcing that if even half of the newly hatched
birds survive the summer, 1977 would be a "spectacular year" for the
crane.[30] In response to the figures, the <u>Washington Post</u> declared in an
editorial that "the whoopers are winging up, up and away from extinction."[31]

Conclusion

Because whooping crane numbers were low before human interference,
there may be some question as to whether the decline of the whooping crane,
unlike that of the Bald Eagle, stems more from humans or from natural

---

[28]"Whooping Cranes," p. 155.

[29]"Death of Whooping Crane Leaves 65 in Existence," <u>New York Times</u>,
June 2, 1977, p. 18. (The <u>Times</u> headline for this story is inaccurate.)

[30]"A Spectacular Year For Whooping Crane," p. 14.

[31]"The Whoopers Flap Back," p. A-18.

Frequently conclusions briefly summarize the points made in the paper. Especially in long or complex papers, the writer may decide that a summary is needed.

This student decided that no such summation was necessary, for his argument was not complex and the points had already been clearly made. He decided instead to end with a value judgment about the material presented. Such an ending leaves the reader not with a flat summary, but with a sense of the significance of the subject.

-14-

selection. However, humans have certainly sped up the decline and should

be <u>human</u> enough to try to abate it. As an editorial in the <u>Christian</u>

<u>Science Monitor</u> once asked, "'Can society, whether through sheer wantoness

or callous neglect, permit the extinction of something beautiful or grand

in nature without risking extermination of something beautiful and grand

in its own character?'"[32]

---

[32]Quoted in Allen, p. 31.

The bibliography is typed on a separate page at the end of your paper. It should list all the works that appear in your footnotes. You should also include in the bibliography any other works that influenced your thinking, even if there are no references to these works in the paper.

The entries are listed alphabetically by the name of the author, with the surname appearing first. If there is more than one author, only the first author's name is inverted. If a work has no author, it is alphabetized by the first word in the title other than *a, an,* or *the.*

Each individual entry is single-spaced, with double spacing between entries. The first line of an entry is not indented (unlike the first line of a footnote). Subsequent lines in an entry are indented approximately five spaces.

Bibliographical entries for books differ from footnote entries in three ways: (1) the author's name is inverted; (2) periods rather than commas and parentheses separate the main units of the entry; and (3) no page numbers are given.

Footnote entry: [6] Robert Porter Allen, *On The Trail of Vanishing Birds* (New York: McGraw-Hill, 1957), p. 44.

Bibliography entry: Allen, Robert Porter. *On The Trail of Vanishing Birds.* New York: McGraw-Hill, 1957.

Bibliographical entries for magazine and newspaper articles differ from footnote entries in three ways: (1) the author's name is inverted; (2) periods rather than commas separate the main units of the entry; and (3) the page numbers for the entire article are listed.

Footnote entry: [9] Fred S. Guthery, "Whoopers in Idaho," *National Parks and Conservation Magazine,* October, 1976, p. 20.

Bibliography entry: Guthery, Fred S. "Whoopers in Idaho." *National Parks and Conservation Magazine,* October, 1976, pp. 18–21.

BIBLIOGRAPHY

Allen, Robert Porter. On the Trail of Vanishing Birds. New York: McGraw-
Hill, 1957.

Barker, Rodney. "A Whooper Rally." Natural History, March 1977,
pp. 22-30.

"Death of Whooping Crane Leaves 65 in Existence," New York Times, June 2,
1977, 18.

Fisher, James, Noel Simon, and Jack Vincent. Wildlife in Danger. New York:
The Viking Press, 1969.

Greenway, James C., Jr. Extinct and Vanishing Birds of the World. 2nd ed.
New York: Dover Publications, 1967.

Guthery, Fred S. "Whoopers in Idaho." National Parks and Conservation
Magazine, October, 1976, pp. 18-21.

"Maryland Wildlife Center Reports Whooping Crane Egg Bonanza of 21." New
York Times, May 31, 1977, p. 32.

McNulty, Faith. The Whooping Crane: The Bird That Defies Extinction. New
York: E. P. Dutton & Co., 1966.

Scarbrough, Linda. "The Ugly Duckling Updated." New York Times Magazine,
November 30, 1975, pp. 88-93.

"A Spectacular Year for Whooping Crane." New York Times, June 23, 1977, p. 14.

"Whooping Cranes." Audubon, September, 1977, p. 155.

"Whooping Cranes Survive Disease Threat." Science News, April 26, 1975,
p. 27.

"The Whoopers Flap Back." Washington Post, October 18, 1977, p. A-18.

Zimmerman, David R. "Captive Breeding: Boon or Boondoggle." Natural
History, December, 1974, pp. 6-8, 10-16, 19.

PART VI
A Writer's Handbook

PUNCTUATION/CAPITALIZATION/ SPELLING

PUNCTUATION

Read this paragraph about a comedienne:

during the weekend we went to see the comedienne judith grant at
club ninety-five have you seen her perform she does remarkably believ-
able impersonations of several well known movie stars bette davis talullah bankhead katharine hepburn and greta garbo among others
the performance took us all young and old alike back into the early
days of the silver screen i had heard that the glories of individual star-
dom had passed that the big movie companies do not invest so heavily
in one actress these days however i had not realized before how much
moviegoers of today may be missing my evening with bette and talullah
and katharine and greta was indeed a revelation to me and my companions the time passed so quickly that it was one o clock in the morning
before we even thought about going home

Did you have a hard time getting through what you just read? If so,
you appreciate already how much punctuation helps you when you
read.

Punctuation divides what you write into logical units so that your
writing will be clearer to your readers. When punctuation is inap-
propriately handled, readers become distracted and confused.
They may miss your meaning while they are struggling with your
punctuation (or lack of it). A careful proofreading for punctuation,
then, is important. Reading your work through aloud once, just for
punctuation, will probably be a good idea, especially if punctuation
is a problem for you. As you read aloud, listen for pauses; many of
them will indicate the need for a break, which punctuation provides.
This method works for checking punctuation because you will hear
the same kinds of voice inflections in writing read aloud as you do
in speech. That is, the voice falls markedly and stops at the end of
a sentence, and there is a minimal pause where a comma is
needed.

Read the following sentences aloud, listening for when and how
long you pause and for falls in your voice.

1. We stayed home yesterday to plant tulips.
2. We stayed home yesterday to plant tulips, even though a light
   rain was falling.

3. We stayed home yesterday, planting tulips and other bulbs, and later we rewarded ourselves by going to the movies.

Some pauses do *not* indicate punctuation. The best advice we can give you for deciding at these points is to ask yourself whether the words on either side of the pause depend so heavily on each other that the link between them should not be broken. Remember: Every punctuation mark is a *break*.

As you proofread aloud, if you hear a pause where you have failed to provide a needed punctuation break, or if you have punctuated where the writing should continue to flow without stopping, go back and correct at those points. You may want to ask someone else to read aloud to you, so that you do not have to concentrate on both reading and listening. Whoever reads must be sure to "read in" the punctuation marks exactly as they appear—or do not appear—on the page, or the reading aloud won't tell you what you need to know.

With a careful reading aloud, you will hear where you have overpunctuated, where the writing needs to continue to flow without a break. If you hear an awkward punctuation pause around a word that should be helping to hold a sentence together ("that" and "than" often serve in this way), or between a verb and the subject it immediately relates to, or between an adjective and the noun right behind it, you will know at once that you have overpunctuated.

Once you have decided which kind of punctuation mark—how long a pause—is needed where, then you may want to experiment some with your punctuation. Perhaps you will want to use a semicolon instead of a period between two closely related complete thoughts, or a dash instead of a comma for a special effect of emphasis.

▪ 1. The period

The period is the most common mark of *terminal* punctuation. Use it to end sentences that make a statement or convey a request.

   a. Jeannie was lonely at first, but she soon came to like having the house to herself.
   b. After dealing with four children, a full-time job, the care of a home, and meal preparation, I am just too tired to sit down and read before I go to bed.
   c. Lucy arrived breathless.
   d. Please arrive fifteen minutes before curtain time.

2. The question mark

The question mark is used as terminal punctuation for questions.

a. Did you know that yogurt originated in Turkey?
b. See that large bird with iridescent green feathers?

 ## 3. The exclamation point

The exclamation point follows expressions of exclamation.

a. Leave that poor terrapin alone!
b. Don't tell me you're still waiting for the parade!
c. We watched the sun set over the Grand Canyon—an awesome spectacle!

Caution: Do not overuse the exclamation point. It is intended to make a statement emphatic; if you use it too freely, the emphasis is lost.

We went to the swamp early, to observe the alligators before they awoke. As we stood on the bank, they began to move slowly—exactly at the moment the sun came up! What strange creatures they are! We felt as if we had stumbled backward in time into a prehistoric era!

Deleting the first and third exclamation points would increase the effect of the second one.

 ## 4. The semicolon

4a. The semicolon may be used instead of a period between two complete statements so closely related you want them to be read together as a single sentence.

   a. My old country school is no longer standing; it has been replaced by a ten-room elementary school and a modern regional high school.
   b. Rosie and Verna, our zoologist friends, are coming into town next week to visit the Bronx Zoo; neither has ever seen a white lion, so we are excited about showing them one.
   c. Joseph wants a job like the one in India, I know; however, he does not want to leave this country.

4b. The semicolon is also used to separate sets of items in a series, with the series themselves punctuated by commas; such semicolons make a sentence easier to read.

There are three major divisions in the new college: Humanities, which includes English, art, speech, philosophy, and drama; Social Sciences, which includes history, psychology, sociology, and political science; and Science, which includes biology, chemistry, geology, physics, and astronomy.

5. The comma

The comma, the punctuation mark that provides most of the punctuation *inside* sentences, has many uses. A relatively weak mark, it punctuates sentence content that needs minimal separation and indicates a brief pause to readers.

5a. In a sentence composed of two complete statements joined by a connector word, use a comma before the connector word.

   a. We were tired and hungry after hiking, *but* we stopped to pick wildflowers before we returned to our car.
   b. The tall man in the shiny red top hat and the rainbow-striped boots led the parade, *and* all of us cheered as he marched by.

Some common connector words: and, but, or, nor, yet, so.

NOTE: The comma may be omitted before the connector word if the two statements are short and misreading cannot occur:

Charles left early *but* Mary stayed till midnight.

Caution: Do not put a comma before a connector word unless there is a complete statement on either side of it:

After seeing the flying saucer, he ran frantically for a telephone *but* accidentally dialed his mother.

5b. Use a comma between items in a series.

   a. We made a fruit salad of oranges, apples, raisins, bananas, and figs. Then we ate, sang, danced, and talked.
   b. Gen teaches dancing in a private school in the city daily, at a dance club in the suburbs weekly, and out on Long Island during the summer.
   c. Jennifer played the flute, William picked his guitar, and the rest of us tried to sing along.

5c. Use a comma to separate most adjectives in a series.

> The awkward, velvety-eyed, shy giraffe entertained us for a long time.

Some adjectives are not separated by commas; such adjectives often designate one of the following characteristics: number, size, age, color, material or substance:

> Polly's mother made six large new green canvas tote bags for Polly's classmates.

If you cannot decide whether to use commas with a series of adjectives, you can test the situation by:

 a. putting *and* between the adjectives, to see whether they sound logical that way:
   the awkward and velvety-eyed and shy giraffe
   but not: six and large and new and green and canvas tote bags
 b. reversing the adjectives, to see whether they sound all right in a different order:
   the shy, velvety-eyed, awkward giraffe
   but not: canvas green new large six tote bags

Caution: Do not put a comma between a final adjective and the noun:

> In the Rothko room of the art gallery, you find yourself surrounded by pure, pulsating, sensuous, color. (incorrect)

5d. Use a comma after an introductory construction:

 a. *Although most mice are not very strong,* we found our refrigerator had been moved three feet from the wall during the night.
 b. *To get to know more people,* you need to become involved in more activities.
 c. *After drinking the vanilla by mistake,* I had a peculiar hangover.
 d. *Fighting for her sense of dignity,* she refused to open her mouth for the force-feeding tube to be inserted.

NOTE: Short introductory constructions do not have to be set off by a comma:

> *Before we swam* we lay in the sun and talked quietly.

But: Be alert to possible misreading. The following short introductory constructions need commas to prevent misreading:

 a. Soon after Nicole was well and happy again.
 b. When the helicopter hit the gas tank broke loose and exploded.
 c. While I watched my father changed the back tire.
 d. If you can afford to go to St. Thomas for Christmas.
 e. By the way things are going very well for me this year.

5e. Use a comma before some concluding constructions.

    a. John is leaving in the morning before breakfast, because he must be at the castle by sunrise.

    b. Three of the dancers decided to skip the afternoon rehearsal, although they knew they might lose their positions in the new production.

    c. Let's sing all the verses, since the program time assigned to us is longer than we had anticipated.

    d. Ellen was rude to the visiting actor, who did not know how to explain her behavior to their hostess.

But: Do not use commas in sentences like these:

    a. The five sisters left the room while their aunt was still trying to argue with them.

    b. We have not seen our pet pigeon since she escaped from the enclosure a week ago.

    c. Beverly called her sister's attention to a lame fawn that was standing beside its mother.

In each of these sentences, the added-on material ("while their aunt was . . . ," "since she escaped . . . ," "that was standing . . .") is essential to complete the meaning of the sentence.

Caution: Be sure to use the comma before a concluding construction if misreading might occur without it:

Charles left early, *for* the boat would not wait. ("Charles left early for the boat . . ." could create a misreading.)

5f. Use a comma to set off parenthetical insertions: transitional words and phrases, opinion indicators, and other miscellaneous inserted material:

    a. The guard told us to step carefully. We proceeded, *therefore,* in Indian file. (transition)

    b. Maple syrup, *I believe,* is a major native product of Vermont. (opinion)

    c. As soon as she heard of Jean's illness, her mother, *of course,* rushed to her daughter's bedside.

    d. Eating raw limpets, *I found out,* is like trying to eat art gum erasers.

    e. The elephants, *according to their trainer,* look forward to their bath in the big pool in their enclosure.

5g. Use a comma to set off some inserted modifiers, and some appositives (words that rename what they follow):

    a. Jack Lucas, *who made those brownies,* lives over by the river.

    b. The vinegar, *which has begun to cloud,* is still useable.

c. One of Adrienne Rich's poems, "Orion," has a special appeal for me. (appositive)

In the above sentences, the material surrounded by commas is not essential for the sentence to be complete; the insertion merely expands what it follows. Because its sentence could stand without it, the insertion is set off by commas.

But: Do not use commas in sentences like these:

a. The man *who made those brownies* lives over by the river.
b. Vinegar *which has begun to cloud* is still useable.
c. Adrienne Rich's poem "Song" appeals to readers of many ages. (appositive)

In these three sentences, the added-in material is essential to the sense of the sentence. (Try reading the sentences without: "who made those brownies"; "which has begun to cloud"; and "Song.") Because the sentence cannot stand without the insertion, the added material should not be separated from the rest of the sentence.

Caution: Be sure to use *two* commas to surround nonessential inserted material; do not forget the second one.

5h. Use a comma to set off quoted material from the rest of a sentence:

a. Ruth asked, "What time does the ferry leave?"
b. In *Working It Out,* Alice Walker comments, "What . . . are we to make of Phillis Wheatley, a slave (and a poet), who owned not even herself?"
c. "That tree looks like a good hiding place for the treasure," he thought to himself.

5i.   Use commas to set off nouns of direct address:

a. *Jim,* come here.
b. You, *sir,* will have to come in later.
c. Hurry up, *Mary.*

5j.   Use commas to set off mild exclamations, such as "yes" or "no," and similar words:

Oh, yes, I will join you for dinner.

5k.   Use commas in dates and addresses:

a. My mother left for Russia on October 13, 1977.
b. June 19, 1979, is the last date you may apply for that grant.

    c. My best friend lives in Silver Spring, Maryland.

    d. Send the letter to Redding Thompson, 93 N. Prospect Street, Burlington, Vermont 05401.

5l. Use commas between contrasted elements in a sentence, and sometimes for emphasis:

    a. She found on the shore only colored pebbles, not the exotic shells she was looking for.

    b. As a stranger in the African desert, I feel not only deaf, but also blind.

5m. Do not overuse the comma.

    a. Do not put a comma between a subject and its verb: Eating pizza and drinking beer, are her favorite pastimes. (incorrect)

    b. Do not put a comma between a verb and its object: After months away from the farm, Michael found, digging potatoes and turnips hard on his back. (incorrect)

    c. Do not put a comma between a final adjective and the noun: The soft, silky, cape flowed gracefully. (incorrect)

    d. Never put a comma after "such as," "like," and similar terms: Some countries, such as Brazil, Mexico, and Chile, schedule their school years quite differently from ours.

    e. Never put a comma before a parenthesis; place it after the parentheses, if the sentence requires a comma there: In *Kind and Usual Punishment* (an exposé of the American penal system), Jessica Mitford describes the disturbing day and night she spent in D.C.D.C. (the District of Columbia's Detention Center for Women).

6. The colon

The colon, a rather formal punctuation mark, has several uses:

6a. to introduce a formal series:

The reasons for a low energy level include the following: poor diet, heavy smoking, inadequate rest, metabolic difficulties, and blood deficiencies.

6b. to direct a reader's attention to the second half of a sentence:

The decline in the public school population is understandable: children born during the last "baby boom" have finished high school by now.

6c. to introduce quoted material:

In an article in *New Times,* Karla Brown observes: "Living in New York is still like living at the hub of the wheel of the world."

7. The dash

The dash, a rather informal mark of punctuation, is used in two major ways:

7a. A single dash helps to emphasize whatever follows it:

I have but one goal on this trip to Ireland—to kiss the Blarney Stone.

7b. A pair of dashes may be used to set off the material between them from the rest of the sentence:

In the 1920s, liberals argued that the opposite of repression—sex education, freedom of talking, feeling, and expressing—would have healthy effects.

Note that commas could have been used instead of these dashes. However, the dash in 7a makes what follows it stand out, and the pair of dashes in 7b make the sentence easier to read than it would have been with commas.

In typing, distinguish dashes from hyphens by typing two hyphens to form a dash.

Caution: Do not overuse dashes. Doing so suggests that you have not constructed your sentences very carefully.

8. The parentheses

Parentheses (singular: parenthesis) are sometimes used around explanatory or other added-in material.

a. The two leading female gymnasts of the world (one Russian, the other German) moved with flawlessly precise timing on the double bars.
b. The hypothalamus (our bodily temperature regulator) sometimes functions less adequately with ageing.
c. May Sarton (1912–   ), author of *The House by the Sea,* lives on the Maine seacoast.

Caution: Don't overuse parentheses. If you tend to put much sentence content inside parentheses, restructure your sentences. When you do so, you may find your parenthetical details not important enough to include.

NOTE: Generally, surrounding inserted material with dashes will make it stand out more; with parentheses, it stands out less.

9. The apostrophe

The apostrophe has three functions: (a) to form the possessive of nouns and of some pronouns; (b) to indicate contraction of words and omission of letters; and (c) to make plurals of numbers, letters, and words used as themselves.

9a. To form the possessive:

    a. Add the apostrophe plus "s" to singular nouns:
       That cat's game with the barn mice is hilarious.
       Smokers should respect the nonsmoker's right to a smoke-free environment.
       Form the possessive of singular nouns ending in "s" in one of two ways: hostess's, hostess'; Frances's, Frances'
    b. Add *only* the apostrophe to plural nouns ending in "s":
       Those cats' games with the barn mice are hilarious.
       Have you seen the Schultzes' new speedboat?

But: Add the apostrophe plus "s" to plural nouns not ending in "s": women's, children's.

    c. Add the apostrophe plus "s" to certain pronouns:
       everybody's, other's, someone else's, no one's, and so on.

But: Omit the apostrophe with the possessive of *personal* pronouns: ours, yours, his, hers, its (it's means "it is"), theirs.

NOTE: There are a few common expressions you hear so often that you may forget that they require an apostrophe. Be alert to them: a day's work, your money's worth, a week's rest, are some examples.

9b. The apostrophe substitutes for deleted letters or words in contractions and omissions:

    a. contractions: it's (it is); don't (do not); who's (who is, or who has);

you've (you have); that's (that is); we'll (we will); can't (cannot); let's (let us go); and so on.

   b. omissions: seven o'clock (seven of the clock); the radical '60s (1960s).

9c. Add the apostrophe plus "s" to make the plurals of numbers, letters, and words used as themselves:

The two "A's," five "9's," and three "of's" on the poster are all printed in ink that glows under black light.

Caution: Sometimes using the apostrophe plus "s" will create a sentence that is hard to read. Watch out for such awkward constructions and recast sentences in which they occur.

   a. Our local newspaper's editorial page's make-up is confusing.
     The make-up of the editorial page of our local newspaper is confusing.
   b. Our barn mice's favorite game is hide and seek with the cat.
     The favorite game of our barn mice is hide and seek with the cat.
   c. I borrowed my father's sister's friend's suitcase.
     I borrowed a suitcase that belongs to my aunt's friend.

Caution: Do not drop in apostrophes where they don't belong:

   a. in the simple (nonpossessive) plurals of nouns:
     Soap opera's are absurd. Corrected: Soap operas . . . .
   b. in the present singular of verbs:
     Janet want's to ride the carousel. Corrected: Janet wants . . . .

■ 10. The hyphen

The hyphen has three major uses:

10a. to divide a word at the end of a line:

Scarves can be used to achieve many different fashionable effects.

10b. to connect the parts of compound words:

double-header, self-reliance, half-moon

10c. to connect two or more words forming a single adjective before a noun:

the long-awaited costume ball, the Nielsen-rated program, the two-year-old child, the well-known acrobat

Exception: When a compound adjective completes a sentence instead of coming before its noun, no hyphen is used: That acrobat is well known in gymnastic circles.

NOTE: For more about how to handle compound words, see "Spelling."

11. Underlining (italics)

Underlining, in either handwriting or typing, equals italics (slanted type) in print.

11a. Underlining is used for titles of major publications and of long literary and musical works:

a. books: Poetic Celebrations, The Web and the Rock, Exploring Canada

b. magazines: Psychology Today, Rolling Stone

c. newspapers: Washington Post, Christian Science Monitor

d. plays: Hedda Gabler, The Zoo Story

e. full-length films: Klute, Sounder, True Grit

f. long poems: The Love Song of J. Alfred Prufrock

g. long musical compositions: Mozart's Little Night Music, Schubert's Trout Quintet

11b. Underlining sets off terms used as themselves inside a sentence:

a. The word pajama originated in the Hindi language.

b. The letter s and the number 5 can be confused if they are not formed carefully.

NOTE: Quotation marks may be used instead of underlining to set off terms used as themselves.

11c. Underlining is sometimes used to give added emphasis to a word or words in a sentence:

While they were hiking, she said to him, "Don't you dare drop that rock on my lunch!"

Caution: You should not often need to use underlining for emphasis in your writing. Strong sentences can stand on their own. Excessive underlining usually suggests hasty, lazy writing; avoid it.

12. Quotation marks

Quotation marks are used in three major ways: (a) to punctuate minor titles; (b) to set off direct quotations; and (c) around dialogue, either spoken or internal.

12a. Minor titles

    a. essays, articles, chapter or section headings: Thoreau's "Civil Disobedience"; Beth Thompson's column "Getting There"; "People and Places" in *Holiday* magazine; "Five Ways to Stop Smoking" in Dr. Jennie Albertson's *Improving Your Health*
    b. short stories: "The Worn Path"
    c. short poems: "Whose Lips I've Kissed"
    d. short musical compositions: Neil Diamond's "Stargazer"
    e. paintings: Helen Frankenthaler's "Red Slash"

12b. Direct quotations:

    a. "I swing out over the earth over and over again," from Audre Lorde's "Love Poem," is one of my favorite lines of poetry.
    b. In her book *In the Shadow of Man,* Jane van Lawick-Goodall says she observed chimps as they "bit the ends off their tools [grass stems] when they became bent," to make them useable again.

12c. Dialogue:

    a. Spoken:
       "Do you like the Alvin Ailey dancers?" John asked Sam.
       "I don't know. I've never seen them perform," replied Sam.
       "Then, let's go! You'll like their exciting choreography, I know," John urged.
       Notice that a new paragraph begins whenever the speaker changes.
    b. Internal:
       "What will my family think if I take up truck-driving?" wondered Alice.

12d. Single quotation marks

Single quotation marks are used when a title or quoted material appears inside a quotation:

    Laurie asked her father, "Do you know anything about T. S. Eliot's poem 'Macavity: The Mystery Cat'?"

12e. Quotation marks with other punctuation marks:
Periods and commas go inside quotation marks:

    a. One of my favorite folksingers is Joni Mitchell; I especially like her "Both Sides Now."
    b. I also like Olivia Newton's "Country Girl," Jim Croce's "Time in a Bottle," and John Denver's "Country Roads."

Semicolons and colons are placed outside quotation marks:

    a. One of Emily Dickinson's riddle poems is "A Narrow Fellow in the Grass"; by the time you finish reading the poem, you can see the snake that is the answer to the riddle.
    b. Ernest Hemingway achieves highly dramatic conflict among the characters in his short story "The Short Happy Life of Francis Macomber": Francis, the weak male; Margot, the strong female; and Robert, the strong male.

Question marks and exclamation points go outside quotation marks—unless the question or the exclamation itself is being quoted, in which case they go inside:

    a. Did you hear her say ,"All aboard"?
    b. Stop smiling and saying, "Yes, yes"!
    c. I wondered aloud, "What shall I do next?"
    d. "No!" Thomas said again to the hungry bear.

Caution: Do not use quotation marks around questionable words in a sentence, or to try to achieve a humorous effect:

    Nancy pointed out to her parents that smoking marijuana was no more harmful than getting "bombed" on alcohol.

Using quotation marks in this way has the unfortunate effect of calling attention to what they surround. If you are tempted to write this kind of sentence, you probably need to look for more precise language.

13. Brackets

Brackets are used when you need to insert a word or words into a quotation.

    In a book about Dr. Mary Walker, I was amazed to read the following statement: "The medal awarded her for service in the [Civil] War was taken back by the United States government."

14. Ellipsis dots

Ellipsis dots (three spaced periods) are substituted for deletions from quoted material.

Original: "When my sons grow up, then, Gentlemen, I ask you to punish them, you hurting them the same as I hurt you, if they seem to you to care for money, or aught else, more than they care for virtue." (Plato, *The Apology of Socrates*)

With ellipsis: Near the end of *The Apology*, Socrates asks the court: "When my sons grow up . . . I ask you to punish them . . . if they seem to you to care for money, or aught else, more than they care for virtue."

If deleted material is at the end of a sentence, then add one more dot to the three, to indicate a period.

To discover how well you understand punctuation after studying this section, punctuate the following sentences:

1. Ruth asked the little girl How old are you

2. Harry please bring pecans walnuts and chestnuts when you come for the weekend we need those I think for between meal snacks

3. One of my favorite short stories is Shirley Jacksons The Lottery which has been filmed for classroom use

4. Its too early to take a taxi to the theater but lets think about going by Johns fathers horsedrawn carriage

5. Have you seen Natalie Smorgavich in Shaws play Major Barbara

6. My Aunt Katherine Jones is in line for a diplomatic appointment but she is reluctant to leave Washington

7. Look at that dancer leap

8. Hi exclaimed Jonathan when he saw the man from next door who was walking his dog in the park

9. My neighbors cat will climb any tree in sight however that habit creates a problem when she cant get back down without a firefighters assistance

10. Whether you like it or not im going to include the quotation To thine own self be true from Shakespeare in my psychology paper asserted Tom

Now punctuate the unpunctuated student paper below, dividing it into paragraphs as you work. Be sure to capitalize letters that begin new sentences. You will have to make some punctuation choices, so you may want to compare your punctuated version with those of your classmates, and to discuss the various effects achieved by different punctuation choices.

> i was suddenly awakened at four o'clock one morning by my wife its time to go she exclaimed gazing across the room and seeing her standing with suitcase in hand it dawned on me that this was the moment for which we had been waiting nine months i sprang out of bed grabbed whatever clothes were available and started dressing while simultaneously calling the doctor ill meet you at the hospital in forty-five minutes was the doctors reply to a very nervous father-to-be on the way to the hospital i tried to remain calm as i tried to remember the training we had received in prepared childbirth classes and the reading we had done in having your baby naturally inhale exhale breathe deeply and slowly i repeated to my wife over and over again as we drove into the city arriving at the hospital i drove right up to the front door and carefully ushered my wife to the admitting office after rushing through much paperwork not really knowing what we were signing we finally made it to the labor room then it began the timing of contractions the breathing in unison and the waiting three long hours later when my wife was fully dilated the doctor sent me out to dress in the delivery room garb a green cap mask gown and shoes once in the delivery room i held my wifes hand and assisted whenever possible twenty short minutes later a beautiful six-pound twelve-ounce girl was born one does not realize how much pain a woman can tolerate or the strength she possesses until he can witness a childbirth i shall always treasure having shared my daughters birth with my wife it was an event i shall not forget

You will find a punctuated version of this paper in the Appendix.

CAPITALIZATION

Usually you know what to capitalize, without much thinking about it. But when you're not quite sure, these rules will help you out.

15. In general, capitalize the names or titles of *specific* places, persons, organizations, historical events, or educational courses.

15a. Capitalize the complete names of specific geographic places:

Spring Street   the *Illinois River*
Grand Island, Nebraska   the *West*
Lake Superior

Also capitalize words that derive from names of specific geographic places:

a *New Yorker*   *Indian* food
French blue jeans

But: Do not capitalize the points of the compass or geographic terms that do not name a specific region:

drive *west* on route 66   a beautiful *river*
the *plains*   the *suburbs*
downtown

15b. Capitalize titles of persons if used with the person's name or as the person's name:

Although she had been poor all her life, *Mother* always kept her dignity.

Professor Stevens   *Uncle* Jake
Mayor Baldwin

But: Do not capitalize titles of persons when the title is not used as a name or part of a name:

Jim's *uncle*   Stevens is a *professor.*
my *mother*   Joe Baldwin, the *mayor*

15c. Capitalize all significant words in the names of specific organizations and institutions:

Girl Scouts of *America*   *Department* of *Commerce*
American Cancer Society   *Largo High School*

But: Do not capitalize words that refer generally to groups or institutions:

steelworkers   the *unemployed*
pacifists   *high school*

15d. Capitalize names of specific historical events and names of historical eras:

the *Civil War*   the *Middle Ages*
the *Age* of *Reason*   the *Nuremberg Trials*

But: Do not capitalize words that refer generally to historical happenings:

war crimes
an ancient *democracy*

industrialism
the rise of *capitalism*

15e. Capitalize the names of specific educational courses:

Math 285
Philosophy 101

English 102

But: Do not capitalize names of subjects in general:

Have you thought of taking philosophy this semester?
Have you completed your math requirement?

But: Do capitalize the word "English," even when it is used to refer to the subject in general. "English" derives from the name of a country, "England," which must be capitalized along with its derivatives.

16. Capitalize the days of the week, months of the year, and holidays:

Friday
September

Thanksgiving

17. Capitalize all of the words in titles except for short and unimportant ones. Capitalize even these if they are the first words of a title:

Soul on Ice
Reader's Digest
The World of Zen
Sex and Power in History

On Death and Dying
"The Lottery"
"All in the Family"

18. Capitalize religious names and terms of especially sacred significance:

God
Buddha
Mosaic law

the *Annunciation*
the *Koran*

But: Do not capitalize the word "god" when used generally:

the Greek *gods*
belief in a *god*

SPELLING

"Anybody who can think of only one way to spell a word is a damn fool." We have heard that remark credited to at least three persons: Mark Twain, Will Rogers, and Andrew Jackson. We would not be surprised to hear it from anyone who has ever tried to write in the English language. Because the spelling of our language is so arbitrary and so unpredictable, you should not allow yourself to feel like a blockhead if you "can't spell." Spelling ability is *not* an index to IQ; some of the smartest people we know can't spell! However, it is true that spelling errors make a piece of writing hard to read. So you will want to look carefully for misspellings as you proofread your writing.

Read the following paragraph:

Most of us know at least one women who is begining colledge in her fourties. Her family may find this new arangement dificult to acommodate to. However, once they become acustomed to it, they frequently speak proudly of her. She, on the other hand, may have to struggle to overcome certian guilt feelings; somehow, the principal of self-development for her own being is hard for her to except, despite the advise of her freinds who have allready traveled the same path. Gradualy, though, she realizes that she truely is a whole person, seperate from her husband and her childern, and she learns to function outside the wife-mother role. Then she can relax, let down her gaurd some, and finaly begin to recomend "comming back to school" to her neighbors. The growth observeable in such women is exciteing to watch; its one of the real pleasures of being in the collage enviroment today.

How many misspelled words did you spot? There are 27. You will find a corrected version of this paragraph in the Appendix. Turn to it and see how well you did. If you as a reader found the misspellings in the above paragraph distracting, you can now appreciate the importance of proofreading for spelling.

As we pointed out in the chapter on writing and rewriting, stopping to worry about spelling while you are writing can do more harm than good because it will hinder the flow of your writing. So ignore spelling as you write; then be sure to attend to it later.

19. Proofreading for spelling

If you often misspell, then you may want to do a separate proof-reading just for spelling. To proofread for spelling, read your writing aloud, making yourself say aloud *exactly* what you wrote down, not merely what you *intended* to write, which no doubt will still be lingering in your head. In proofreading for spelling, you must train your eye to pay equal attention to each individual letter of a word, rather than reading groups of words the way you usually read. If you meant to write "preserve," but you wrote "perserve," then you must read *"per*serve." "Unusal' does not spell "unusual," nor does "quite" spell "quiet," nor can "conscience" mean "conscious."

If you handwrite your papers, be sure every letter of a word will look to a reader like what you meant it to be; otherwise, illegibility can be taken for misspelling. If you type your work, be especially alert to typographical errors, which can be read as spelling errors.

20. Improving your spelling

Once you learn to spot your spelling errors, you will begin to recognize your "spelling demons"—words that consistently trip you up. Make a list of these on a 3 × 5 card—or a 4 × 6 or a 6 × 8, if you are tormented by a horde of demons—and keep it handy when you write. This way, you will save yourself the time and trouble of looking them up. Almost everybody has some spelling demons. One of us, for example, never can remember how to spell these words: *guarantee, obsession,* and *license.*

If you misspell many words in addition to your demons, we urge you to buy a spelling dictionary. Spelling dictionaries give spelling and word divisions only, so that it is easy to locate words in them. Two spelling dictionaries we might recommend are *Webster's New World 33,000 Word Book* (Collins, Williams & World Publishing Company, 1971) and *Instant Spelling Dictionary: 25,000 Words* (Career Institute, Dept. 899-66, 555 E. Lange Street, Mundelein, IL 60060, 1967).

Your regular dictionary can help you with spelling in a way you may not be aware of. Most hardbound dictionaries and some paper-back ones feature a section on spelling rules. Look there if you need help with such spelling dilemmas as how to form irregular plurals (children, mice); how to form the plurals of words ending in

-y and -ey (ferry, ferries; donkeys); how to add prefixes and suffixes (*re*negotiate, final*ly*); and so on.

How to handle compound words (new words composed of two or more old words) is also clarified in your regular dictionary. If a compound word should be written all together, it will be divided by only the syllable-division marker, a dot in the middle of the line: fel·low·ship. If the new word is hyphenated, a tiny hyphen will appear between its old words: self-con·fi·dence. If the compound word remains two separate words, there will be an empty space between the original words: cross sec·tion.

Because our language changes, you may find compound words treated differently in different dictionaries. Don't fret about that. The one caution we suggest here is that you not set up a compound word so that deciphering it creates a problem for your reader. "Cross section" may be "cross-section" in some dictionaries. Just don't write it "crosssection"; all those s's in a row are hard to read!

Over the years people with spelling problems have devised various mnemonics (pronounced: knee mahn' icks) to help them remember how to spell certain confusing words. "Mnemonic," from Greek, means "a memory aid." Probably the most common mnemonic is the one that goes "i before e, except after c"—to help us remember how to spell "believe," "sieve," "receive," and so on. Here are some others you might find useful:

1. *truly* a handful (five letters, for "truly," equals a handful of five fingers)
2. A good *secret*ary keeps a secret.
3. George Elliott's old grandmother rode a pig home yesterday— to spell "geography."

You can make up mnemonics to help you remember how to spell your demon words, as we have done for one of ours:

obsession: Oscar banned Sally's elephants every sunny Saturday in Owen's neighborhood.

Mnemonics are often easier to remember if they are funny, so play around some as you devise yours.

21. Sound-alike words

We want to give you some special help with one particular kind of spelling problem: that of words that sound alike, either exactly or approximately, but that have different meanings. It is easy to confuse such words, and you may need some "meaning aids" to keep them straight. So we provide below a list of some of these trouble-makers, with example sentences:

1.	accept (verb)	Will you *accept* the offer?
	except (preposition)	Put all *except* the spoiled ones into the basket.
2.	advice (noun)	Give me some *advice.*
	advise (verb)	I'll be glad to *advise* you.
3.	affect (verb)	Will it *affect* my promotion possibilities?
	effect (noun)	The *effect* of the collision was slight.
4.	already (adverb)	They have *already* come.
	all ready	I am *all ready* to go. (means "completely")
5.	altogether (adverb)	Carolyn was *altogether* wrong.
	all together	They are *all together* at the station already. (means "everyone gathered")
6.	capital	What is the *capital* of Brazil? (place)
	capital	Marie has a large amount of *capital* invested in that office building. (money)
	capitol	Maryland's State House, in Annapolis, is the oldest *capitol* in the United States. (building)
7.	choose	Be sure to *choose* the best.
	chose	Yesterday she *chose* a desk for her study.
8.	cloths	Those silk *cloths* come from Taiwan.
	clothes	Put the *clothes* in the dryer.
9.	coarse (adjective)	The texture of those rugs is too *coarse.*
	course (noun)	Is that *course* required for your degree?
10.	conscience (noun)	His *conscience* troubled him because he had lied.
	conscious (adjective)	I was still *conscious* when the dentist began to drill.

11. desert (noun)	The sands of the *desert* sparkled in the sun.
desert (verb)	Did you *desert* your friends at the party?
dessert (noun)	We had grasshopper pie for *dessert*.
12. effect	See "affect."
13. except	See "accept."
14. fair (noun)	Let's go to the county *fair* this fall.
fair (adjective)	She is a very *fair* executive.
fare (noun)	The bus *fare* has gone up.
15. formally	We dressed *formally* for the costume ball.
formerly	*Formerly* he worked as a fire-fighter.
16. forth (adverb)	Step *forth* and assert yourself.
fourth (adjective)	Beth sat in the *fourth* row (from "four")
17. hear (verb)	Did you *hear* Frank play "Tally Ho" on his horn?
here (adverb)	The parade should begin *here*.
18. its (possessive pronoun)	*Its* head is small for its body.
it's (it is)	*It's* perfect weather for skiing.
19. know (verb)	I *know* everybody in the class.
no	His answer was *"no"*—in *no* uncertain terms.
20. later (adverb)	We will follow you *later*.
latter (adjective)	The *latter* third of the concert was too modern for my taste.
21. lead (noun)	That basket is as heavy as *lead*.
lead (verb, present)	Thomas will *lead* the way.
led (verb, past)	It's Thomas' turn, because Kate *led* yesterday.
22. lose (verb)	"Did you *lose* my turtle?" asked Jimmy.
loose (adjective)	The name of the bar is The *Loose* Goose.
23. no	See "know."
24. passed (verb)	James *passed* the long, difficult test.

past (noun)	That happened so far in the *past* I wish we could forget it.
past (adjective)	The *past* few days have been hectic.
25. peace	That group works hard for world *peace.*
piece	Give me a *piece* of cheesecake.
26. personal (adjective)	Linda considers that her *personal* business.
personnel (noun)	Isn't it strange that all the *personnel* in that company have red hair?
27. precede	Let Richard *precede* you in the line. (go before)
proceed	Please *proceed* to the end of the block. (go forward)
28. principal (noun)	The *principal* was in his office. (person)
principal (noun)	The *principal* was $12,000. (money)
principal (adjective)	Their *principal* food was rice. (meaning "major")
principle (noun)	The *principles* Esther lives by are honesty and dependability. (rule, code of behavior)
29. quiet (adjective)	It was *quiet* in the house.
quite (adverb)	It was *quite* dark outside.
30. right (adjective)	You were quite *right* to tell John the truth.
right (noun)	All members have a *right* to their own opinions.
write (verb)	Louie is going to *write* his paper on computers in the home.
31. role	Sam will play the *role* of Helmer in "A Doll's House."
roll	He called the *roll* quickly.
32. sense (noun)	Most dogs have a *sense* of smell.
sense (verb)	Did you *sense* some hostility on Jenny's part?
since (conjunction)	*Since* your pet iguana will be on the train, Jake won't go.

since (preposition)	I have not talked with Betsy *since* yesterday.
33. stationery (noun)	Eleanor wrote on lavender *stationery.*
stationary (adjective)	Her desk is *stationary* in that corner.
34. than (used to compare)	Charlotte is more reflective *than* I.
then (adverb of time)	Jasper turned red and *then* left the room.
35. there (introductory word and adverb of place) their (possessive) they're (they are)	*There* are young people who, as soon as *they're* old enough to drive, think they should have a car of *their* own. Many want to keep *their* cars on the school grounds, over *there* near the playing field.
36. through (preposition) threw (verb)	Timing her jump precisely, Sandy *threw* the ball *through* the hoop.
37. to	Is Ellen planning *to* go *to* the ballet?
too	I want some frozen raspberry yogurt *too.* (means "also") It is *too* late to worry now about whether your costume is *too* loose.
two	Ed has *two* valuable comic books I want.
38. weather (noun)	The clear *weather* makes today just right for exploring the valley.
whether (conjunction)	David didn't know *whether* to laugh or to cry.
39. where (adverb of place) were (verb)	*Where were* you when the rest of us left for the art gallery?
40. whose	*Whose* pocket is housing a croaking frog?
who's (who is, who has)	*Who's* coming scuba-diving with us?

41. woman (singular)

Harriet Tubman, a somewhat fragile *woman,* was neverthe-less a major figure in the Un-derground Railway during the Civil War.

women (plural)

Are you taking the course *Women* in Art?

42. your (possessive pronoun)
you're (you are)

You're likely to lose *your* coat if you take it off in this trolley car.

REVISING PROBLEM SENTENCES

frag

22. Write complete sentences.

Don't treat fragments of sentences as if they were complete sentences.

   a. There is a great need for female doctors. Especially in obstetrics and gynecology.
   There is a great need for female doctors, especially in obstetrics and gynecology.
   b. Jim's gaily wrapped package sat waiting in the closet. Safely hidden from inquisitive little fingers.
   Jim's gaily wrapped package sat waiting in the closet, safely hidden from inquisitive little fingers.
   c. Europe's rail system is quick, cheap, and efficient. While European roads are primitive.
   Europe's rail system is quick, cheap, and efficient, while European roads are primitive.
   d. The school has been dubbed SERE. An acronym for survival, evasion, resistance, and escape.
   The school has been dubbed SERE, an acronym for survival, evasion, resistance, and escape.

Exception: Sentence fragments are permissible when used deliberately, for emphasis:

The plane takes off with a mighty roar. Off toward Vietnam.

I sometimes think as I look at my child: "I love you, but you remind me of my mistakes and I can't bear to look at you. Or talk to you. Or think about you."

Johnson felt he could release his frustrations on his wife because he felt at home with her. Ordinarily they got along well, and talking with her about his unhappiness with his job and with life in general was a source of release for him. But not this day.

run-on/cs

23. Avoid run-on sentences and comma splices.

Do not run together two complete statements. Do not "splice" together two complete statements with a comma.

Two complete statements can be joined together in one sentence in *only* two ways:

1. with a connector word (and, but, or, nor, for, so, yet)
2. with a semicolon.

There are four possible ways to correct run-on sentences or comma splices:

1. Split the two statements into two separate sentences.
   a. I don't mind cooking, in fact I enjoy it.
      I don't mind cooking. In fact, I enjoy it.
   b. The worst thing about Hell is that there will be no one to turn to, you will be all alone.
      The worst thing about Hell is that there will be no one to turn to. You will be all alone.

2. Put a connector word (and, but, or, nor, for, so, yet) between the two statements.
   a. I have thirty more years before retirement, by then I should have reached my goal.
      I have thirty more years before retirement, and by then I should have reached my goal.
   b. Jim said it looked snug around the waist, I thought it looked perfect.
      Jim said it looked snug around the waist, but I thought it looked perfect.

3. Insert a semicolon between the two statements.
   a. He could not respond it seemed hopeless.
      He could not respond; it seemed hopeless.
   b. Water conditions of the soil can be a real source of trouble when camping, however, your camp should be located close to a spring of running water.
      Water conditions of the soil can be a real source of trouble when camping; however, your camp should be located close to a spring of running water.

4. Restructure the sentence.
   a. The plains Indians were a trusting people, many of the tribes didn't even have a word for "lie."
      The plains Indians were so trusting that many of the tribes didn't even have a word for "lie."

b. This is why there are so many robberies, murders, and rapes, people are just bored.
Many robberies, murders, and rapes are committed out of boredom.

mix

24. Rewrite mixed-up sentences.

Mixed-up sentences are ones that got out of control as you were writing them. They began in one way, then ended in a way that didn't quite fit the beginning. You can think of them as having the head of one sentence and the tail of another. Here is an example:

If I can help out just by listening to a child's small but pressing problems gives me satisfaction.

The "head" of this sentence is "If I can help out just by listening to a child's small but pressing problems." The "tail" is "gives me satisfaction." The problem is that the head and tail don't go together.

To revise a mixed-up sentence you can change the tail to fit the head:

If I can help out just by listening to a child's small but pressing problems, I am satisfied.

Or you can change the head to fit the tail:

Just listening to a child's small but pressing problems gives me satisfaction.

Sometimes, though, a sentence will be so badly mixed up that you can't even find its head and its tail. What should you do then? Just throw it out, then try again to express your idea—this time in a clear, straightforward sentence.

a. I found that getting involved in working with students on their reading problems a new and enlightening experience.
Helping students with their reading problems was a new and enlightening experience for me.

b. I think that would be the most important thing about a job is satisfaction.
The most important thing about a job, for me, is the satisfaction I receive from it.

c. Not being able to go to her mother and talk to her the way she once did and the love for her husband not being returned, made her feel very depressed.
Her husband no longer loved her, and she could no longer talk over personal problems with her mother. Her isolation made her feel very depressed.

d. At one point I gave up completely deciding whether or not to commit suicide, to end my life at the age of twenty.
At the age of twenty, I decided to end my life.

An occasional mixed-up sentence is nothing to worry about. Just rewrite it when you discover it. But if many of your sentences get out of control, you have a problem that needs to be tackled head on.

Try, either by yourself or with the help of your instructor, to discover *why* you are writing so many mixed-up sentences. If you can find the causes of your problem, you'll be that much closer to a solution. Here is a list of some common causes, each of which suggests its own cure:

Cause: You're trying to write in a style that is more formal and complex than you can handle.

Cure: Write in a simpler, more direct style.

Cause: Your only purpose for writing is that you have to complete an assignment. Attempting to spin something out of nothing, you wind up in a tangle of words and phrases.

Cure: Choose writing topics that are more "real" for you—on subjects you know something about. And as you write, focus on writing for readers who want to hear what you have to say.

Cause: You treat writing as a one-step process. Once you start writing, you just plunge forward, even when you can feel sentences escaping from your control.

Cure: Change your writing habits. Practice writing the way professionals do—use a several-step process involving false starts and lots of crossing-out and rephrasing. Control your sentences instead of letting them go off on their own.

Cause: You're not sure what sentence structures are acceptable in written English. You know that certain "loose" sentence structures are all right in spoken English, but you're not sure which structures will work in written English.

Cure: This cure will take time—a whole semester at least. Purchase a workbook or work through programmed materials on the basic sentence patterns of written English. Your instruc-

tor can advise you on books and materials available at your
school.

25. Avoid confusing shifts.

If you begin writing in the present tense, don't make a confusing
shift to the past. Or if you are using one pronoun, such as "I," don't
shift to another, such as "you." Or if you begin writing in the active
voice, don't shift to the passive voice.

a. We left early to go to the circus. Once there, we wander around,
eat popcorn, and some of us get lost.
We left early to go to the circus. Once there, we wandered around,
ate popcorn, and some of us got lost.

b. The other members of the team must accept all decisions made by
the leader, even if that means they won't make it to the top. You
must be willing to trust the leader without question.
The other members of the team must accept all decisions made by
the leader, even if that means they won't make it to the top. They
must be willing to trust the leader without question.

c. The teacher focuses on main events. Trivia is included only when it
helps the student understand the material.
The teacher focuses on main events. She includes trivia only when
it helps the student understand the material.

NOTE: For more about confusing shifts, see chapter 10.

om

26. Do not omit words that are needed.

Sometimes, especially when you are trying to avoid repetition,
you may be tempted to omit words that are necessary for grammatical completeness. Resist the temptation. Your readers need to
understand how the parts of your sentence fit together.

a. I knew then that everything would be all right, but there would be
other patients just like her.
I knew then that everything would be all right, but that there would
be other patients just like her.

b. In my opinion her dependence on tranquilizers is no healthier than
the alcoholic or the addict.

In my opinion her dependence on tranquilizers is no healthier than the alcoholic's dependence on alcohol or the addict's need for a fix.

c. If your hair is long, don't be surprised when the Japanese barber wraps a few curlers here and there and a good dousing with hair spray.
If your hair is long, don't be surprised when the Japanese barber wraps a few curlers here and there and gives you a good dousing with hair spray.

d. Dave saw his four-year-old brother was moving too close to the cliff.
Dave saw that his four-year-old brother was moving too close to the cliff.

e. Having grown up in the ghetto, Teresa was both delighted and uneasy about her scholarship to Harvard.
Having grown up in the ghetto, Teresa was both delighted with and uneasy about her scholarship to Harvard.

NOTE: If you frequently omit words, turn to the handbook section on "Dialect Interference: Problems with Omitted Words." (38)

mod

27. Place modifiers close to the words they modify.

A modifier is a word or group of words that gives readers additional information about some other word in the sentence. In general, keep your modifiers close to the words they modify.

a. A rope was hanging from the ceiling to swing on.
A rope to swing on was hanging from the ceiling.

b. Having lost respect for her, I only felt an empty numbness towards her.
Having lost respect for her, I felt only an empty numbness towards her.

c. Lloyd decided on his way to the office to buy flowers.
On his way to the office, Lloyd decided to buy flowers.

d. The Marlboro ads depict a man on a horse smoking a cigarette.
The Marlboro ads depict a man on horseback smoking a cigarette.

dng

28. Avoid dangling modifiers.

A modifier is a word or group of words that gives readers additional information about some other word in the sentence. A modifier is said to "dangle" when the writer forgets to include the word that it modifies. When a modifier dangles, readers are tempted to attach it to some other word that does appear in the sentence. The result is confusing and sometimes humorous. Notice, for example, how you are tempted to misread this sentence: "Twisting around the mast, the cook had difficulty grabbing its tail."

a. Already failing one test, my spirits were low.
   Since I had already failed one test, my spirits were low.
b. While running an EEG one day, the pens started clacking and throwing ink about the room.
   While I was running an EEG one day, the pens started clacking and throwing ink about the room.
c. Gazing from the hillside, the early morning fog blanketed the slough like a damp overcoat.
   Gazing from the hillside, I watched as the early morning fog blanketed the slough like a damp overcoat.
d. Seeing her standing with suitcase in hand, it dawned on me that this was the moment for which we had been waiting nine months.
   When I saw her standing with suitcase in hand, it dawned on me that this was the moment for which we had been waiting nine months.
e. To swim properly, each stroke should be timed.
   To swim properly, you should time each stroke.
f. When playing tennis, concentration is important.
   Concentration is important in playing tennis.

S-V

29. Match your subjects and verbs.

Subjects and their verbs should "agree" in number. If the subject is singular, the verb should be singular. If the subject is plural, the verb should be plural.

This sounds like a simple enough rule, and for the most part you've probably mastered it. But you may sometimes have trouble with it. When you do, here are the most likely sources of your problem:

1. You're not sure what the subject of the sentence is.
2. You're not sure whether the subject is singular or plural.
3. You speak a dialect that differs slightly from standard English.

We will treat these different sources of the problem one at a time.

29a. You're not sure what the subject of the sentence is.

a. If several words come between the subject and the verb, you may mistake a noun close to the verb for the subject.

   1. The large boxes of mixed candy was on sale.
      The large *boxes* of mixed candy were on sale.
   2. The role of the police officer in these shows seem stereo-typed.
      The *role* of the police officer in these shows seems stereo-typed.

b. If the subject follows the verb (reversing the usual order), you may mistake a noun that comes before the verb for the subject of the sentence.

   1. Behind the defensive line is several young linebackers.
      Behind the defensive line are several young *linebackers.*
   2. Hiding in the corner behind the plants are the long-sought-after runaway child.
      Hiding in the corner behind the plants is the long-sought-after runaway *child.*

c. Sentences beginning with "There is" or "There are" pre-sent a special problem because they seem to have no sub-ject. Actually the subject follows the "There is" or "There are" construction.

   1. There is not many people on Assateague Island.
      There are not many *people* on Assateague Island.
   2. There wasn't even enough chairs to go around.
      There weren't even enough *chairs* to go around.

29b. You're not sure whether the subject is singular or plural.

a. When the subject of the sentence is a collective noun like "committee" or "team" or "jury," do you treat the noun as singular or plural? The answer depends on the meaning you intend. Usually you will want readers to view the group as one unit, so you will treat the noun as singular:

   The committee was more successful than we had hoped.
   Our team is expected to win.

But occasionally you may want readers to view the group as a number of individuals. Then you'll treat the noun as plural:

   Unable so far to agree on a verdict, the jury continue to de-bate the case.

b. Are pronouns like *each, one, none, either, neither, any, every, whoever,* and *somebody* singular or plural? In casual speech many people treat them as plurals. But in writing, especially in formal writing, these words have traditionally been treated as singular. There is some evidence that the traditional rule may be changing, but in the meantime you should probably play it safe. Even if you would usually say "each of them were," you will find it safer to write "each of them was."

1. Whoever are going should be ready by six o'clock.
   Whoever *is* going should be ready by six o'clock.
2. Each of the twelve stamps are worth fifty dollars.
   Each of the twelve stamps *is* worth fifty dollars.
3. Everybody in the local jail were released.
   Everybody in the local jail *was* released.

c. If the subject of the sentence is compound (two subjects connected by *and, or,* or *nor*), do you treat the compound subject as singular or plural? The answer is fairly complicated. Let's begin with the easy rule: When the two parts of the compound subject are connected with *and,* you always treat the subject as plural.

My mother's natural ability and her desire to help others *have* led to a career as a psychic medium.

And now the more complex rule: When the two parts of the compound subject are connected with *or* or *nor,* you match the verb with the part of the subject that's closest to it. If that part of the subject is singular, your verb should be singular.

Neither the students nor their instructor *was* able to find the classroom.

If that part of the subject is plural, the verb should be plural.

Neither the instructor nor her students *were* able to find the classroom.

29c. You speak a dialect that differs slightly from mainstream (standard) English.

If you make a great many errors in subject-verb agreement, dialect interference is almost certainly the source of most of your problem. For advice, turn to the handbook section on "Dialect Interference: Problems with '-s' Endings." (37)

n-p

30. Match your nouns and pronouns.

Pronouns are words that substitute for nouns. Each pronoun should agree in number with its antecedent (the noun it refers to). Use singular pronouns to refer to singular nouns, plural pronouns to refer to plural nouns.

> The sermon reminded us that even though temptations to be unkind are great, we must learn to resist it.
>
> The sermon reminded us that even though temptations to be unkind are great, we must learn to resist *them.*

For the most part you probably follow this rule quite easily, without even thinking about it. But in certain situations you may run into problems. Let's talk about those situations, one at a time.

30a. Many of your problems with pronoun-antecedent agreement may arise because you do not want to discriminate against women.

Traditionally it was acceptable to write "The average student is worried about *his* grades"; but this sort of sentence, which ignores half the human race, is becoming less and less acceptable. In an effort to avoid such unacceptable sentences, you may be tempted to use a plural pronoun: "The average student is concerned about *their* grades." But this sentence is not acceptable in formal writing, because the plural *their* doesn't agree with the singular *student.*

The correct form is "The average student is concerned about *his or her* grades." This sentence is socially acceptable, because it includes both men and women, and it is grammatically acceptable, because the singular "his or her" agrees with the singular "student."

However, too many repetitions of *his or her* can begin to sound awkward. To avoid such awkwardness, you can recast your sentences. You can write "The average student is worried about grades" or "Students are usually worried about grades."

problem sentences:	*acceptable revised versions:*
If an individual on approved leave wishes to continue hospitalization coverage, they must pay the full premium.	If an individual on approved leave wishes to continue hospitalization coverage, he or she must pay the full premium.

Persons on approved leave who wish to continue hospitalization coverage must pay the full premium.

When a person goes to the hospital, they are put on a schedule that is convenient for the hospital staff.	When a person goes to the hospital, he or she is put on a schedule that is convenient for the hospital staff. Patients are put on schedules that are convenient for the hospital staff.

30b. You may be uncertain whether words like *anyone, somebody, each, either,* and *everybody* should be treated as singular or plural.

Should you write "Everyone must cast his or her vote in person" or "Everyone must cast their vote in person"? Many people treat these words as plural, especially in informal speech and writing. In formal writing, however, these words have been traditionally viewed as singular. Although informal practice seems to be changing the formal rule, you'll find it safer to follow the formal rule for now. Write "Everyone must cast his or her vote in person."

If "his or her" begins to sound awkward to you, you might write "Voters must cast their votes in person" or "You must vote in person" or "All votes must be cast in person."

problem sentences:	*acceptable revised versions:*
Everyone was told to make sure they attended class on Friday.	Everyone was told to make sure he or she attended class on Friday. All the students were told to make sure they attended class on Friday.
Has anyone lost their glove?	Has anyone lost his or her glove? Has anyone lost a glove?
Each of us wanted their fair share.	Each of us wanted his or her fair share. All of us wanted our fair share.

30c. If the noun you're referring to is a collective one like *committee, jury,* or *audience,* do you treat the noun as singular or plural?

Your meaning will determine which way you will treat it. If you are speaking of the group as a single unit, write "The committee announced its decision." But if you want to focus on the group as a collection of individuals, write "The committee argued over their decision all afternoon."

ref.

31. Make pronoun references clear.

Pronouns are words that substitute for nouns. They are a kind of shorthand. In a sentence like "When the queen issued the order, she assumed everyone would obey it," the pronouns *she* and *it* are simply shorthand for the nouns *queen* and *order.*

Make sure that your readers will understand just what noun each pronoun refers to. Most of the time your pronoun references will be clear, but occasionally you may slip up. When you do, here are the most likely sources of your problem:

1. Your pronoun does not have a noun to refer to.
2. Your pronoun could possibly refer to two different nouns.
3. Your pronoun is too far away from the noun to which it refers.

We will treat these different sources of the problem one at a time.

31a. Your pronoun does not have a noun to refer to.

a. The course consists of seven weekly sessions, each two hours long. *They* guarantee that you will increase your reading speed and comprehension.
    The course consists of seven weekly sessions, each two hours long. The instructors guarantee that you will increase your reading speed and comprehension.

b. Many people watch soap operas as a form of relaxation. Like Monday night football games, *this* provides viewers with a relaxing escape from everyday problems.
    Many people watch soap operas as a form of relaxation. Like watching Monday night football games, watching soap operas provides viewers with a relaxing escape from everyday concerns.

c. In the encyclopedia *it* states that only eight out of one hundred snakes are poisonous.
    The encyclopedia states that only eight out of one hundred snakes are poisonous.

d. "Like a Winding Sheet" is about a black man who feels victimized by white people; the story shows how much friction *it* causes between him and his wife.

"Like a Winding Sheet" is about a black man who feels victimized by white people; the story shows how much friction these
feelings cause between him and his wife.

31b. Your pronoun could possibly refer to two different nouns.

 a. When Jack put the sculpture on the table, *it* broke.
  The table broke when Jack put the sculpture on it.
        OR
  The sculpture broke when Jack put it on the table.
 b. Mary Ellen said to Pamela that *she* was wrong to have repeated
  the rumor.
  Mary Ellen apologized to Pamela for having repeated the rumor.
        OR
  Mary Ellen reprimanded Pamela for having repeated the rumor.

31c. Your pronoun is too far away from the noun to which it refers.

 a. Her two teenaged girls and her eight-year-old son were causing
  problems. Sometimes all three children would refuse to go to
  school, and they frequently stayed out late at night. *He* had become the leader of a street gang.

  Her two teenaged girls and her eight-year-old son were causing
  problems. Sometimes all three children would refuse to go to
  school, and they frequently stayed out late at night. The boy had
  become the leader of a street gang.

 b. Though they are presented as keepers of justice, the police on
  many television programs are cold-hearted killers. In one epi-
  sode last week I saw a person choked, another run down by a
  squad car, and four people shot to death. Instead of trying to
  solve a situation, *they* seem to shoot first and ask questions later.

  Though they are presented as keepers of justice, the police on
  many television programs are cold-hearted killers. In one epi-
  sode last week I saw a person choked, another run down by a
  squad car, and four people shot to death. Instead of trying to
  solve a situation, the police on these programs seem to shoot
  first and ask questions later.

//

32. Put parallel content in parallel form.

Sentence parts that have parallel (similar) functions should be
expressed in parallel (similar) structures. When you put parallel
sentence parts in unparallel form, the form fights the meaning.
Readers will be grateful when the form of your sentences supports
their meaning.

 a. This summer I plan to work a little, go to school, see some old friends, as well as just sitting around.
 This summer I plan to work a little, go to school, see some old friends, and just sit around.

 b. I have been accused of being rough, hardheaded, and a thoughtless individual.
 I have been accused of being rough, hardheaded, and thoughtless.

 c. A person may pursue a goal at college, at a trade school, a military career, or in industry.
 A person may pursue a goal at college, at a trade school, in the military, or in industry.

NOTE: For more about parallel sentence structure, see chapters 10, 11, and 14.

33. Write in the active voice.

 When a sentence is written in the active voice, the subject performs the action; in passive voice sentences, the subject receives the action. "Carlos read the novel" is written in the active voice. "The novel was read by Carlos" is written in the passive voice. So is "The novel was read thoroughly."
 In general, prefer the active voice to the passive; it is more direct and forceful.

 a. The skills I need to master will be worked on.
 I will work on the skills I need to master.

 b. Finally, after two hours of bumbling, the pie was completed by Harriet.
 Finally, after two hours of bumbling, Harriet completed the pie.

 c. *I'm OK, You're OK* is a book worth reading. Time should be taken to read it thoroughly. Much self-confidence may be gained.
 I'm OK, You're OK is a book worth reading. Those who take time to read it thoroughly may gain much self-confidence.

Exceptions: Though you should usually write in the active voice, you might sensibly choose to write in the passive voice when:

 a. You do not know the actor of the sentence:
 It was determined that her brain cells were slowly being destroyed.

 b. You wish to focus on the action, not the actor:
 You are shown how to pace through a book at a rate two or more times your normal reading speed.

   c. The receiver of the action is more important than the actor:
     Roots, according to the paper, has been seen by approximately
     30 million people.

wordy

34. Tighten wordy sentences.

A wordy sentence is one that can be trimmed *without losing any meaning.* Sometimes you can tighten wordy sentences simply by deleting excess words; other times you'll need to restructure the sentence.

   a. Some of the mentally retarded can be taught to lead productive lives through training.
     Some of the mentally retarded can be trained to lead productive lives.
   b. A choice I made that seemed to surprise almost everyone I knew was when I separated from my husband and filed for divorce.
     When I separated from my husband and filed for divorce, I surprised almost everyone.
   c. The basic principle of a parochial school mainly involves that of receiving a good education along with discipline.
     Parochial schools provide a good education and a healthy dose of discipline.
   d. The males are classically known as being dumb jocks.
     The males are stereotyped as dumb jocks.
   e. Having a physical education major involves taking many science courses.
     Physical education majors must take many science courses.

NOTE: For more about wordiness, see chapter 12.

ob

35. Avoid overburdened sentences.

   a. This paper is a salute to all black women all over the nation who have suffered through almost unendurable hardships trying to keep their families together as a strong and united group in the face of a relentless oppression that confronted them in their day-to-day lives.
     This paper is a salute to all the black women of America who have suffered deeply as they tried to keep their families together in the face of relentless, day-to-day oppression.

b. As I walked through the front door, after nearly breaking my neck on what I thought were steps, only to find that they were rotten and infested with small white termites, I was stunned by the smell of death.

As I walked through the front door, after stumbling on the rotten, termite-infested steps, I was stunned by the smell of death.

Overburdened sentences are usually long, but long sentences aren't necessarily overburdened. When a sentence is overburdened, readers have trouble seeing how the parts relate to one another. When a long sentence is well-structured, the relationships among its parts are immediately clear to readers:

Every afternoon that I am at home and not otherwise occupied, I sneak down into the basement at one-thirty and hide there in the semi-darkness until three o'clock doing something that I don't really like to talk about.

NOTE: If you often write overburdened sentences, turn to the section on doublespeak in chapter 12.

DIALECT INTERFERENCE

This chapter is intended to help writers whose spoken dialect is interfering with their written English. A dialect, as you may already know, is a variety of spoken language typical of a regional or social group. For example, if you are from Appalachia, you may speak "Appalachian English," or if you're black, you may speak a dialect known as "Black English."

Writing, as you know, is nearly always done in standard English, a language accessible to the vast majority of English-speaking people. Dialects differ from standard English in two important ways, both of which can cause interference when a dialect speaker writes. First, a dialect has a system of pronunciation slightly different from that of standard English. Second, a dialect also has its own system of grammar that differs in small but noticeable ways from the grammar of standard English.

If you speak a dialect, your pronunciation may sometimes interfere with your writing. For example, if your dialect allows -ed to be dropped from the ends of words in speech, you may tend to omit -eds when you write. Grammatical differences between a dialect and standard English can also interfere with your writing. The grammar of your dialect may allow a sentence like "We on time for once" or "Harry type fifty words a minute," when standard written English requires "We are on time for once" or "Harry types fifty words a minute."

This chapter details common differences between some spoken dialects and standard written English. If you speak a dialect, you're probably already aware of some of these differences. Most dialect speakers are able to shift back and forth, depending on the situation, between dialect speech and standard speech. In very formal situations, or when speaking to people who don't speak the dialect, there's a tendency to shift to a more standard English. You can take advantage of whatever ability you already have to shift into standard English as you work to clear up writing problems caused by dialect interference. And you can use this chapter to increase that ability even further.

As you read this chapter you will notice that we assume that dialect English is "different from," not "inferior to" standard English. Years ago nearly everyone thought that dialect speech was just sloppy—that it differed from spoken standard English in totally unpredictable ways. But within the last twenty years linguists (scientists who study the ways people actually speak) have been steadily proving that the language of dialect speakers has a high degree of regularity. One linguist, William Labov, sums up these discoveries in a thought-provoking essay, "The Logic of Nonstandard English."* There he argues that nonstandard English is not illogical; it is just different from standard English. Nearly all linguists and a growing number of English professors agree with Labov.

As you work to conquer writing problems caused by dialect interference, don't allow yourself to lose confidence. The fact that you have these problems is *not* evidence that your mind works in illogical ways. It is merely evidence that your spoken dialect is interfering with your written English.

36. Problems with -*ed* Endings

Some writers have a problem with -*ed* endings of past tense verbs. They write "Lurleen *walk* home from school yesterday" instead of "Lurleen *walked* home." Or they write "As a supervisor, I am *charge* with the responsibility of evaluating my subordinates" or "After school the children were *suppose* to go straight home," when they should have written *"charged* with" and *"were supposed."* Occasionally a writer with this problem will add an -*ed* ending when it's not needed. One student, for example, wrote "A traffic violator was *founded* hung in his cell." The past tense of the verb "find" is "found," not "founded," but this student was so used to being corrected for leaving off -*ed*s that he threw in an extra one just to be safe.

The -*ed* problem is caused by an important difference between speaking and writing. Linguists (scientists who study how people actually speak) have discovered that nearly all speakers of English fail to pronounce -*ed* endings at least some of the time, and that some speakers drop their -*ed*s more often than others. Most speakers don't even notice that they have done this. The context of their sentences usually makes the past tense clear, so dropping -*ed*s in speech really doesn't matter much. But in written English those -*ed*s become conspicuous by their absence; a reader, unlike a listener, consciously misses them. If you tend to omit -*ed* endings in your writing, you need to become more aware of this difference between spoken and written English.

---

* William Labov, "The Logic of Nonstandard English," *Georgetown Monographs on Language and Linguistics,* vol. 22, 1969, pp. 1–22, 26–31.

Just being aware of the difference will help you some, and more experience in both reading and writing will reinforce your awareness. But luckily there is a faster way to attack the problem. The same linguists* who discovered that everyone drops at least some -ed endings in speech also discovered that people tend to drop these endings less frequently when they are speaking in formal situations. The most formal situation of all, they discovered, was reading out loud. Even if you drop many -ed endings in casual speech, you will tend to pronounce them when you read aloud. A possible solution to your problem, then, is to read your rough draft *out loud,* using a formal reading voice.

For practice, try reading these sentences out loud in a formal-sounding voice. *Don't* be careful to read exactly what's on the page, as you ordinarily would when proofreading. Read the sentences the way you would say them in a very formal voice.

The child is begging for attention and love which is deny her or him.
The agency assists the batter wife or husband with temporary housing and counseling.
She was scare out of her wits.
My grandmother use to run a hotel in Denver.
Last week I ask if he could get tickets for the Superbowl.

Did a formal reading voice help you to catch one -ed problem in each sentence? Did you read *denied* instead of *deny; battered wife* instead of *batter wife; scared* instead of *scare; used* instead of *use;* and *asked* instead of *ask?* If you read in the missing -eds, fine. A formal, out-loud reading of your rough drafts should help to correct your problem.

It's possible that you found some of the missing -eds but overlooked others. Linguists tell us that we're more likely to pronounce these word endings in some situations than in others. If the word following the -ed begins with a vowel (a,e,i,o,u), for example, we are more likely to pronounce the -ed than if the following word begins with a consonant. This matter is too technical for us to go into, but we mention it so you will understand why it is possible to catch some -ed problems and yet miss others.

If you have the -ed problem, don't let it bother you as you write your rough drafts. Just focus on what you have to say and keep

---

* Wm. Labov, *The Social Stratification of English in New York City* (Washington, D.C.: Center for Applied Linguistics, 1966). Walt Wolfram and Ralph Fasold, *The Study of Social Dialects in American English* (Englewood Cliffs, N.J.: Prentice-Hall, 1974).

your words flowing. There will be time enough later to fill in those missing -eds.

Proofread the following sentences for any -ed problems. Remember to use a formal, out-loud reading voice as you proofread.

1. Some of the children could be consider undernourished.
2. It was mention to me during the intermission.
3. Most of the characters have die by the end of the play.
4. I was surprise at the way he responded.
5. He beated her up so badly that he was thrown in jail.
6. Everything about the place has change since last year.
7. I already explain it.
8. The cost of bread has increase because of the increase cost of flour.
9. Though it was below freezing, I walk three miles to the hospital.
10. It's suppose to last for a lifetime, but it broke after a week.
11. He looked like a scare rabbit.
12. It happen to her when she was only eight years old.
13. Jack talk about the situation and then try to clear up the problem.
14. The story capture my imagination.
15. The police follow him until he stop and pull over to the side of the road.

37. Problems with -s Endings

If you have a problem with -s endings, it may be caused by dialect interference. Actually there are three distinct ways in which a spoken dialect can lead to -s problems in written English. Let's treat them one at a time.

We'll begin with verbs. Two linguists, Ralph Fasold and Walt Wolfram,* tell us that dialect speakers omit the -s endings from some verbs for grammatical reasons. When a dialect speaker says "He talk too much for his own good" instead of "He talks too much for his own good," the -s has been omitted because the grammar of the dialect doesn't require it. It's not that the dialect speaker fails to pronounce the -s. The -s is not there to be pronounced.

---

* *The Study of Social Dialects in American English* (Englewood Cliffs, N.J.: Prentice-Hall, 1974), p. 154.

Let us show you how present-tense verbs of one dialect differ from those of standard English. In the following chart we show on the left how the present tense of "to work" is marked in the dialect; on the right is the standard English marking of the same verb:

the dialect		*standard English*	
I work	we work	I work	we work
you work	you work	you work	you work
he/she work	they work	he/she works	they work

Notice that in the dialect the forms of the verb have been regularized: the verb is *work* throughout. But in standard English, the third person singular (he/she/it) is irregular: *works* instead of *work*.

In another dialect, the markings of present-tense verbs differ from the standard English markings in this way:

the dialect		*standard English*	
I work	we work	I work	we work
you work	you work	you work	you work
he/she works	the men works	he/she works	the men work
	the women works		the women work

This dialect has extended the rule of standard English. In standard English, only the third person singular (he/she/it) verb is marked with an -*s*; in the dialect, the third person singular *and* plural verbs are sometimes marked with an -*s*.

Occasionally a writer who is conscious of leaving -*s* endings off of verbs may supply them where they don't belong, as in "I goes to the movies at least once a week." This may be "hypercorrection"—overcorrecting the dialect in an effort to be safe. Standard English requires the -*s* ending for present-tense verbs in the third person singular *only:*

I go	we go
you go	you go
he/she/it goes	they go

Though most -*s* problems have to do with verbs, two other kinds of dialect interference may also create a problem. In at least one dialect, possession is not shown by *s* plus an apostrophe: "She welcomed her husband death." Standard written English requires both the apostrophe and the *s* to indicate possession: "She welcomed her husband's death." If you find yourself omitting the apostrophe and the *s*, as in "Harry car" or "Richard Wright story" or "Alice friend," make the corrections as you proofread: "Harry's car," "Richard Wright's story," "Alice's friend."

Some dialect speakers occasionally omit the -s ending from plural nouns, as in "He bought six book" or "They were my friend" or "I had to work two job to support my family." Standard English requires an -s to mark most plural nouns: "six books," "my friends," "two jobs." There are certain exceptions, however, that can cause problems for dialect speakers, since the exceptions may lead to hypercorrection. Speakers who are conscious of leaving the -s endings off of nouns sometimes add them unnecessarily, as in *childrens, womens, peoples, feets.* The standard English plurals of these irregular nouns are not marked with -s: *children, women, people, feet.*

In spite of all this talk about -s endings, we'd like to caution you not to worry about -s's as you write your rough draft. Save your concern for the proofreading stage of the writing process. If you are plagued with the problem, you might do one last proofreading just to catch those slippery s's.

Proofread the following sentences for problems with -s endings:

1. The girl father was a doctor.
2. He seem to be doing well.
3. The story illustrate how one man, Howard, overcame his physical handicap.
4. In most instance the people do not pay attention to his sermons.
5. Poe stories can be read in one sitting.
6. Al travel to South Carolina once every two weeks.
7. Whenever he get a chance, he like to try to speak French.
8. Though I am forty years old, many time I am called a "girl."
9. The average farmer expenses have doubled in the past ten years.
10. The movie last only twenty minutes.
11. The film give the viewer a new way of looking at the Civil War.
12. Old peoples are not respected in today world.
13. Steve main problem is that he can't spell.
14. Many new career have opened up in the medical field.
15. He believe in justice for all peoples.

38. Problems with Omitted Words

Most writers carelessly omit a word every once in a while, like this:

It would be far more pleasant for if I could be accepted on the same basis as Charlie.

The writer meant to write "pleasant for *me*," but forgot to write the *me*. Perhaps this was just a slip of the pen, or maybe the writer's thoughts were racing ahead of his pen. But whatever the cause, careless omissions like these are easy enough to catch with careful proofreading.

There are other omissions, however, that are not quite so easy to catch. These are omissions that can be traced to dialect interference. In some dialects certain helping verbs required by standard English may be omitted. For example, standard English requires "I have gone there" or "I've gone there," but some dialects allow the *have* or the *'ve* to be omitted: "I gone there." Linguists Ralph Fasold and Walt Wolfram* have an interesting explanation for this difference between the dialect and standard English. It turns out that if standard English allows a contraction (for example, *I've* for "I have," *he'll* for "he will," or *they're* for "they are"), then the dialect sometimes omits the helping verb altogether. It's as if the dialect had "contracted" the contraction down to nothing.

Below we list several sentences with omissions that resulted from dialect interference. For each sentence, we then list two versions that are acceptable in standard written English.

dialect	*standard English*
I gone there lots of times.	I've gone there lots of times.
	I have gone there lots of times.
He go there tomorrow.	He'll go there tomorrow.
	He will go there tomorrow.
They over there all the time.	They're over there all the time.
	They are over there all the time.
He good.	He's good.
	He is good.
She be promoted next month.	She'll be promoted next month.
	She will be promoted next month.

Proofread the following sentences for omissions.

1. It a subject most people don't want to talk about.
2. You're nervous because you been in school only a short time.
3. I don't think it fair.

---

* *The Study of Social Dialects in American English* (Englewood Cliffs, N.J.: Prentice-Hall, 1974), p. 158.

4. Do you know someone who be good for the job?
5. They can't read as well as they supposed to.
6. In the opening lines, he saying that he afraid of death.
7. He be here in a few minutes.
8. In the movie she displaying all her talents.
9. Before you know it, it full of fish.
10. She mainly a career woman.

39. Miscellaneous Problems

39a. Standard English requires the use of the word *an* before nouns that begin with vowels (a, e, i, o, u). Some spoken dialects do not.

dialect	*standard English*
a orange, *a* apple	*an* orange, *an* apple

39b. Standard English does not allow the repetition of the subject of the sentence, as do some dialects.

dialect	*standard English*
That teacher, *she* likes me.	That teacher likes me.
My father, *he* works in Detroit.	My father works in Detroit.

39c. Standard English requires the word *there* instead of *it* in sentences like this one, which are acceptable in some dialects: "It's a man in my class that I like very much."

dialect	*standard English*
It's a supermarket at the end of the street.	*There's* a supermarket at the end of the street.
Is it a Methodist church in this town?	*Is there* a Methodist church in this town?

39d. Standard English does not allow the use of *they* to indicate possession, as do some dialects. Standard English uses *their*.

dialect	*standard English*
Mary and Mike brought *they* stereo to our house.	Mary and Mike brought *their* stereo to our house.

The three little kittens lost	The three little kittens lost
they mittens.	*their* mittens.

39e. Standard English requires the words *whether* and *if* in sentences like the following:

dialect	*standard English*
I wonder is he going.	I wonder *if* he is going.
Ask him can you do it.	Ask him *whether* you can do it.

39f. Standard English does not permit the double negatives that are allowed in some dialects.

NOTE: In standard English the word *hardly* counts as a negative.

dialect	*standard English*
They don't know nothing about it.	They don't know anything about it.
I can't hardly believe it.	I can hardly believe it.

39g. Standard English does not recognize a use of the verb *be* that occurs in at least one dialect.

In this dialect *be* can be used to refer to an action stretched out in time. A simple translation into standard English is not possible, as can be seen from the following examples:

dialect	*standard English*
He be working hard.	Does *not* mean "He is working hard." Means "He works hard habitually."
She be sick.	Does *not* mean "She is sick." Means "She has been sick for some time and continues to be sick."
They be waiting for me to make a mistake.	Does *not* mean "They are waiting for me to make a mistake." Means "Habitually, they have been waiting and continue to wait for me to make a mistake."

NOTE: This use of the verb *be* should not be confused with the dialect rule allowing contractions to be dropped in a sentence like "They be here soon," which means "They'll be here soon." See the section on "Problems with Omitted Words" under "Dialect Interference" for further information. (38)

Proofread the following sentences for problems caused by dialect interference.

1. Some of the student work full time.
2. Jill was dress up for the party.
3. Where you been lately?
4. As far as I'm concern, he's innocent.
5. I'd like to know who stole they car.
6. Her childrens were born two year apart.
7. My job keep me very busy.
8. Did you see a ostrich at the zoo?
9. They be ready in a few minutes.
10. I worried unnecessarily because my answer prove to be correct.
11. Jack been living there since 1975.
12. Student with good grades can get tutoring jobs.
13. The carp is place on a board and cook in the oven for an hour.
14. Your sister, did she win the tennis match?
15. I feel faint. Is it a place where I can sit down?
16. There are two basic method of preparing hard shell crabs.
17. Larry founded out too late.
18. If you give him a raise, he be happy.
19. It doesn't seem like the kind of story that Flannery O'Connor usually write.
20. Ask him is it suppose to rain tomorrow.
21. Suzanne be sick.
22. When she was young my daughter ask me all kinds of strange questions.
23. Their argument don't amount to nothing.
24. Last week she fix up my brother room for my grandmother.
25. This story tell about a young man who destroys a house.

PART VII
A List of Writing Topics

WRITING TOPICS

A. THE WORLD OF WORK

1. Describe your job as it is. Then explain how the job could be made more meaningful to you. How could it be changed to make you feel more dignified, more responsible, more important, and so on?

2. Explain any difficulties that may be involved in getting into the profession or vocation you've chosen. Describe the obstacles that lie in your way.

3. Do you like the work you are doing? Why or why not?

4. If you know what work you'd like to do in the future, explain why this sort of work appeals to you.

5. Describe someone you know who is trapped in a profession or a job which he or she finds wholly unsatisfactory. How does his or her work affect the rest of that person's life? (This person could be yourself, of course.)

6. Interview someone who does work that she or he finds interesting or exciting. Shape the results of your interview into a paper focused as you choose.

7. Have you rejected a career you might have liked because pursuing it seems too demanding, with too many hassles and barriers to overcome? Explain.

8. Have you encountered any difficulties at work because of competition with someone of another race or sex, or has this happened to anyone you know? Write about the feelings involved or the resolution of the situation, or both.

9. A problem for working mothers is adequate child care. Investigate what, if anything, your community is doing about child care and

report what you learn. Include suggestions for further action in your paper if you like.

10. What kinds of work do you think your talents, your personality, and your temperament suit you for?

11. Do you think homosexuals should be barred from any jobs? If so, what jobs would you specify, and why?

12. Examine in a paper some popular stereotypes or images of persons in your chosen profession. Comment on how you feel about these.

13. Write about the way a particular job has been glamorized. Contrast the job's image with reality.

14. If you have ever talked with a school or college counselor who seemed prejudiced against your pursuing the work you want to do because "men (or women) don't usually do that sort of work," describe how the counseling session went.

15. Are there features of your job which encourage you to treat customers or clients as though they were not really people? (For example, a nurse or a doctor might be tempted to look at a person as a disease or a cluster of symptoms.) If your job encourages you to so treat the people you come in contact with, does this fact affect you in any way?

16. Is college necessary to get a job that pays well?

17. Do some reading about the rate of unemployment among different age groups. Why does whatever variation you find exist—and how does this or how will this affect you or someone close to you?

18. If you feel that you have been discriminated against, either as a minority person or as a woman, in the world of work—in hiring, in assignments, in promotion, in firing, and so forth—describe the situation. How did you handle it? Were you satisfied with your handling of it? If not, what do you wish you had done differently?

19. What effect does prolonged joblessness have on a person's self-image? If possible, make this topic come alive by talking with someone who has been out of work for a long time.

20. Interview someone who lived through the Great Depression. Shape this topic as you see fit.

21. To what extent does the world of work you inhabit allow you to be a human being? In what ways, if any, does your job tend to dehumanize you?

22. Did or do you have difficulty finding role models of the same sex as yourself in the work you want to do? Where and how have you sought such models? Where else might you look? How much do you feel you need such reinforcement?

23. Have you, or has anyone you know, ever been the victim of "reverse discrimination"—in hiring, promotion, firing, and so forth—because of not being either a member of a minority group or a woman? If you know of such an experience, write about it, and include how you feel about this issue.

24. In the world of work, such concepts as flexitime, share-a-job, and other innovations to better fit the scheduling needs of a variety of persons are becoming popular. Try to talk with someone who is working under such an arrangement, and write a paper about some specific ways in which such practices meet human needs. Or, if you know of arguments sometimes used by employers against instituting such practices, try to counter those arguments.

B. EDUCATION

1. Robert Frost said, "We come to college to get over our littlemindedness." How, if at all, does this observation relate to your experience with college so far? Cite specific examples of ways in which you feel "expanded"—if you do.

2. Describe something specific about your child's schooling that you either approve or disapprove of. If you choose to work with the former, explain why you feel good about what you describe. If you choose the latter, try to think through in your paper what steps you might take to remedy the situation.

3. Choose an instructor—other than your freshman English instructor —from whom you are taking a course this semester. Describe in detail one class period (an actual one) in such a way as to communicate either your admiration or your distaste for his or her teaching style. No names, please.

4. If you have attended both parochial and public school, write a paper in which you express your feelings about both. If you like, continue your paper with a discussion of how you would like to see some elements of one kind of school incorporated into the other.

5. What courses are you planning to take as electives? How, if at all, do you foresee your selections being related to your use of leisure time, both now and in the future?

6. An ancient Greek scholar defined students as "lamps to be lighted, rather than vessels to be filled." A contemporary thinker from the East says, "Not to imitate—but to discover—that is education—is it not?" What do you think of these definitions? How, if at all, do they fit your learning experiences at college so far?

7. Write an objective letter to one of your instructors suggesting changes he or she should make in his or her teaching. Assume that the instructor is interested in improving.

8. Have you ever taken a course taught primarily with programmed (self-teaching) materials—through either machines or books? If so, did you enjoy the course? Why or why not? How effective did you feel the method was as a learning experience?

9. Write a paper in which you either support or argue against one of the following statements found in an article entitled, "Some Common Beliefs about Education": (a) "Teaching is telling." (b) "Answers are more important than questions." (c) "Learning is preparing to live."

10. Choose a course which you're enjoying (other than freshman English!). In a paper, convince a friend to sign up for it next semester.

11. Why are you in college? Do some really hard self-examination before you write this paper; it could be a very important one for you.

12. If you've attended school in another country, contrast some aspect of that country's educational system with an aspect of ours.

13. If one of your instructors gave a lecture this week, summarize it for a friend who missed class.

14. Comment in a paper on the following: Someone once asked the Greek philosopher Aristotle: "What's the difference between being educated and being uneducated?" Aristotle replied: "The same difference as between being alive and being dead." What do you think Aristotle meant? Would you agree or disagree with him? Relate his comment to *your* experience with education.

15. Accompany an instructor (or an administrator) through at least half of his or her day. What did you learn about this person and his or her job?

C. RELIGION

1. Write a 50- to 100-word summary of last week's sermon, commenting on it if you wish.

2. If you are a Jew or a Christian, describe your concept of God to a person from another culture—someone completely unfamiliar with the Judeo-Christian tradition.

3. What kind of religious instruction, if any, do you plan to provide for your children?

4. What is the value of prayer, as you see it?

5. Do you disagree with your church's position on any important issue? Defend your own position on that issue.

6. Should prayer be allowed in public schools?

7. Should women be ordained?

8. If you have recently converted to a religion (or to atheism), explain what led you to convert.

9. If your religious beliefs differ from those of your parents, contrast the two sets of beliefs.

10. Take a careful look at the Ten Commandments (Exodus, chapter 20). Which of these commandments do you feel are important rules for twentieth-century Americans to live by? Why? Or which are rules you personally want to live by? Why?

11. What is your attitude toward the concepts of heaven and hell?

12. Write a humorous description of either heaven or hell.

13. Talk with someone who is heavily involved in an Eastern religion or in the Jesus Movement. Write about your conversation.

14. If your religious beliefs have remained generally the same since childhood, have you examined those beliefs independently, on your own? If you have not, and you feel any need or desire to do so, write a paper in which you conduct such an examination.

15. Read some portion of Mark Twain's *Letters to the Earth*, a religious satire, and comment on it in a paper. Attach to your paper a xeroxed copy of the portion you read.

16. Alfred North Whitehead, British mathematician and philosopher, says that religion is "what we do with our solitude." Write a paper in which you either support or refute that statement.

17. Read about Situation Ethics (see, for example, books on the subject by Thomas Fletcher and James Pike), and make a statement about how that approach to "living religiously" strikes you *for your own life*.

18. Are the women and the men in your church expected to serve it in different kinds of ways, or are all areas of participation equalized? Discuss how you view whatever situation does exist in your own church.

19. Is your church racially segregated in any way? If so, discuss how you feel about this. If you are against such segregation, in what way are you actively involved in opposing it?

20. If you have firsthand experience with some non-Protestant or non-Catholic religion in America (for example, Quaker, American Indian, Black Muslim, Jewish), explain some of the basic tenets of your religion to someone who knows nothing about it.

21. Read Herman Hesse's *Siddhartha*, a short novel about a young Indian searching for spiritual understanding. Write a character study of the young Siddhartha.

22. Examine the story of Adam and Eve in Genesis from a feminist viewpoint. Be sure to look at *both* accounts of the creation of man and woman, the one at the end of chapter 1 and the one at the beginning of chapter 2. Focus on some portion of the whole Adam and Eve story, and write a feminist analysis of it.

23. Write a paper in which you compare the Judeo-Christian account of the Creation (in Genesis) with the account in some other religion—perhaps Hindu or Mormon or American Indian. Ask a librarian to help you locate other accounts.

D. VIOLENCE AND STRESS

1. Write about an experience, either positive or negative, that you have had with guns.

2. Write about how violence is glamorized in the media. Use specific television programs, advertisements, films, newspaper items, or comic strips to illustrate your insights.

3. If you have served in a war, write about a personal experience with violence.

4. Argue that marijuana can be a healthy escape from stress. Or argue that it is a dangerous kind of escapism.

5. How might a family provide harmless outlets for the aggressive impulses of children? Of adults?

6. If you have seen a violent movie recently, describe the movie in a way that emphasizes the violence—to show how ridiculous the violence is, or how sordid or how painful.

7. Do you usually try to *avoid* stress? If so, examine in a paper what such avoidance may cost you in missed opportunities or any other loss.

8. Describe a burst of anger that someone recently loosed on you. How did *you* feel? How do you explain the other person's behavior?

9. Discuss a decision that you must make in the near future—one that is causing you considerable anxiety and stress.

10. Are fear and hatred two sides of the same coin? If you think they are, develop a paper on whatever connection you see between them. Use some real-life examples to clarify your theory.

11. There have been many complaints about violence in the news media. In your opinion, should unpleasant, disgusting or painful pictures appear in newspapers or on television?

12. If you use sports, taking a walk or a leisurely bath, working in the yard, or some other specific measure to relieve stress, write about how the activity helps you, including how you first discovered it as a stress reliever.

13. A number of modern phenomena are cited as possible causes of the high level of violence in contemporary society—among them noise pollution, urban density (too little living and breathing space for individuals), and violence in the various media. Select one such possible contributing factor, preferably one you yourself have had to deal with, and discuss how its effect might be diminished.

14. Some people hold that rape is a crime of violence (caused by hostility and anger), rather than a crime of sexual passion. Analyze this interpretation of rape.

15. If you see a rape as a crime of violence (see topic 14), what steps could be taken to reduce the incidence of this crime?

16. Discuss the possible relation between personal hostility and public violence.

17. If you tend to repress frustration and anger instead of externalizing them, do you see any danger in that practice? If violent explosions are not your style, can you think of other, constructive ways of relieving yourself of such stress?

18. Movies in which women are abused in some way have increased in recent years. Although such films are often advertised as being "sexy," they may in fact have more to do with violence than with sex (or love). If you have seen any movies that might be analyzed in this way, write about one of them as an expression of violence.

19. Write a humorous essay in which you show that certain fairy tales, or some other stories intended for children, are perversely violent.

E. THE ARTS AND CREATIVITY

1. Take your reader on a tour of an art museum you have visited. Write the paper to encourage a visit by your reader.

2. If you are in a position to encourage creativity in other persons in any way, how do you go about doing so?

3. Write about the achievements of a favorite artist, musician, or writer. Explain why the work of this particular person especially

appeals to you. Or explain why you think his or her accomplishment is especially significant.

4. Argue that your city should establish a special high school for the arts.

5. If you plan to enter the world of art—for example, as a painter, sculptor, musician, dancer, actor, or writer—describe the frustrations and difficulties you anticipate. Or describe the joys. Or weigh the advantages against the disadvantages, and explain your decision either for or against such a career.

6. Discuss your positive feelings about some art form—music, literature, the visual arts, dance, or theater. Write from the viewpoint of either a performer/participant or an appreciative observer.

7. Some people would discount the artistic contributions of various artists—writers, painters, dancers, and so on—because of the sometimes unorthodox ways in which they conduct their personal lives. How does this position strike you? Argue either for or against this viewpoint, citing specific artists in your argument.

8. If you can recall the first time you went to professional theater, describe your experience to someone who has never been, with the idea of encouraging that person to see a play.

9. If listening to classical music is a fulfilling experience for you, describe what happens during the experience, and why it is important to you.

10. Have you ever felt "taken out of yourself" while looking at some piece of visual art—a painting, a piece of sculpture, or a photograph, for example? If so, describe the experience.

11. Some people do not acknowledge that photography is an art form. If you are especially interested in photography, defend it as art.

12. During periods of recession, when schools trim their budgets, activities related to the arts are often among the first eliminated. Either support or argue against such priorities in education.

13. A Persian poem advises: "If you have but two pence in your dole/ Spend one for a loaf of bread/The other for hyacinths to feed your soul." Argue either for or against following this advice.

14. In our country, there are many scholarship opportunities for students with high academic standing or athletic prowess, but far fewer for those who show promise or creativity in the arts. Would you or would you not encourage more such endowments for artistic development?

15. If you are especially interested in the cultural opportunities your community does—or does not—offer, what can you do to increase such opportunities?

F. ECOLOGY AND NATURAL LIVING

1. Describe your neighborhood as it is. Then describe how you would improve it if you had the power to make it more beautiful and more livable. Use enough details so that your reader can visualize the changes you suggest.

2. One of the by-products of nuclear energy is plutonium in a form readily usable for creating a devastating bomb. In light of that fact, argue either for or against the production of nuclear energy.

3. If you are particularly concerned about the preservation of our natural resources for any reason or purpose, what are you doing to contribute to or promote such conservation? If you are not now doing anything, what might you do?

4. If you are happy in the neighborhood where you live, explain why. Take care not to be so emotional in your description and your support that a reader might lose respect for your writing on account of its oversentimentalizing.

5. It is not at all clear that nuclear power plants now in operation include adequate safeguards against dangerous pollution of our living environment. In light of that fact, argue for or against the production of nuclear energy. If you argue against production, be sure to inform yourself about the advantages of nuclear energy, so that you can counter them.

6. If you or someone you know is utilizing solar energy in any way, describe that utilization.

7. Write an article about a natural foods store in your community.

8. Criticize the food served by a particular school, hospital, or other institution—from a nutritional standpoint.

9. Select some area other than your own neighborhood and describe how you would redesign it to make it more pleasant and functional for human beings. You might work with one block, part of one street, a shopping center, or an entire residential area.

10. How would ordinary Americans have to change their living habits if our government were to decide seriously to combat pollution and environmental decay?

11. Give your reader advice on vegetable gardening.

12. If you are especially interested in solar energy, write a paper explaining how you would use it in a house, a place of business, or some other structure.

13. Write a critique of your school cafeteria, a fast-food chain, or a local restaurant.

14. Sometimes a piece of land is considered for zoning either for industrial purposes or as a national park. Discuss the factors that you feel should take priority when such zoning decisions are made.
15. Tell your reader how to care for some particular variety of indoor plant.
16. Describe soul food (or some other specialized kind of food) to someone completely unfamiliar with it.
17. Write a critique of your local supermarket.
18. Do you know anyone who has "returned to the land" to live? How does he or she feel about this new way of life?
19. Do you know anyone who "moved to the land" and then decided to return to city or suburban life? Why did he or she return?
20. Show your reader that he or she can save money, or be better off nutritionally, or both, by substituting fresh foods for canned, frozen, or ready-mix foods.
21. If you or anyone you know has been involved in a wilderness survival program, such as Outward Bound, describe the program and the participant's response to it.
22. Read some of *Small Is Beautiful* by E. F. Schumacher, a book about appropriate technology, and apply his theory to a specific instance, arguing either in support of or against Schumacher. The theory might be phrased: What is needed is not mindless growth, but programs that are tailored to the culture, resources, and aspirations of a particular region.

G. DEATH AND DYING

1. If you fear death, either describe your fear or attempt to explain why it exists.
2. If you do not fear death, explain why.
3. If you have ever had a close call with death, describe the experience, trying to focus on your reaction to it.
4. How would you inform a child of the death of a loved one? Write from personal experience if possible.
5. How do you think you would react to the news that you had only one year to live? What would you do with that year?
6. Do you think there are any situations in which suicide is a rational act?
7. Write about the death of someone you loved, if you can do that without oversentimentalizing.

8. Choose a religion such as Judaism, Christianity, Hinduism, Buddhism, or Unitarianism and explain how that religion deals with the fact of death.

9. Talk with someone who has worked on a hotline. Ask him or her about the reasons people seem to have for considering suicide.

10. If you had a friend or a relative who was suffering a great deal—say from an automobile accident or from cancer—what would you do for or say to him or her?

11. Should parents have the power to decide whether a deformed or mentally defective child should be allowed to live?

12. Should a child be allowed to visit his or her dying parent in the hospital?

13. Write out instructions for how your body is to be handled after your death—a traditional funeral, a memorial service, cremation, donation to medical research, or whatever.

14. Albert Camus has written that there is only one genuine philosophical problem: whether to commit suicide. He claims that if you think seriously about this question, you either commit suicide or you will have discovered a reason for living. If you have thought seriously about Camus's question and have not chosen suicide, why not?

15. Patients suffering from terminal cancer are sometimes given LSD under special supervision. How do you feel about this practice?

16. If you have ever known someone who knew he or she was dying, describe that person's resistance to and/or acceptance of the fact of death.

17. Describe a funeral that you attended recently, so that your reader will understand how you felt about the ceremony.

18. Is suicide immoral? Why or why not?

19. Have you ever known anyone who was dying? Describe your own reaction to his or her impending death. What did you do and say?

20. If you plan to work with the sick and dying (as a nurse, doctor, hospital technician, clergyman, or whatever), what do you think you can do to ease the suffering of a patient?

21. Should passive euthanasia be legalized? Passive euthanasia involves *allowing* someone to die, by withholding certain medication or by not utilizing life-continuing machines, for example.

22. Should active euthanasia be legalized? Active euthanasia involves *helping* someone to die, by administering certain drugs, or by "pulling the tubes," for example.

23. If you know of a culture other than our own that has an attitude toward death that interests you, write about that attitude.

24. Read the first seven chapters of Elisabeth Kubler-Ross's well-known book *On Death and Dying*. Summarize what she says for someone who has not read the book.
25. Would you rather die in a hospital or at home? Why?
26. If you could be alive to write your own obituary, what would you want it to say? What are you actually doing in your day-to-day life to help guarantee that obituary for yourself?

H. JUSTICE

1. Write about some inequity in our judicial system. Use at least one true anecdote to illustrate the inequity.
2. What, if anything, are prisons good for?
3. Learn what you can about the movement for prisoners' rights, if you can get a lead on this issue. Write a paper about your feelings on the issue. Should persons being punished for lawbreaking *have* any civil rights? If so, how extensive should they be?
4. Try to find out what kind of vocational rehabilitation is offered to prisoners (both men and women) in a facility near you. Is it realistic, in view of the employment likely to be available to such a person once he or she has been released?
5. If you can talk to someone who works in either a public or a private employment agency about the particular difficulties an exprisoner has in finding employment, write a paper on your findings. How do you think prejudice against exprisoners could be decreased?
6. Have you ever been in jail? If so, write about the impact of this experience on you.
7. Show that comparable activities are unjustly labeled as "lawful" or "criminal," depending on a person's status (age, social position, sex, color, religion, professional position, and so on).
8. Write about a time when you were the victim of a crime.
9. Interview a police officer—or better yet, accompany the officer on his or her beat. What did you learn about the officer, or the job, or both?
10. Why are our prisons filled with a disproportionate number of black persons?
11. Write about the theme of justice in the Book of Job, from the Old Testament. Why does Job question God's justice? What conclusions, if any, does the author come to about God's justice? (Warning: the reading is difficult.)

12. A profound question raised by philosophers, theologians, and creative writers is, "Why do good men suffer?" If you have a pat, easy, conventional answer, skip this topic—great minds have anguished over it. But if you've given the question serious thought, put your speculations on paper, even if you come up with no conclusions.

13. Read Albert Camus's *The Plague*, a difficult and depressing novel. Write about the author's view on cosmic justice.

14. In what areas of your life are you called upon to act as judge (for example, as a parent or as a supervisor)? What problems do you face in being just?

15. Write about revenge. Why is it such a powerful human emotion? You should definitely narrow this topic in some way. For example, you could write about vengeance in a movie you've seen, or about vengeance in Vietnam, or about a personal experience with vengeance.

16. Do you believe in capital punishment? If so, for what specific crimes? And what are your arguments for it?

17. If you do not believe in capital punishment, what do you see as appropriate retribution for those who commit heinous crimes—for example, a three-time murderer or a person convicted of rape several times? Defend your answer as if you were arguing with someone who did believe in capital punishment in such instances.

18. Read enough in *The Crime of Punishment* by Karl Menninger to be able to explain in a paper Menninger's concept of how scapegoating figures in our crime and punishment system.

19. What alternatives to our present punishment system of committing lawbreakers to traditional "holding facilities"—local jails, state and federal prisons, and so on—can you think of? Try to find out about some of these alternatives—halfway houses, provisions for families to continue to live together, adoption of paroled persons into a regular family home, and so forth—and report on your findings. Would you favor more widespread use of such alternatives? If so, how would you promote their use?

I. SPORTS/EXERCISE

1. If you are very good at a team sport, summarize your qualifications to impress a coach or a scholarship committee.

2. If you've coached a team, describe the rewards and frustrations of the experience.

3. Write about the physical dangers of some popular sport such as football.

4. Describe the violence of some sport such as ice hockey.

5. Argue that schools should emphasize sports that any individual can participate in and benefit from throughout his or her life (for example, swimming, bowling, tennis), instead of such sports as football and basketball.

6. Should high school (or college) sports programs spend as much money on girls' sports as on boys'?

7. Write about the high cost of some sport such as skiing.

8. Write a letter to your local TV news program suggesting any improvements you'd like to see in their sports coverage. Or write a letter praising their sports coverage.

9. Explain why you admire a favorite sports figure.

10. Write about the extreme discipline required for ballet as a dance form, or for a sport like gymnastics.

11. Write about some program that uses sports or physical activity as therapy for persons with physical, mental, or social handicaps.

12. Write a humorous description of a sport.

13. If you're familiar with a sport popular in another culture, such as cricket, describe the sport to American readers.

14. Write a paper about the exaggerated language of sportscasters and sports reporters.

15. Show that major league sports have become big business—that "the name of the game" is money.

16. Show that there is a correlation between feeling in control of one's body (often acquired through good physical education training in youth) and a general feeling of self-confidence. Describe persons you know as both positive and negative examples to support your point; (don't use real names).

17. Think about whether your lifestyle involves enough physical activity at work or during your leisure time to keep you healthy. If it does not, write a paper about a plan you could follow to remedy this situation.

J. GROWING OLD

1. Write a paper about someone you know who has aged in a way that you admire and respect.

2. *The Coming of Age*, a book by Simone de Beauvoir, contains an interesting chapter on "old age in historical societies." Read this chapter and summarize it for someone who hasn't the time to read it.

3. We live in a relatively age-segregated society. Examine both the advantages and the disadvantages of this segregation.

4. We hear much about the disadvantages of growing old. Talk to some older person (65 or more) about some possible *advantages* of age. Write a paper about these advantages.

5. Be alert to how older people (about 60 or older) are portrayed on television. Does stereotyping occur? Watch enough situation comedies and similar programs to be able to describe two or three stereotypes.

6. Find out whether your college has a continuing education program for senior citizens. If it does, try to get some retired person you know, who seems to need new interests in life, involved in the program. Follow this person's participation in the program long enough to be able to write up an evaluation of how well the program served the person.

7. If you know of some especially good community program for senior citizens, describe that program to readers who might be interested in taking advantage of it.

8. Write about a close friendship you have with someone who is much older (or younger) than you are. What have you gained from this friendship that you could not have received from someone your own age?

9. Describe someone you know (over 65) who defies the commonly accepted assumption that old age is horrible.

10. Do you think about growing old? If you do, what inner resources are you developing against the inevitable diminishing of your physical resources as you age?

K. RACE AND ETHNIC IDENTITY

1. Describe someone you know who has lost his or her ethnic character in the attempt to assimilate himself or herself into the mainstream of American culture.

2. Write a jazzy description of "soul."

3. Write a positive description of your ethnic background—Italian, Polish, Irish, and so on.

4. Write about features of your ethnic background that you are (or were) ashamed of.

5. If you have had an experience of interracial or intercultural dating, write about that experience.

6. If you experience a culture conflict between your world of work or school and the world of your friends, describe your feeling of being trapped in the middle. Do you feel like a chameleon changing color to fit your surroundings? Or do you function smoothly in both worlds?

7. Describe a stereotype of any ethnic group of people, and then assess its accuracy.

8. Have you ever been stereotyped? Describe how you felt.

9. What picture of American Indians, black Americans, Italian Americans, Southern whites, Chinese, or other minority group is presented in movies or television dramas, or both? Limit this topic radically, perhaps by discussing the image of one of these groups as presented in one film or one TV series.

10. It is often said that the liberation struggle of the black woman and the white woman differ. If you are a woman: Whichever race you are, talk about this question with a woman of the other race, and report your findings in a paper.

L. MEN AND WOMEN

1. Write about the way a television series depicts male-female relationships.

2. If you have lived in another culture, contrast the position of women in that culture with the status of women in our own. Or simply focus on the position of women in the other culture.

3. Should priests be allowed to marry? Should nuns?

4. Should prostitution be legalized?

5. Write about the extremes to which some women will go to look beautiful.

6. Describe unfair tactics used by members of one sex to gain power over members of the opposite sex.

7. Do we need men's liberation?

8. Argue that men will benefit as much as women from women's liberation.

9. Are you acquainted with any couples in which the woman has a career and the man maintains the home (and looks after the children, if there are any)? If so, how does this arrangement strike you? Interview such a couple if you can. Shape your paper, from the interview, with whatever focus most interests you.

10. Would you consider living in an arrangement like the one described above? Why or why not?

11. If you are a woman, do you experience any conflicts or guilt about full-time wife-motherhood or full-time career or a combination of both? If so, how do you deal with these feelings?

M. MARRIAGE AND OTHER LIVING ARRANGEMENTS

1. What do you expect from marriage? Which of your expectations do you think are reasonable, and which are not?

2. If you've been married for some time, write a recommitment vow.

3. Write a marriage contract or a "temporary alliance" contract. Do this jointly with your partner.

4. Contrast the traditional roles of husband and wife with the new roles.

5. Compare and contrast your expectations of marriage with the reality.

6. If you would rather live with your partner unmarried, explain why you feel this way.

7. If you would rather marry than live together unmarried, explain why you feel this way.

8. Argue that homosexuality is (or is not) a sickness.

9. Argue that homosexuality is (or is not) immoral.

10. Describe the gay scene in your community, if you know enough to do so accurately.

11. Does one partner in a marriage have to be "boss"? Or can power and responsibility be shared?

12. Write about the problems of being married to a person of another faith.

13. Write about the problems of interracial or intercultural marriage.

14. What effect does divorce have on a woman who has not worked outside the home and who has no marketable skills?

15. How are men hurt by present divorce rulings?

16. Under what conditions, if any, should alimony be awarded to either spouse?

17. What is the position of your religion on the matter of divorce? To what extent do you agree?

18. If you know a gay couple who will talk freely with you, describe their day-to-day life together in a paper.

N. PARENTS AND CHILDREN

1. Do you plan to have children? Why or why not?

2. Which features of your personality suit you for parenthood? Which do not?

3. Describe the power relationship between you and one of your parents. How does your parent exercise power, and how do you wield it?

4. Try to imagine yourself as your own parent. What would you be worried about? What would you be proud of?

5. Describe someone you know who is, in your opinion, a bad parent, and explain why you so consider him or her.

6. Describe someone you know who is an ideal (or close to ideal) parent, and explain why you see him or her so positively.

7. Interview one of your parents on a particularly touchy subject, making a special effort to really *hear* what he or she is saying. Report on the experience.

8. Describe some older person in your family whom you would like to emulate as you grow older. Or describe someone you would not like to pattern yourself after.

9. Describe your efforts to make yourself independent of your parents.

10. Write a paper in which you discuss several ways in which parents might "program" their children toward stereotypical sex roles through their child-rearing practices.

11. Find out about family life in another culture, preferably by talking to someone who has experienced it firsthand. Report on your findings in an interesting, readable style.

12. How do you and your husband or wife divide child-rearing responsibilities? How satisfactory is this arrangement?

13. Write a character sketch of one of your children.

14. Write a love letter to one of your children, showing that child why you are glad you had him or her.

15. Show that it is easier for parents to gratify their children materially than spiritually.

16. Analyze as honestly as you can your motives for having had children, or for wanting to have them.

17. Contrast your expectations of motherhood (or fatherhood) with the reality as you have experienced it.

18. Are you sometimes too possessive of your children? If so, have you found ways of overcoming or minimizing this possessiveness?

19. Explain your philosophy of discipline, giving real examples of the kinds of rewards and punishments that you find workable and acceptable.

20. Should we have government-supported day care centers?

21. Do children lack certain basic rights in our society?

22. Do children have too many rights in our permissive society?

23. Write a paper based on the following statement: If you think raising a toddler is hard, wait until your child is a teen-ager.

24. Child abuse—what are its causes and what can be done about it? (You might want to deal with only one-half of this topic.)

25. What responsibilities do you think children have as their parents grow old?

26. Do you approve of interracial adoption? Why or why not?

27. Argue that in the event of divorce women should nearly always gain custody of the child, or that men should gain custody much more often than they do at present.

28. Write about the difficulties or satisfactions (or both) of being a single parent.

PART VIII
A Collection of Student Papers

STUDENT PAPERS

1. IRISH VS. AMERICAN EDUCATION

During my junior year of high school my family moved from a suburban
American community to a small village in rural Ireland. The change was a
very pleasant one once we got over the initial cultural shock, and we learned
a great deal from the visit. My biggest discoveries came from being enrolled
in the local convent, a school that was very different from my old high
school. The difference lay not in the subjects that were taught, but rather
in the way they were taught and the surroundings and atmosphere they
were taught in.

In contrast to my ordinary brick high school, the convent was a Gothic
mansion with tall, narrow windows and doors, vaulted ceilings and endless,
winding corridors. Included in the school uniforms were soft slippers that
wouldn't mar the marble floors or teak staircases. Not only were our steps
hushed, but the gloomy, ancient decor intimidated us into speaking in
whispers when walking along passageways. To run or yell in a hallway was
unthinkable.

Unlike its American counterpart, the convent was badly heated and had
almost none of the educational facilities or equipment believed necessary
in America. There was no cafeteria or food service. There were no science
labs (although my biology teacher *did* bring a dead frog one day and dis-
sected it for us). The home economics department consisted of one stove
and seven sinks. There was no library, really, just a box of paperback books
that the English teacher let us borrow from. There was one record player
for the entire school and a tape recorder that dated from World War II.

Strangely enough, instead of being academically inferior to my American
high school, the Irish convent was superior. In my class at home *Love
Story* was considered pretty heavy reading, so imagine my surprise at finding Irish students who could recite passages from *War and Peace*. In high
school we complained about having to study "Romeo and Juliet" in one
semester, whereas in Ireland we simultaneously studied "Macbeth" and

Dickens' *Hard Times,* in addition to writing a composition a day in English class. In high school I didn't even begin algebra until the ninth grade, while at the convent seventh graders (or their Irish equivalent) were doing calculus and trigonometry.

Not that the Irish were completely superior in educational standards. Many of the students at the convent had never even heard of chemistry, much less sex education. They knew by heart the exploits of Cuculain (a legendary Irish warrior) but knew nothing of Freud or Marx or any religion but their own. The average Irish student seemed to have a firm knowledge of the classics but was out of touch with the world of today.

The main reason for this contrast may be the way the classes were taught. In America the teacher is usually approachable and his or her teaching style is informal. The students feel relaxed and very often daily life is discussed, ranging anywhere from politics to personal problems. Unfortunately, some people take advantage of this and waste hours and hours of class time to the detriment of other students.

At the convent there was no disruption, no disorder, no wasted time. Classes ran smoothly and on a tight schedule. Unfortunately, this made for dull, regimented classes where tension ran very high. We stood when asked questions and fired off the answer as quickly as possible, never asking questions for fear of being singled out and drilled for lacking knowledge.

After experiencing these two systems of teaching, I am not sure which is the better one. Perhaps a combination of the two would be the best way —a system in which there is order and discipline but without suppression and fear.

2. IT WAS HALLOWEEN NIGHT

It was Halloween night. My husband was out for the evening, and all the kids were accounted for. I had distributed the ritual goodies to the ghosts and goblins who rang the bell, put the baby to bed, and settled down to read *Ragtime.* From the rec room downstairs came the booming beat of hard rock played at full volume, courtesy of my son, Pat, and his friends. At about ten o'clock, the stereo was mercifully quiet and they trooped out. Pat stopped to ask if he could go to Jack's house, two blocks away. "Okay," I said, "but don't be too late." Less than an hour later he was dead.

At around midnight in the police station, two detectives tried to piece together for his father and me what had happened. A carful of teenagers . . . A curve on a wet road . . . A blowout . . . Perhaps some beer . . . Ambulance . . . Helicopter . . . Trauma Center . . . . I listened without really hearing. I drank hot coffee, but it could not warm the icy numbness within me.

He was our second child. Born in the Indian summer of our fourth year of marriage, it was his impending arrival that made us decide to take the plunge and buy a house. I had hoped during that pregnancy that the baby would be a girl, but we were delighted with a healthy and beautiful second son. We named him for his grandfathers and took him home to meet his toddling older brother.

He grew up tall and straight; a bright student who did well in his sophomore classes. He loved the sea, and talked of becoming an oceanographer. He liked basketball, boats, biology and peanut butter, not necessarily in that order. He was, at once, very ordinary and very special. Now, incredibly, he was gone.

Death came like a thief in the night. He was so much a part of us; then, with no warning, he was snatched away, and with him all the hopes, the dreams, the plans. I wanted to cry, but could not. I felt nothing but that awful, empty coldness.

As the days and months passed, I tried to put his death into some kind of perspective. I searched for answers and found none. I wanted an explanation, but none was forthcoming. I accepted, with eternal gratitude, the love and support of family and friends, and through them I found a measure of peace.

I came to the realization that all any of us really has that is enduring is what we give to each other. Patrick gave us love and joy and hope, and these we still have. My only wish is that he knows, somehow, how very much we loved him, and how glad we are to have shared his life.

3. SOUL

Look, white brother, ya got no soul. No brother, I am not referring to your heart. I mean real down-to-earth soul. Nah man, I am not talking about soul food, like chittlings, hamhocks or pigs feet. I am talking 'bout soul, ya know? Rockin', grindin', windin', bindin', bumpin' soul. No, Lester, I do not mean to exercise. Brother, I am talking about something hip, mean, bad, out-a-sight. Lester, I did not say anything about a hippopotamus who can not see. Lester, you must be some type of nut. Lester, you are impossible. For heaven's sake, let's forget the whole thing.

LESTER! Why, why, why, must you think of going to church, because I mention the word heaven? Look, brother—and I say brother because brother is soul. No, Lester, I am not looking for my soul brother. Hey, cat, you are a trip. Lester, cat is only a word for man. Trip is only a phrase that pays. You dig? O.K. Let's start from the beginning. Brother, finger-snapping, do-it-to-it, movin'-and-a-groovin', yeh-yeh baby, hey-hey babe is soulful soul. Solid? Lester, what makes you think of a baby trying to snap his fingers. Man, your head is on lop-side-ed. Stop, Lester. I was only playing wit' ya. You can't screw your head back on straight. Lester, stop, stop! You are a real nut. No, Lester, I won't crack you open. O.K., Lester, lesson no. 1, don't take things so seriously. It's all a part of soul. Get hip, will ya? Mellow, man, mellow—take it in stride—cruise on, brother—more power to ya. Keep trying, LESTER, ya bound to overcome.

4. "POPSICLE"

It makes me laugh to hear you say that we "spoil" Chris because she's
handicapped—that we give her whatever she wants. Let me tell you what
the procedure is in teaching a 3-year-old deaf child one word.

One of the tools you need is a small table and chairs set so that the child
can get up and down easily. Children, generally, are unable to sit still for
long periods of time and get frustrated if they have difficulty climbing up
and down when they need a break. Deaf children have a particular problem
here since they do not expend the energy the rest of us do in talking.

Another necessary tool is a set of 3 × 5 cards that contain pictures of the
words that Chris has already mastered; i.e., pictures of her mom, dad and
sister, and pictures of a cat and a dog. The other tools you will need are a
lot of patience and a ready smile. Since deaf children cannot hear the tone
of your voice, they "listen" to your expression and depend on your pleased
response for reinforcement.

Okay, you're ready to start the warm-up exercises. Sit in one of the little
chairs across from Chris. Show her each picture whose word she has already
mastered; praise her when she says the word.

Now you're ready for the new word—"popsicle."

1) Show her the picture of a popsicle.

2) Say "popsicle," slowly and distinctly.

3) Hold the palm of her hand in front of your mouth and say pah, pah,
pah (so she can feel the puff of air coming from your mouth).

4) Repeat step 3 until she's mastered "pop."

5) Again hold her hand in front of your mouth while you make an
exaggerated "s" sound. She must see how your teeth are positioned and
feel that the "sssss" produces air from your mouth.

6) For the "c" sound, place one of her hands in front of your mouth so
she can feel the air. Place her other hand on your throat so she can feel
the sound you make. Show her how to place her tongue on the roof of her
mouth to get the hard "c" effect.

7) Repeat step 6 until she's mastered "kah."

8) Now practice the s-c sounds together, "sica," using the same methods as in steps 5 and 6.

9) For the "l" sound, show Chris how you roll your tongue to get the
"la" sound. Hold her hand against your throat so that she "feels" the
sound.

10) Now you're ready to put it all together. Show her the picture of
the popsicle, place her hand on your throat and say "pop si cul," exaggerat-
ing every syllable.

You may not get through all 10 steps in one day. If she gets tired, push
her further than she wants to go, but not to the point where she's frustrated.
Or to the point where you're frustrated either. For if you aren't happy and
smiling, you'll lose her for sure.

When at last she masters the word "popsicle," give her a popsicle. After you've both gone through "popsicle" every day for 2 or 3 weeks, every time Chris says "popsicle" you will both want to celebrate the victory. What better way to let her know she's got the idea, than by giving her a popsicle?

Imagine this process with every word Chris learns, and maybe you'll understand why we tend to give her everything she asks for. Everything she asks for is to be celebrated.

5. CHARLIE'S CARRY-OUT

Located on Nine Points Road, just outside the District of Columbia, is a small carry-out that, while offering sub-standard seafood fare to the public, does a booming business: Charlie's Carry-Out—an all-night stop for the hungry and the lonely. I recall my last late-hour attempt to beat my own hunger at Charlie's.

As I pulled into Charlie's parking lot, my car caught one of the cardboard boxes lying around and dragged it while I circled looking for a space where I could see my car from the inside. The noise made several drunks turn and stare. Off to one side were three kids about sixteen years old teasing an old man. One of them had grabbed a ragged glove from the man, and a game of keep-away was going well for the kids. I parked next to the trash cans where I saw an old woman digging through the trash, occasionally stopping to polish off a leftover piece of fish.

Reaching the front door, I stepped over several people who were either sleeping or passed out. One of them was spitting blood so I stopped briefly at the pay phone to call an ambulance for him. Hanging up the greasy receiver, I called to the fat man in the dirty T-shirt to make mine a fish sandwich with extra hot sauce. Without a word Charlie picked up another piece of fish and tossed it into the grease, from several feet away.

Before my sandwich was done, the ambulance had come and gone, the guy outside had gotten his ragged glove back, and someone's angry wife had thrown a brick through the windshield of their new Oldsmobile. Dirty Charlie handed me my sandwich in exchange for $1.05, in advance, and out the door I headed. As I drove off, I looked back and saw one customer throw his sandwich across the counter at Charlie. The sandwich dropped to the floor and I remember wondering how Charlie was going to tell the difference between that sandwich and the rest of the scraps on the floor. I wished I had ordered the crabcakes instead.

6. NIGHTCLUB CIRCUIT

Many people think nightclub musicians have a life of glamour—such an easy and exciting job! This is a misconception. Being the wife of a professional piano player allows me not only to observe, but to be involved in the difficulties of this "glamorous" occupation.

Behind the four or five pleasing hours of entertainment that a musician is paid for are numerous hours of rehearsal. Each song must be done uniformly with the other members of the band—not only instrumentally but vocally as well. Any off-key notes are unaffordable. To get this tight sound, every detail of each song must be memorized.

Buying and maintaining their equipment requires quite an expenditure for the musicians. Hundreds of dollars are spent just for an instrument. Each instrument (except drums) then needs an amplifier and a head, to produce the precise volume and sound needed for nightclubs. Amplifiers and heads also run hundreds of dollars apiece. Other necessary equipment—microphones for the vocalists, a PA board (the broadcast transmitter), and speaker cabinets—can total over a thousand dollars.

Since this heavy equipment is transported from club to club and receives excessive use, blown tubes and fuses and wornout cords must be replaced frequently. A piano needs to be kept in tune. For this, the pianist either pays thirty to forty dollars per tuning or buys a $400 strobotuner and learns how to tune.

Appearance and attitude are important factors on the nightclub stage. Most club managers require band members to wear uniforms—at their own expense. Since the main reason for a band's existence is to keep the customers happy and drinking, many band members try to develop split personalities to please the wide variety of customers. Socializing becomes an important part of the entertainment (often to the distress of band members' spouses).

Many clubs offer variety music, so that a nightclub band has to develop a large repertoire. They may be expected to play disco, the top forty, rock and roll, country western—or even a polka or a waltz. More rehearsal time, then, is needed to perfect this range of music.

There is seldom job security in the life of nightclub musicians. They may get lucky and be booked as a house band—but this will last only as long as the crowd stays with them. Usually they are booked a week or a weekend at a time, and consequently are constantly looking for the next job.

As you can now see, nightclub musicians have a more difficult occupation than appears on the surface. And yet an enthusiastic fever usually holds them to their business—always wondering if they will "make it big."

7. BORROWINGS FROM BLACK CULTURE

Although the sixties saw blacks struggling to attain civil rights, they are still a long way from the equality they need. However, for a group that has been oppressed in this country for two hundred odd years, the black population has been socially significant. Blacks have influenced the white middle class by their modes of dress, language, music, and dance.

There was a time when the African look was threatening to whites. But times changed. In the sixties love beads became a unique means of expression for blacks and whites alike. Whether made of elephants' ivory tusks or plain old plastic, beads were commonplace. Dashikis also started a style of their own, along with bandeaux and shawls. And the Afro hairstyle has become popular with Caucasian men as well as women.

The English language has picked up so many words from "Black English"—as it is sometimes referred to—that even Henry Higgins would find decoding difficult these days. How can anyone accurately explain the meaning of *soul food*, or *boogie*, or *funky*, yet these words are frequently heard. Nouns which originated in Black English and slipped into our everyday conversation include *dude* (male), *bama* (someone who doesn't dress well), *brother* (friend), *blood* (fellow black), and *honky* (white person). Some adjectives that many of us are familiar with are *solid* (good), *bad* (great), *phat* (well built), *cool* (no problems, all right), *hip* (up to date), and *uptight* (nervous). Verbs which have achieved considerable acceptability are *jam* (improvise), *rap* (converse), *jive* (exaggerate), and *hassle* (badger). Phrases also abound: *dig it, strung out, old lady*, and *out of sight* are all mainstays.

Black music has also been a trend setter. Starting with rhythm and blues, this music developed into a rage yet to die down—rock and roll. Black musicians who helped create rock include Muddy Waters, Chuck Berry, and Little Richard. Later came black vocal groups which helped develop the sound known as "soul music": the Temptations, the Supremes, the Miracles, and the Four Tops. Recently we have been introduced to disco, as interpreted by Van McCoy, Natalie Cole, and the Tramps. Other forms of music developed by black artists which have come to appeal to white ears include jazz, reggae, acid rock, and funk.

One of the stereotypes of blacks is that they all have rhythm and can dance. This, of course, is a fallacy. But they must be credited with introducing many new steps. The Twist, the Funky Chicken, and the Locomotion are black dances from some years back. More recently have come the Robot, the Hustle, and many variations of disco. These steps have been adapted, improved, and literally sold to whites.

Clearly black culture has had much influence on the mainstream culture in our country. Blacks have given as well as received customs to help develop the style that is known as American.

8. A SUICIDE

Thursday morning Kathy left her home to shop for the rope that she would place around her own throat. Kathy never went back home that day. Her body was found hanging in a maintenance storage room ten days later.

During her absence her friends and neighbors speculated on where Kathy might be. Some people felt she could have run away with a lover. Others thought she might have met with foul play. Everyone hoped she was alive.

Her body was discovered by a maintenance man. The blood had long since dried and caked around her mouth, and her eyes still bore the make-up she had applied that last Thursday morning. The maintenance man felt weakened by his tragic discovery and was given the day off.

Kathy's family was notified by the police. Kathy's elderly father was spared the means by which she had taken her life. Her daughter Julie wanted to be the one to identify the body. She was escorted by a private detective who had been hired to investigate Kathy's disappearance. Julie refused offers by friends to accompany her to the morgue. Julie's most vivid memory of her mother at the morgue was that she had a "serene face and was still wearing her eyeglasses."

Kathy's suicide touched my family's lives. Kathy had lived next door for two years. We had shared her problems and fears. Kathy had loved my children. I was very fond of Kathy and her daughters. I don't know what makes a person make the final decision to kill herself. With Kathy, it must have been many things. I was in shock when Julie told me what her mother had done. But one of Kathy's biggest problems was she worried all the time. She would even create situations to worry over.

In forty-four years, Kathy had never learned to cope with life. She imagined her children didn't care enough about her. She incessantly whined at her daughters, who eventually became immune to her guilt-ridden recriminations. She felt her parents had neglected her as a child, and she convinced herself they were to blame for all her present problems.

As a final attempt to get her friends' and loved ones' pity, she went out and bought a book about tieing knots, including the hangman's noose. Her suicide note said she took her own life, "to bring my scattered family together." Kathy never realized her family had always been close. She was the one who separated herself from them.

I can't help being angry with Kathy. She used a brutal method to kill herself, knowing her long absence would terrify her aged parents and prolong their agony. She left a sixteen-year-old daughter with severe adolescent problems who might now feel the way to cope with life is to run away or to end it all with suicide.

Not all suicides are this senseless. Some persons, like teenagers, have no resources, little experience, and usually feel no one cares enough to help them. Kathy, however, caused damage and pain to others dependent on her. Most important, Kathy is going to miss a lot of living, but then Kathy missed a lot of life when she was alive.

9. SO HE'S DRIVING YOU CRAZY

So he's driving you crazy? That soft, rosy bundle of joy you welcomed into your life just a short time ago has, seemingly overnight, become an iron-willed perpetual motion machine. He has the curiosity of a cat, the agility of a mountain goat and more energy than most power plants are capable of producing. He's faster than a speeding bullet, more powerful than a locomotive, and today he learned to climb the shiny new fence that just set you back $800. Take heart, dear friend. Do not despair. Save your strength, because things are definitely going to get worse. The "terrible twos" can't hold a candle to the traumatic teens.

This is not to say that the care and feeding of young children is not a difficult, time-consuming task. Your aching back and weary step are living proof of that. But, after all, how much trouble can a three-year-old really get into? How far from home can he get? By the time he is fourteen, there will be hours on end when you really have no idea where he is. No matter how good your lines of communication may be, all you really know about a teen-ager's whereabouts is what he tells you when he leaves the house.

Of course your child would not lie to you. He really does plan to go to Tommy's house. Indeed, he does. But, therein lies the rub! He and Tommy, finding things dull there, go on to Jim's, and then to the drugstore, the ballfield, Charlie's, the library, back to the drugstore and, finally, hours later, home—where you, his innocent parent, greet him and ask if he had a nice time at Tommy's.

All of this is, of course, compounded when, at the magic age of sixteen, the State decides he is mature and responsible enough to drive a car. The State, however, does not know him as well as you do. He is also not driving the State's car. He is driving yours. And who do you think will be up calling the hospitals when he is an hour late getting home? Not the good old Department of Motor Vehicles, that's for sure!

What all this really means is that now when he leaves home to go to Tommy's, he will drive. And when he and Tommy get bored, they will seek adventure at (you hope) speeds up to 55 mph. The wonderful world of the Capital Beltway will open to your Precious Baby, and the wonderful world of Lady Clairol will open to you as you discover at least ten new gray hairs every morning.

One of the biggest traumas of the toddler years is toilet-training. I have seen strong women—and stronger men—reduced to quivering heaps while trying to coax their Little Darling into the bathroom. Years later, these same people will spend an equal number of hours pleading with them to come out.

While the rest of the family lines up in the hall with soap, towels, shampoo, etc., the Crown Prince is using the last drop of hot water for his shower and will be at least another twenty minutes blow-drying his hair. One parent I know read *War and Peace* waiting to take a shower while her offspring lounged in the tub shrinking his jeans; and while cold showers are certainly invigorating, too many too often are not conducive to pleasant intra-family relations.

"But," you protest, "at least teen-agers eat. My toddler will surely come down with malnutrition, beri-beri or bubonic plague if I don't convince him to eat something!" Relax. By the time he is fifteen, he will be eating everything in sight that isn't either nailed down or still moving. In ten years your

grocery bill is bound to make you see those times when you finally got him
to eat two green beans and a bite of roast beef as the good old days they
really were. I predict that at some time during your child's teen years you
will seriously consider the purchase of (a) a cow; (b) a peanut farm; (c)
stock in the McDonald Corporation; or (d) all of the above.

Of course, while he is doing all this eating, he is growing at a fantastic
rate. Right out of the clothes you paid $100 for last week. It is not enough
that his clothes keep him warm and dry. They must be "in." Unfortunately,
what is "in" is usually expensive. There is no point in buying what is "in"
when it is on sale, because by that time it is most assuredly "out," and will
remain unworn in the closet until you donate it to Goodwill.

I do hope that the foregoing has not been too discouraging for you. Do
press on in the marvelous adventure of parenthood. You have not yet begun
to fight. While coping with teen-agers can be an exercise in frustration, the
rewards are many and varied. A team of scientists at Harvard is working
under a Federal grant conducting research to determine just what those rewards are—and when they find out they have promised I'll be the first to
know.

10. WATER-SKIING TO SIGNALS

One of the most important factors in water-skiing is the communication
link between the boat and the skier. To ensure that both skier and driver
know what is going to happen, a series of signals have been developed. They
are as follows:

In gear and hit it: When the skier is in the water ready to go up on the
skis, he or she shouts "In gear" to the driver, who puts the engine in gear.
As the boat moves away, the slack rope is drawn tight. The skier then yells
"Hit it" and the driver throttles forward, pulling the skier out of the water.
Use of these commands provides for a safe start without any sudden jerks
and without tow ropes tangling around the skier's arms or legs.

Okay signal: After a fall, the skier slaps both hands over his or her head as
soon as it's clear there is no injury. The use of two arms is important, as a
one-arm wave could be misinterpreted as a wave for help, or it might be
thought that the other arm is injured and cannot be raised.

Take me home: When the skier pats the top of his or her head, it means
"That's enough and let's return to the dock."

Turn: When either the skier or the driver circles an arm above his or her
head in either direction, the need for a turn is being indicated.

Speed okay: An "O" made with the thumb and index finger is a sign that
the skier is satisfied with the speed of the boat.

Speed up: The "thumbs up" gesture is used by the skier to indicate a need
or a desire for more speed.

Slow down: The thumbs down gesture is used by the skier to indicate
that less speed is needed.

Cut the engine: A "slit the throat" motion with the arm indicates that the boat is to be stopped. This signal can be used by driver, skier or observer. At the time of this signal the skier assumes a position directly behind the boat between the two wakes.

Some skiers develop additional signals for even more effective communication between the skier and the boat. For instance, the observer may hold his or her arms extended to signal the skier to straighten his or her arms. If additional signals are developed, all those involved with the skier should be familiar with them. In any case, the signals listed above should be retained, as they are universal in the water-skiing world and can be correctly interpreted just about anywhere.

11. A WARNING

After drinking the last drop of wine out of the jug, my friends and I left the park raising hell. The jug was the last of six fifths of wine that ten of us had drunk.

We had gotten drunk mourning over the death of our friend, Larry, who was killed in a robbery earlier in that week. We were pissy drunk, walking down the streets crying, calling Larry's name out loud, when a friend drove up. He told us to pile in his car so he could take us home. He knew we were in no condition to get home safely.

As he drove us home, we were stalled on a narrow street by a double-parked automobile. There were two men in the automobile, and another one was standing outside the car, talking to a girl, with the car door opened. We asked them politely to "get the hell out of the street." They politely ignored us in return. The second time we demanded that they move that contraption or be moved. They then called us a few nasty names. So John, one of my closest friends, and I got out of the car to see just what the problem was. As I approached the brother standing by the car door, he swung a wild punch at me, hitting me twice in the jaw. I didn't feel a thing. I was so drunk, I was numb from top to bottom. I then grabbed him by his shirt, threw him down, and began kicking him. John grabbed the man who was trying to get out of the car to help. We all began to fight in the middle of the street, when the third man in their car got out with a pistol in his hand. He fired the gun in the air to scare us off. As we backed off, the man shot at us.

John and I ran back to our car to escape from being shot. The three men hopped in their car and skidded off, sideswiping three parked cars. We pulled off right behind them, in the opposite direction, knowing the police would soon be there, looking to lock someone up.

As we left the scene, we noticed blood all over everything in our car. It was apparent that someone in the car was hurt, cut, or even shot. Instantly I thought John had been shot. I told him to check himself for gunshots because I had heard sometimes you can be shot and not know it. But there was no way he could, with ten drunks in one car. So we stopped the car after we were a good distance from the scene.

As we started to unload so John could inspect himself, I felt very weak. I fell out of the car flat on my face. I then knew it was me who had been shot. I tried to get up, but I was too weak. As the blood began to pour heavily out of my arm my friends began to panic. I started thinking about Larry's death, and how the gunshot wound killed him. The thought of death frightened me, and triggered pains in my chest. I thought I was going to die. With the loss of a lot of blood, I passed out.

When I woke up, I was in the hospital with all kinds of tubes running from me. I was told by my mother that I was in critical condition for five days. I do not remember any of those five days. Except that the police were there when I woke, asking me all kinds of questions. They had caught the man that shot me. The police wanted me to press charges against him, but I didn't. I felt I was the cause, as much as he was.

I came very close to dying in this incident. I saw it as a warning that something worse might happen the next time.

12. RE-ENTRY

Have you ever been out of circulation for twenty-three years and tried, all of a sudden, to re-enter the working world? What happened to you while you were folding all that laundry? Does weekly sorting of forty-two pairs of underpants sharpen your literary skills? And what about office machines? What's come on the market since you left your field? Ah, your typing speed! You were a whiz at one time. You were valued . . . at one time.

You're older now, your looks have faded, your skills are jaded. You have acquired a lot of wisdom and have had many years to reflect upon yourself. But does anyone out there know about you? No, you've been on the shelf too long. Your figure is gone, your hair is gray.

You could give good recommendations. Joe Campbell would give you one, but he is dead now. You had a good job at the lab, but they merged with another company and now no one would know you.

You read the want ads and circled those that sounded good. And when you applied, you learned . . . oh, what you learned. So much has changed. Attitudes, style of dress, and those machines. Everyone is so young, so chic, so self-assured. All of a sudden your confidence wanes. You wish you hadn't come. You could stay home and do arts and crafts, go to lunch with friends; there's nothing there to make you feel insecure. And those damned tests. You don't remember taking so many tests to apply for a job years ago. No one ever gave you an intelligence test, typing, sure, and maybe a little capitalization, but no one ever threw biblical quotes or parables at you. This time it was psychological evaluation from the minute the personnel manager laid eyes on you. Never mind that you passed the typing and the shorthand, even with your rusty skills; no, that's not good enough. Now they're going to psyche you out.

After the interview you say to yourself, "I'm in, I know I'm in." You wait all day for the call. He said he'd call by 4 P.M. Wednesday. No call. You wait. You go over and over what you said in the interview. The doubt begins. Maybe they want a sex symbol, a young chick, an ornament.

"I probably failed the intelligence test; what *were* those questions? I'm lousy at math, I bet that's what did me in. I'm too old. That's it . . . gray hair. I wore a dress; everyone else had a pants suit on. I must have looked too matronly, not with it."

You can't stand it any longer. You call. They found someone else; could they keep your application on file? (Probably file 13.) Now you're down, so far down. It took so much nerve to try and you weren't good enough. Where did you go wrong?

You busy yourself around the house, dig up another project. You want to try again but it is so hard. So you take up bread-baking instead. After the hurt dies down you begin to read the want ads again. But you have all kinds of excuses for not being able to make it that week. Dentist appointment on Monday afternoon; can't afford any more Clairol until payday. If you try hard enough, you'll find an excuse for every day of the week.

You call a few places to see if they're hiring. You get a snippy kid on the end of the line. She's too young to know what you're going through. And you wonder why they place such ill-trained people as personnel receptionists.

You'll crochet an afghan; that will take up your time. One for each of the kids. You're good at that. They'll like it; they'll appreciate you.

Finally, one more ad, one more interview. Now you're getting mad and you know you're worth something. If job A didn't want you then you'll have to sell yourself this next time. What do they know!

You go in and ask for Carol. She is young, attractive. Politely she leads you into a cubby hole to fill out an application. There are a lot of people there filling out applications. The doubts rise to the surface again. You struggle for control. The woman next to you makes a silly remark; your confidence starts to return.

Carol asks you to take a typing test. You've never seen an IBM Executive before. You can't find the switch. You have to ask. Damn! You finally finish. Carol proofs your work. Two errors and a score of 57 words per minute. You figured yourself for 80. She suggests the shorthand test. You haven't used it in twenty-three years but you decide to play all your chips. You pass, perfect score.

Your confidence is on the march again. You're waiting. Carol directs you to the manager's office. The interview is easier this time. The tests were expected. He is a nice, polished, plastic man; you can't read him. They'll let you know by the 15th.

Again the agony of waiting. This time you won't let it hurt. You busy yourself. You clean, rearrange a room. You wait. The call finally comes—

you get the job. All of a sudden you're not too old, too gray, too matronly or too out of it. You're in.

13. A DANGEROUS STATE OF MIND

I once served as an aide to one of our most powerful senators. That senator made me more aware than I had ever been before that some of our white leaders are still victims of an early nineteenth-century mentality: they're still stereotyping black people.

I don't think I will ever forget one time when I was in the senator's presence. I had been assigned to drive him from his senate office to Washington National Airport. As soon as he got into the car, I could feel his apprehension. He couldn't decide what to say to me or how to say it. He shook my hand and said, "Good afternoon, young man." Then he sat silently for a few seconds. Finally, he began by asking me my age, my educational background, and my place of birth. I wondered if he was going to ask me if I liked girls; he didn't, and I breathed a sigh of relief.

For approximately two miles, we drove in total silence. Then the senator began telling me about a friendship he and his wife had with a "colored girl" who had been a classmate of his daughter at a prestigious university. According to the senator, whenever he and his wife visited their daughter, they would always request the presence of the "colored girl." She would play the piano and sing while he and his family had a merry time. I sat there behind the steering wheel, listening, but not hearing. When we finally reached our destination, I breathed another sigh of relief.

My drive back to my office was not a pleasant one. I wondered to myself: What was the senator telling me? Was he saying that all black people had musical talent? Was he saying that his only exposure to black people had been on a master-servant level? I finally concluded that the senator was still living in the early nineteenth century when black slaves would sing and dance while their masters drank whiskey and clapped their hands. A dangerous state of mind for a modern-day senator, I thought to myself.

14. THE YOUGHIOGHENY RIVER AND ME

Standing in the early morning light of October in Chiopyle National Park, I studied the swollen river below me. The water level was higher than usual, from heavy rainfall. And this was to be the day of my first white water rapids trip.

For weeks I had looked forward to today. Now the cool mountain air and the swollen river had sobered my thoughts. I was about to ride the white water rapids of the Youghiogheny River in an eight-foot rubber raft. The added element of the danger of high water chilled my spine. Did I really want to get into that raft?

Our group waited anxiously while the park ranger determined whether it would be safe for us to undertake our six-mile trip. We were to go. In silence, my team carried our four-person raft to the river's edge and launched it. The water was cold and once again I felt goose bumps crawl along my spine.

Nervously our team paddled our raft across the river to meet with the guide and the other members of the expedition, for final instructions. Our procession of rafts moved out of the shallows and glided down the river.

We approached the first rapid swiftly. Water sprayed over the front of the raft but we went through without difficulty. The second rapid was a repeat performance. Like most novices, we began to congratulate ourselves on our expertise. But our confidence was to be short-lived. We approached the third rapid from the right side of the river. We were to traverse the river, make a hard right turn, then shoot through the jutting rocks. Just as we were about to go into our turn, the current overwhelmed us. Desperately, we tried to turn hard right, but the river had other plans for us. We were dashed against the rocks and I was tossed to the bottom of the raft.

Lying in eight inches of water, entangled with my paddle, I struggled to rise. The raft was tilted crazily and we were in danger of being swamped. With mighty force the swirling waters lifted us and sent us spinning off the rocks. We shot the third rapid backward, totally out of control, tossed around like wet laundry in the spin cycle of a washing machine. We caromed off of the rocks, completely at the mercy of the river until it yielded and carried us into stiller waters. Only then did we regain control of our raft. We grinned sheepishly at each other in embarrassment as we bailed water.

We paddled to the shoreline to rejoin our group. As I watched the other teams maneuver their rafts through the rapid, I slowly regained my composure, but I knew now that completing this rafting adventure would be no easy feat.

15. AN EEG EMERGENCY

While I was running an EEG (electroencephalogram) one day, the pens started clacking and throwing ink around the room. I knew then that I was in trouble. My patient was having a seizure. Pressing the alarm button, I ran to the patient to immobilize her. Poor little thing, she was only four years old.

Within seconds, three other members of my clinic rushed into the room. The physician started giving instructions, technicians rushed about, while the patient lay there helpless. As I drew the medication, the physician prepared her arm for the injection. When he gave the medication, a soft hush fell over the room. Slowly the pens stopped swaying and clacking. The patient's movements calmed. I knew then that everything would be all right, for this child, this time—but that there would be other patients in my life just like her.

16. WHO GOES TO THE RACES?

A favorite pastime of mine is observing people, and my favorite place to observe is at the horse races. After about fifteen encounters with the racing crowd, I discovered that there are four distinct groups of people that appear at the track: the once-a-year group, the professionals, the clubhouse bunch, and the welfare and unemployed group.

The largest group at the track are the ones that show up once a year. They know little about horses or betting. They rely strictly on racetrack gimmick sheets and newspaper predictions for selecting possible winners. If that doesn't work they use intuition, favorite numbers, colors, or appealing names. They bet larger amounts as the day goes along, gambling on every race, including the long-shot bets on exactas and daily doubles. Of course, the vast majority go home broke and frustrated.

A more subtle and quiet group are the professionals. They follow the horses from track to track and live in campers and motor homes. Many are married couples, some are retired, and all are easily spotted with their lunch sacks, thermos jugs, and binoculars. Since most are familiar with one another, they section themselves off in a particular area of the stadium. All rely on the racing form and on personal knowledge of each horse, jockey, and track in making the proper bet. They bet only on the smart races, and rarely on the favorites. Never do they bet on exactas or daily doubles. More often than not they either break even or go home winners.

In addition, there exists the clubhouse group. They can be found either at the cocktail lounge or in the restaurant, usually involved in business transactions. They rarely see a race in person and do their betting via the waiter. It's difficult to tell whether they go home sad, happy, or in between. They are just there.

The most interesting members of the race track population are the unemployed and welfare group. They won't be found in the clubhouse, but right down at the rail next to the finish line. It is here one can discover the real emotion of the racetrack—the screaming, the cursing, and the pushing. They are not sportsmen. Betting at the races is not a game for them, but a battle for survival. If they lose they must borrow enough money to carry them until the next check comes in, and then, of course, they head right back to the track. This particular group arrives at the track beaten and leaves beaten.

I have probably lost more money than I have won at the track, but observing these four interesting groups of people makes it all worthwhile.

17. LIGHT ACTION TODAY IN SOUTH VIET NAM

Damn, I wish Bill hadn't done that, gotten his head blown open like that. Dumb ass, now he's dead, but at least he's out of this hell. When there's this much lead flying around, you'd better keep your head down.

Ha, what a contrast to this morning when we dug in. We figured this patrol was going to be a breeze. Intelligence had said this was a "light-contact" area.

Bill, Rich and I were a gun-team—and a good one at that. Bill set up the machine gun while Rich and I filled sandbags. Other men from the company took up positions around the perimeter of our encampment.

It started around four in the humid afternoon. Beyond our defense perimeter a reconnaissance patrol started to draw enemy small-arms fire. The unit had called for air support and the helicopter gunships were coming in low, their rocket and machine-gun fire shredding the jungle. By sunset the fire-fight had escalated into a pitched battle.

But now it was too dark for the gunships; they couldn't hit what they couldn't see. The enemy was repaying us in spades now; the night was their time and they knew it.

When a bright rocket flare turned the black night into an eerie, yellowish day, I tried not to look at Bill. He's dead. Not a thing I can do now, not for him. But Rich, where the hell is Rich? He had yelled that we were low on ammo and had dashed off to scrounge up some. But how long ago was that? Five minutes? Five hours? Might as well have been five years.

Now I'm alone in this hole. Bill is dead and Rich is gone but I'm here. I don't want to die. I want to go home, back to the world. I want to be clean, I want to soak in a hot tub, I want to sleep in clean linen and hold on to a soft, warm woman. But I'm here. I stink—in my grimy fatigues lying in a damp hole. And this damned gun is not my woman. Oh God, I don't want to die; not now, not today, not ever.

Another flare lights up the night. There is plenty of movement out there. They're coming now. Hundreds of them are rushing our lines, yelling and screaming. Their short-range rockets are blasting into our bunkers. After each explosion, huge chunks of earth and small bits of men are thrown into the air. Horrible screams pierce the night. Wounded men are moaning and crying all around me.

The attackers press our lines relentlessly. Now they overrun our outer defense lines. Nothing slows them. They keep coming and coming.

Am I hitting any of them? I see some falling, but more materialize out of the dark, filling the gaps almost immediately. Drop, you bastards! Drop! They're closer now, too close. And they keep coming.

Closer . . . and closer.

Oh, Jesus, not now. Please, not now.

Dateline Saigon—United States Army spokesmen here said there was light action today in South Viet Nam. "Generally a real quiet day," said Captain J. Pollick, "a little skirmish here and there." Allied forces suffered "minor losses" while Viet Cong and North Vietnamese losses were put at "well over 2000."

In Paris, it was reported that peace talks between the United States and North Viet Nam broke down after a dispute concerning the shape of the negotiating table. Conflict was also reported on the number of flags that each side should be able to display and also . . . .

18. BETTER TO DIE AT HOME

I look upon the benefits of modern science with mixed emotions. When a person is deteriorating due to old age or the ravages of a fatal illness, it is not a blessing to have life prolonged with the aid of mechanical assistance. If all hope for a meaningful life is gone, it is better to die at home in peace, surrounded by one's family.

Those individuals taken care of at home are attended by their family and friends, who try to make the patient's last days as comfortable as possible. They can see their children and grandchildren, who are sometimes not permitted to visit in a hospital. My father was taken care of at home before he passed away from cancer. I recall that he enjoyed the family visits, and that we were able to spend more time with him than we were able to in the hospital. My mother prepared the foods that he could eat, the way he liked them. He had drugs for pain, but was not encumbered with tubes and other medical apparatus. Both of my grandmothers also died at home, and I recall visiting them in their last days when I was a little girl.

In contrast, when a person goes to the hospital he or she is put on a schedule that is convenient for the staff. The patient doesn't see the family except at visiting hours. Unless one has a private nurse, the patient is left unattended for hours. In the hospital, one feels like a statistic. Just another case to be cataloged.

At 5 a.m., the clattering of the carts carrying water pitchers awakens patients. If one is able to eat solid food, the diet in the hospital is not the type to tempt one's appetite. The patient is fed intravenously when unable to eat solid food. Many kinds of tubes are attached to the patient for various purposes. Blood is tested often. In addition, many other kinds of tests are run and the patient is X-rayed frequently. The patient feels like a pin cushion. The patient may be on the verge of death, but tests are performed to collect scientific data to benefit science. The tests are expensive. However, most people hospitalized have medical insurance or medicare, so the hospital staff does not hesitate to take as many tests as possible; they know the bill will be paid one way or another.

Hospitals are concerned with keeping the heart beating, not with the dignity of life. The 83-year-old father of a friend of mine, who had a slow-growing cancer of the prostate and whose veins were collapsing due to old age, was treated by the hospital staff as a collection of symptoms, not as a person. The nurses insisted on checking his blood pressure often, even though he found this very painful. In addition, they took blood tests every day, in spite of the fact that they had difficulty finding his veins. Before he died, he also had to endure the torture of being X-rayed to check the progress of the cancer. Mercifully, he died after being in the hospital only a few weeks. Unfortunately, an 89-year-old aunt of mine suffered for seven months in the hospital before she died. She went in and out of comas, had pneumonia a couple of times and was pulled back to life to suffer more. She was a shrunken senile old lady begging for death when she died.

This is not the kind of end I wish to have. I believe a person should die with some dignity. At home one has some control over one's surroundings, and feels like a human being. There is a lot to the saying "There's no place like home."

19. TIME OUT

Howard Cosell is not the only offender. Most television sports announcers set my teeth on edge. I enjoy televised professional sports, especially football, but I cannot understand the low quality of sports broadcasting provided by the networks. I could forgive the numerous technical errors and the consistently mispronounced names, if the persistent running commentary was tolerable. Every Sunday during football season, overstatements abound, clichés cascade, and "touching" anecdotes turn this viewer's stomach.

Each rookie who displays any talent is proclaimed a future Hall of Fame nominee. Each participating team becomes the "toughest, meanest, and most interesting to watch." Any pass completion is "fantastic," and every call by an official is "controversial." A second stringer, having a good day, is said to be the "most underrated player in the league."

The local fans each week are dubbed "the most loyal in the world" and "the best to be found in any stadium." The head coach always seems to be "the most respected man around" and has always "done a great job with the boys." According to the exaggerations of our announcers, there are no adequate athletes performing well, only superb superstars gaining glory.

During the pre-game chit-chat, the weather is described as "picture perfect" or "unbearably miserable." Even the elements are not allowed to remain ho-hum in television land.

Quarterbacks are "men of great courage" and specialty teams are "suicide squads." Every person on the field is "a real man" with "a lot of heart." If a team is losing by twenty-eight points in the fourth quarter, we are instructed not to "count this team out" because these "tough competitors" have been known to "turn it around."

Even more offensive than the overstatements and clichés are the maudlin personal stories that sportscasters force upon us. When they deplete their supply of handy statistics, they turn to pathos. The viewer is informed that a certain hulking linebacker was a sissy in second grade. Another bought "dear old mom" her dream house with his first playoff bonus. We hear vivid descriptions of previous injuries, and suffer through some poor guy's "excruciatingly painful" experience with a pulled groin muscle. Billy Kilmer, who was not expected to walk after his car accident, has a daughter with cerebral palsy for whom he "plays his heart out" weekly. O. J. Simpson is enduring a period of great stress. He wants to be near his family in California, but is forced by his contract to earn millions in Buffalo.

If players are aware of these gushy interludes, they must find them embarrassing. All this "True Confession" trivia is being broadcast to a national audience who tuned in to hear football action, not soap opera. "Dear old mom" might be watching, and might not want her neighbors to realize that she doesn't make her own mortgage payments.

I would prefer objective, impersonal announcing. I'd like valid appraisals of athletic ability and relevant statistics. Descriptions should contain honest adjectives and fewer trite phrases. Why not allow the reality of a well-played game to project its own excitement, and let the tension of the competition provide the color. It doesn't seem like an unreasonable request. I wonder if Howard and friends could stop chattering long enough to consider it?

20. JOURNEY OUT OF MY BODY

I have experienced something that let me know more about death than a lifetime of reading and theorizing could. One morning, quite unintentionally, I became dissociated from my body. It happened shortly after I had finished reading Robert Monroe's *Journeys Out of the Body*.

I woke up to a gentle rain, on a gray morning. It was nine-thirty. I glanced at my clock and then drifted back into what seemed to be very peaceful, but light, sleep. The next thing I knew, my body was vibrating slightly, as if an electric current was flowing through my veins. This slight sensation grew to an unpleasant surge of electricity-like energy which set my legs convulsing beneath the sheets. It felt as though I was running in a race, kicking and sweating profusely, but when I looked to the foot of the bed, I was astonished to see that my legs were very still. The sheets had not moved.

At this point I began to experience fear, and in hopes that some light would help bring me to my senses, I groped for the switch on my reading lamp. My hand could not turn the switch. It seemed as if my hand had gone right through the lamp. This frightened me even more. I inspected the switch, hoping that it was broken to account for my inability to make it work, but it wasn't. I looked at the switch from the top, then from the bottom, then from the inside of the lamp. When all this failed to explain why the light didn't click on, I followed the cord to the wall socket. The cord was securely plugged in. I saw the plug from the front, then from *inside* the wall socket.

By this time I was so shaken that I gave up the struggle, and surrendered to whatever was to happen. In one timeless instant, I found myself back in my body, sitting up in bed and staring at my hands. There was no sweat on my body, nor any sign of a struggle. The wall socket that I had inspected so thoroughly was still hidden behind a large trunk—where it had been for years.

This journeying out of my body has happened to me twice since the first time, and each time was just as frightening as the first. It is a very real state-of-being, as certain as walking down the street, or conversing with a friend. I know it's not dreaming. I know I'm not dreaming right now, and I am no less certain while I am experiencing separation from my body. I have told very few people about all this, but since it last occurred well over a year ago, it's much easier for me to talk about now.

There's yet another part to this experience. That's the part that feels good while the whole thing is happening, a feeling of unity with all things that disappears when I come back. I don't think I've ever felt so much joy—coupled with a feeling of fear that I won't come back. Yet, when I do come back, I feel as though something has been lost. Every time I have this experience, I stay longer. I may never have it again on a temporary basis. But I know I will have it again someday. And I won't be afraid, because if this is what death feels like, I'm sure I'll have no desire to hang on to this life when my time comes to die.

APPENDIX

SOME EXERCISE ANSWERS

1. Translations of euphemisms in exercise 5 of chapter 12.

Euphemism:	*Translation:*
1. adult entertainment	pornography
2. correctional facility	jail, prison, detention center
3. culturally deprived child	child raised in poverty
4. deteriorating residential section	slum
5. downsized car	small, economy car
6. encore telecast	TV re-run
7. Egyptological pornoglyphic sacrophagi	graffiti on a mummy
8. engage the enemy on all sides	to be ambushed
9. expired, passed away, left us	died
10. for motion discomfort	for travel sickness, nausea
11. grief therapist	undertaker
12. inner city	ghetto
13. inoperative statement	a lie
14. nervous wetness	sweat
15. powder room	women's toilet
16. preowned automobile	used car
17. protective reaction strike	bombing
18. twilight years	old age

2. Punctuated version of student paper at end of section on Punctuation:

I was suddenly awakened at four o'clock one morning by my wife. "It's time to go!" she exclaimed.

Gazing across the room and seeing her standing with suitcase in hand, it dawned on me that this was the moment for which we had been waiting nine months. I sprang out of bed, grabbed whatever clothes were available and started dressing, while simultaneously calling the doctor.

"I'll meet you at the hospital in forty-five minutes," was the doctor's reply to a very nervous father-to-be. On the way to the hospital I tried to remain calm, as I tried to remember the training we had received in prepared childbirth classes and the reading we had done in *Having Your Baby Naturally.*

"Inhale, exhale, breathe deeply and slowly," I repeated to my wife over and over again as we drove into the city.

Arriving at the hospital, I drove right up to the front door and carefully ushered my wife to the admitting office. After rushing through much paperwork (not really knowing what we were signing), we finally made it to the labor room. Then it began: the timing of contractions, the breathing in unison, and the waiting. Three long hours later, when my wife was fully dilated, the doctor sent me out to dress in the delivery room garb—a green cap, mask, gown and shoes. Once in the delivery room, I held my wife's hand and assisted whenever possible. Twenty short minutes later a beautiful six-pound, twelve-ounce girl was born.

One does not realize how much pain a woman can tolerate or the strength she possesses—until he can witness a childbirth. I shall always treasure having shared my daughter's birth with my wife; it was an event I shall not forget.

3. Corrections for paragraph containing misspelled words in Spelling section:

Most of us know at least one woman who is beginning college in her forties. Her family may find this new arrangement difficult to accommodate to. However, once they become accustomed to it, they frequently speak proudly of her. She, on the other hand, may have to struggle to overcome certain guilt feelings; somehow, the principle of self-development for her own being is hard for her to accept, despite the advice of her friends who have already traveled the same path. Gradually, though, she realizes that she truly is a whole person, separate from her husband and her children, and she learns to function outside the wife-mother role.. Then she can relax, let down her guard some, and finally begin to recommend "coming back to school" to her neighbors. The growth observable in such women is exciting to watch; it's one of the real pleasures of being in the college environment today.

SOURCES OF QUOTED MATERIAL

Page

3 James Gould Cozzens, *Time* (September 2, 1957).
4 Toni Morrison, quoted by Mel Watkins, "Talk with Toni Morrison," *New York Times Book Review* (September 11, 1977).
4 Anne Tyler, "Because I Want More Than One Life," *Washington Post* (August 15, 1976), p. G-7.
5 Carson McCullers, *Playbill* (October 28, 1957).
5 Van Wyck Brooks, source unknown.
6 Jacques Barzun, *On Writing, Editing, and Publishing* (Chicago: University of Chicago Press, 1971), p. 12.
6 Barzun, *On Writing*, p. 5.
7 Flannery O'Connor, source unknown.
7 William Carlos Williams, "How to Write," *New Directions in Prose and Poetry*, edited by James Laughlin (New York: New Directions, 1936), p. 45.
7 Virginia Woolf, source unknown.
7 P. G. Wodehouse, *Collier's* (August 31, 1956).
7 Albert van Nostrand, quoted in Edward B. Fiske, " 'Functional Writing' Course Catching On at College Level," *New York Times* (November 24, 1976), p. 59M.
7 William Faulkner, quoted in Donald M. Murray, *A Writer Teaches Writing* (Boston: Houghton Mifflin, 1968), p. 235.
7 Anne Tyler, "Because I Want More Than One Life," *Washington Post* (August 15, 1976), p. G-1.
8 Sinclair Lewis, quoted in Donald M. Murray, *A Writer Teaches Writing* (Boston: Houghton Mifflin, 1968), p. 240.
8 Lancelot Law Whyte, "Where Do Those Bright Ideas Come From?" *Harper's* (July, 1951).
9 Joan Didion, "Why I Write," *New York Times Book Review* (December 5, 1976), p. 2.

Page

9   Henry Miller, *The Wisdom of the Heart* (New York: New Directions, 1941).
9   Anne Tyler, "Because I Want More Than One Life," *Washington Post* (August 15, 1976), p. G-7.
11 Toni Morrison, interviewed by Karen De Witt, *Washington Post* (September 30, 1977), p. C-1.
14 Gene Olson, *Sweet Agony* (Grants Pass, Ore.: Windyridge Press, 1972), p. 35.
19 Ezra Pound, *ABC of Reading* (New York: New Directions, 1960), p. 62.
19 Samuel Johnson, quoted in *Bartlett's Unfamiliar Quotations*, edited by Leonard Louis Levinson (Chicago: Cowles Book Co., 1971), p. 334.
19 Bernard de Voto, source unknown.
19 Louis Brandeis, source unknown.
19 James Michener, source unknown.
20 Ernest Hemingway, quoted in Samuel Putnam, *Paris Was Our Mistress: Memoirs of a Lost and Found Generation* (Carbondale, Ill.: Southern Illinois University Press, 1970).
20 Ben Lucien Berman, quoted in Donald M. Murray, *A Writer Teaches Writing* (Boston: Houghton Mifflin, 1968), p. 232.
20 Dorothy Parker, *Writers at Work: The Paris Review Interviews (First Series)*, edited by George Plimpton (New York: Viking Press, 1959), p. 79.
20 John Updike, quoted in Donald M. Murray, *A Writer Teaches Writing* (Boston: Houghton Mifflin, 1968), p. 244.
20 Raphael Hamilton, quoted in an interview by Michael V. Uschan, *Washington Post* (September 4, 1977).
21 John Steinbeck, *John Steinbeck: A Life in Letters*, edited by Elaine Steinbeck and Robert Wallsten (New York: Viking Press, 1975).
22 Jonathan Swift, *On Poetry* (1712).
35 Walker Gibson, *The Limits of Language* (New York: Hill and Wang, 1962), p. 104.
40 Gerald Levin, *Prose Models*, 3rd ed. (New York: Harcourt Brace Jovanovich, 1975), p. 161.
40 Mary McCarthy, *Writers at Work: The Paris Review Interviews (Second Series)*, edited by George Plimpton (New York: Viking Press, 1963), p. 302.
40 Anthony Burgess, *Writers at Work: The Paris Review Interviews (Fourth Series)*, edited by George Plimpton (New York: Viking Press, 1976), p. 326.
41 Wayne C. Booth, "The Rhetorical Stance," *College Composition and Communication* 14 (1963), p. 139.
42 Elizabeth Bowen, quoted in Donald M. Murray, *A Writer Teaches Writing* (Boston: Houghton Mifflin, 1968), p. 232.
43 Kenneth Turan, "Smokey's Enduring Appeal," *Washington Post* (November 10, 1976), p. B-1.
44 B. D. Colen, "S. Bear, Fire Fighter," *Washington Post* (November 10, 1976), p. B-1.

Page

46 Sojourner Truth, "Ain't I a Woman?" in Jacqueline Bernard, *Journey Toward Freedom: The Story of Sojourner Truth* (New York: Grosset & Dunlap, 1967).

47 Imamu Amiri Baraka, "Expressive Language," *Home* (New York: William Morrow, 1966), p. 171.

47 José Ángel Gutiérrez, "Mexicanos Need to Control Their Own Destinies," *Pain and Promise: The Chicano Today*, edited by Edward Simmen (New York: New American Library, 1972), pp. 252–53.

50 Mary Orovan, "Humanizing English" (Hackensack, N.J.: Art & Copy, n.d.).

50 Benjamin Whorf, quoted in Mary Orovan, "Humanizing English" (Hackensack, N.J.: Art & Copy, n.d.).

51 William H. Green, "Singular Pronouns and Sexual Politics," *College Composition and Communication* (May 1977), pp. 150–53.

57 H.E.W. *Training Manual #7*: "Getting Your Ideas Across Through Writing," p. 42.

70 Sholem Asch, *New York Herald Tribune* (November 6, 1955).

73 Stuart Chase, "Writing Nonfiction," *On Writing, by Writers*, edited by William W. West (Boston: Ginn, 1966).

78 W. Somerset Maugham, quoted in *A Treasury of Humorous Quotations*, edited by Herbert V. Prochnow and Herbert V. Prochnow, Jr. (New York: Harper and Row, 1969), p. 367.

78 E. B. White, source unknown.

78 Darcy O'Brien, source unknown.

78 Ivan Turgenev, quoted in *The Viking Book of Aphorisms*, edited by W. H. Auden and Louis Kronenberger (New York: Viking Press, 1962), p. 277.

78 Emile Chartier Alain, source unknown.

78 Georges Simenon, source unknown.

78 Henry David Thoreau, *Journals*, July 14, 1852.

79 *Zen Flesh, Zen Bones*, edited by Paul Reps (Garden City, N.Y.: Doubleday), pp. 30–31.

79 Patrick Dennis (Edward Everett Tanner), *Vogue* (February 15, 1956).

80 Donald M. Murray, *A Writer Teaches Writing* (Boston: Houghton Mifflin, 1968), p. 51.

87 Mortimer J. Adler and Charles Van Doren, *How to Read a Book* (New York: Simon and Schuster, 1972), p. 90.

89 Cyril H. Knoblauch, quoted in Edward B. Fiske, " 'Functional Writing' Course Catching On at College Level," *New York Times* (November 24, 1976), p. 59M.

90 Rudolf Flesch, *The Art of Readable Writing* (New York: Collier MacMillan Publishers, 1949), pp. 58–59.

90 Donald M. Murray, *A Writer Teaches Writing* (Boston: Houghton Mifflin, 1968), p. 7.

90 Rudolf Flesch, *The Art of Readable Writing* (New York: Collier MacMillan Publishers, 1949), pp. 58–59.

91 Donald Hall, *Writing Well* (Boston: Little, Brown, 1973), p. 143.

91 Hall, *Writing Well*, p. 144.

Page

108 Jo Goodwin Parker, "What Is Poverty?" in *America's Other Children: Public Schools Outside Suburbia* (Norman, Okla: University of Oklahoma Press, 1971).

117 Henry David Thoreau, "Sunday," A *Week on the Concord and Merrimac Rivers* (1849).

130 Eldridge Cleaver, *Soul on Ice* (New York: Dell, 1968), pp. 6, 18, 38.

131 Joan Didion, "Why I Write," *New York Times Book Review* (December 5, 1976), pp. 2, 98.

132 Mark Twain, source unknown.

133 George Orwell, "Politics and the English Language," *Shooting an Elephant and Other Essays* (New York: Harcourt Brace Jovanovich, 1974).

135 Wallace Stevens, "Adagia," *Opus Posthumous* (New York: Alfred A. Knopf, 1957), p. 169.

137 John O'Hayre, *Gobbledygook Has Gotta Go* (Washington, D.C.: Department of Interior, 1966).

144 Editorial about Queen Elizabeth's Silver Jubilee, *Washington Post* (June 14, 1977), p. A-18.

149 Flannery O'Connor, *Mystery and Manners: Occasional Prose*, edited by Robert and Sally Fitzgerald (New York: Farrar, Straus, and Giroux, 1969), p. 67.

154 Raymond Barrio, *The Plum Plum Pickers* (New York: Harper & Row, 1971).

154 Annie Dillard, *Pilgrim at Tinker Creek* (New York: Bantam Books, 1974).

154 Frank Walters, *The Man Who Killed the Deer* (Chicago: Swallow Press, 1970).

155 *Sappho: A New Translation*, translated by Mary Barnard (Berkeley and Los Angeles: University of California Press, 1966), fragment 3.

157 Jane van Lawick-Goodall, *The Shadow of Man* (Boston: Houghton Mifflin, 1971), p. 32.

163 Ernest Hemingway, *Death in the Afternoon* (New York: Charles Scribner's Sons, 1932), p. 2.

170 Edgar Allan Poe, "The Fall of the House of Usher," *The Rinehart Book of Short Stories*, edited by C. L. Cline (New York: Rinehart and Company, 1952), p. 1.

170 Albert Camus, *The Stranger*, translated by Stuart Gilbert (New York: Alfred A. Knopf, 1946), p. 1.

202 "Sputnik Plus 20: The U.S. on Top," *Newsweek* (October 10, 1977), p. 54.

INDEX

Abbreviations and Symbols for Marking Student Papers

ambig	ambiguous meaning
appr	inappropriate language (Ch. 5)
awk	awkward phrasing
cap	capitalize (HB 15–18)
coh	improve coherence (Ch. 10)
cs	comma splice (HB 23)
di	dialect interference (HB 36–39)
dng	dangling modifier (HB 28)
focus	off the focus (Ch. 6)
frag	sentence fragment (HB 22)
lc	lower case needed (HB 15–18)
log	confused logic
mix	mixed-up sentence (HB 24)
mod	misplaced modifier (HB 27)
n-p	noun-pronoun agreement (HB 30)
ob	overburdened sentence (HB 35)
om	omission (HB 26)
p	punctuation (HB 1–14)
p-a	passive/active voice (HB 33)
p-v	point of view (Ch. 10, HB 25)
ref	faulty pronoun reference (HB 31)
run-on	run-on sentence (HB 23)
shift	confusing shift (HB 25)
sp	spelling (HB 19–21)
s-v	subject-verb agreement (HB 29)
tense	verb tense
thesis	thesis statement (Ch. 6)
trans.	transition needed (Ch. 10)
trite	weak word, or cliché (Ch. 12)
ts	topic sentence (Ch. 9)
var	sentence variety needed (Ch. 11)
w	wordiness (Ch. 12, HB 34)
ww	wrong word
X	obvious error
//	parallel structure (HB 32)
¶	paragraph break (Ch. 9)
⌒	fasten together
∧	something omitted
∼	transpose

NOTE: HB means Handbook